PSYCHOLOGY MADE SIMPLE

Alison Thomas-Cottingham, Ph.D.
Rider University

Illustrated by Scott Nurkin

BOOKS

A Made Simple Book
Broadway Books
New York

Produced by The Philip Lief Group, Inc.

Printed in the United States of America

Produced by The Philip Lief Group, Inc.
Managing Editors: Judy Linden, Lynne Kirk, Hope Gatto, Jill Korot.
Design: Annie Jeon.

MADE SIMPLE BOOKS and BROADWAY BOOKS are
trademarks of Broadway Books, a division of Random House, Inc.

Visit our Web site at www.broadwaybooks.com.

First Broadway Books trade paperback edition published 1960.

Library of Congress Cataloging-in-Publication Data
Thomas-Cottingham, Alison.
   Psychology made simple / Alison Thomas-Cottingham ; illustrated by
   Scott Nurkin.
       p. cm.—(Made simple series)
   Includes bibliographical references and index.
   ISBN 0-7679-1543-7
   1. Psychology—Textbooks. I. Title. II. Made simple (Broadway Books)
BF121.T395 2004
150—dc22   2003069741

10 9 8 7 6 5 4 3

ACKNOWLEDGMENTS

I thank those who supported me during the completion of this project: my husband and biggest fan, Robert Cottingham, Jr.; my children, Robert III and Alison Josephine; my mother, Alice Jean Thomas; my mother- and father-in-law, Gwendolyn and Robert Cottingham, Sr.; and my sister-in-law, Paige Cottingham-Streater. Your love and support are invaluable to me, and I truly could not have done this without you.

I would also like to thank those special friends who helped in times of need: Pat Crawford, Stephanie Golski, India Larrier, and Adrian and Anita Simmons.

Finally, I would like to thank Frances Chamberlain for her expertise and assistance with the writing of this book, and Judy Linden, Jill Korot, C. Lynne Kirk, and Hope Gatto at The Philip Lief Group for providing me with the opportunity to share my love of psychology.

This book is dedicated to the memory of my father, the late Major Thomas, whose hard work and commitment to my pursuits enabled me to study psychology.

CONTENTS

INTRODUCTION

Welcome to *Psychology Made Simple*, an easy-to-follow guide that sheds new light on the broad field of psychology. No matter what your interest in psychology is, this book will offer classic theories, summaries of fascinating studies, and updated information that will help you in your quest for knowledge of this subject. Read it through for a basic understanding of the field of psychology, or refer to it time and again, as you would any reference book, for easy-to-understand explanations of various concepts.

Psychology Made Simple is comprised of fourteen chapters, starting with the basics of psychology, exploring research methods, looking at the various components of an individual that influence behavior, and carrying through to social psychology, the influence that other individuals or groups have on the behavior of the individual.

The book was written with the understanding that psychology is a science with various fields of specialty, but materials in these fields often overlap. Therefore, an integrative approach has been taken; topics and concepts are woven throughout the book. For example, one of the enduring issues in psychology—the person versus situation debate—first appears in chapter 1 and surfaces again in chapter 10.

Chapter 1 focuses on the question, "What is psychology?" At its most basic, psychology is a science, and the goal of this science is to understand behavior. In this chapter, you will learn about the many subfields of psychology,

careers in psychology, and enduring issues in the field.

In chapter 2, "Statistics and Research Methods in Psychology," the techniques that allow psychologists to conduct experiments and make decisions about behavior will be explored.

Chapter 3 studies the brain and behavior. The brain is small, about the size of two fists placed together, but is an incredibly important organ that controls many of our behaviors.

Chapter 4 focuses on sensation and perception. Sensation—sight, sound, smell, taste, and touch—and the perception of our personal interpretations of sensory stimulation require the mind to process the information it receives and transform it into something meaningful. It's an amazing process that is integral to our understanding of human behavior.

In chapter 5, we move from the biological and concrete to more abstract concepts. We can't see cognitions, motivations, and expressions of emotion, learning or memory, but we can assess all of these through the study of the behaviors with which they are associated. Chapter 5 is on cognition, and it covers problem solving, decision making, and language. Every day we are asked to solve problems and make decisions. Cognitive psychologists who have worked in this area have created strategies to improve our abilities to solve problems and make decisions. Language, which we use almost nonstop during our waking hours, and the acquisition of language are also explored.

Chapter 6 examines motivations—why do people behave the way they do, and how can an understanding of emotions lead to an understanding of behavior?

Chapter 7 covers learning and memory. Learning is defined as a permanent change, and sometimes this manifests as a permanent change in behavior. We will focus on behaviorism and learning. Without memory, there is no learning. We will discuss a major theory of learning—the information processing model—and how we assess memory, the accuracy of our memories, and forgetting.

Chapters 8 and 9 focus on life span development. Chapter 8 covers conception, infancy, and childhood; chapter 9 covers adolescence and adulthood. Each chapter emphasizes changes in physical, cognitive, and social development at differing periods in one's life. This area of psychology has gained popularity as our population ages, and scientists understand that development does not end at age twenty-one.

Chapter 10 is the first in our attempt to understand the whole individual. We cover the main theories of personality in psychology. These theories are organized by psychological perspective or orientation. We also revisit the person-situation debate. Is personality the stable construct some propose it to be, or do we change our way of being and behaving depending on the situation?

Chapter 11 discusses assessment, with an emphasis on a variety of psychological tests used to assess and diagnose problematic behaviors.

Chapter 12 focuses on mental disorders, using the *Diagnostic and Statistical Manual* (DSM) of the American Psychiatric Association as our resource. This very important book is used by mental health professionals to gain insight into the diagnosis and treatment of many disorders.

Chapter 13 focuses on treatment, not just of the most severe disorders but also of problems that range widely in severity. The emphasis here is on differing types of approaches to treatment, all of which are based on differing orientations or perspectives in psychology.

Finally, in chapter 14, we take a look at the whole individual and the influence that other individuals and/or groups have on the behavior of the individual.

At the end of each chapter is a section entitled "Test Your Recall and Recognition." These tests were created so that you can conduct an assessment of your own learning and memory. After this section, you will find a list of resources where you may find out more about material covered in the chapter. These include books, Web sites, videos, and DVDs.

As an educator who has taught psychology at the undergraduate level for more than ten years, a researcher who has studied health psychology for five years, and a clinician who has conducted individual, couples, and group therapy for ten years, I can state unequivocally that there is little else so critical to our success in the world than an understanding of our behaviors, learning styles, and motivations. Let *Psychology Made Simple* guide you through the complicated science of human behavior. It will give you new insights into how you behave as well as into the personalities and behaviors of others around you.

WHAT IS PSYCHOLOGY?

KEY TERMS

psychology, perspective/orientation, psychodynamic, behavioral, humanistic, physiological, gestalt, cognitive, sociocultural

Chances are you picked up this book because you wondered what psychology is really about. Or perhaps you wanted to gain some insight into yourself or someone else. Maybe you find psychology mysterious, or you aren't sure what it really encompasses.

This chapter is written to answer the fundamental but complex question: What is psychology?

Psychology is defined as the scientific study of behavior and mental processes, or the science of behavior. Although this definition is accurate, you will soon see that psychology is much more than that. It encompasses a wide range of study. Although discussions of psychology can venture into many different areas, psychology can also be explained in terms that are easy to understand.

HISTORY OF PSYCHOLOGY

The study of psychology dates back to the beginning of recorded history. People have long attempted to understand themselves and those around them. What drives thought? What shapes human behavior? Early philosophers grappled with these questions. Although we define modern psychology as twentieth

century psychology, there were great scientists and thinkers before 1900. Plato and Aristotle pondered issues regarding mind, body, spirit, and soul, and the philosopher René Descartes proposed that mind and body were two separate parts of a person. The father of medicine, Hippocrates, examined the connection between mind and body.

Wilhelm Wundt (1832–1920) created the first psychological laboratory in 1879. He wanted to treat psychology as a science—to study it through laboratory research. He is credited with the development of an approach known as *structuralism*. According to this approach, the mind can be separated and studied as distinct components. Around the same time, William James (1842–1910) developed other ideas about psychology. James's approach is known as *functionalism*. It focuses on the what and why of the working of the mind. These two scientists opened the door to what we refer to as modern psychology.

Psychology is a broad and diverse field of study. Within psychology, there are different ways of thinking that we will refer to as *orientation*, or *perspective*. The history of the science is best understood in the context of these varying orientations. Although it may sound as though these perspectives are separate and distinct, there is some overlap. For example, cognitive and behavioral psychologists have come together to develop a perspective simply known as *cognitive/ behavioral* psychology.

WHAT IS PERSPECTIVE/ ORIENTATION?

A psychological orientation helps to guide a psychologist's thinking. An orientation/ perspective or school of psychology serves as a lens that influences how the psychologist views a particular situation. For example, think of how the world would look to you if you were to wear green-tinted sunglasses, versus gray-tinted sunglasses, versus blue-tinted sunglasses. Each pair of glasses would provide a different view of your world.

The psychologist who embraces a psychodynamic perspective will have a view that differs from the psychologist who favors a humanistic perspective. We will look at seven different psychological orientations: psychodynamic, behavioral, humanistic, physiological, gestalt, cognitive, and sociocultural. Although these perspectives are presented as distinct and separate ways of thinking, most psychologists do not adhere to just one perspective. Many psychologists will tell you that they wear a different lens depending on the circumstance. These psychologists would refer to themselves as eclectic (rather than behavioral, for instance).

Psychodynamic Perspective

When many people think of psychology, they think of Sigmund Freud (1856–1939) and his cigar. It is interesting to know that Freud was not trained as a psychologist, but as a medical doctor. Nevertheless, he can be credited with the development of the psychodynamic perspective, which emphasizes the influence of early childhood experiences on adjustment in adulthood. Psychodynamic perspective also explores the role of the unconscious in everyday lives. People are not aware of the uncon-

PERSPECTIVES IN MODERN PSYCHOLOGY

- **Psychodynamic**—emphasizing the importance of early childhood experiences and the unconscious in our everyday lives
- **Behavioral**—focusing on the behaviors that can be seen by others
- **Humanistic**—focusing on the individual as someone with potential who is constantly striving to reach that potential; therapy is based on the individual's free will and unique qualities
- **Physiological**—examining the connection between the body and mental health
- **Gestalt**—focusing on the individual's perceptions of the world
- **Cognitive**—purporting that behaviors are influenced by our perspective or our thoughts about a particular situation
- **Sociocultural**—looking at the ways that culture, race/ethnicity, age, habitat, religious affiliation, socioeconomic status, class, and other factors determine our behaviors and beliefs

scious, but according to Freud, it influences who they are and what they do.

Behavioral Perspective

There are several pioneers in the development of the behavioral perspective. The term *behaviorism* was coined by a scientist named John Watson (1878–1958). Behaviorism focuses on behaviors that can be seen. Some refer to these behaviors as public events, and they are the opposite of the private events that occur in the unconscious (one focus of the psychodynamic perspective). Behaviorism asserts that behaviors are influenced by environment. Another pioneer in this field was Ivan Pavlov (1849–1936), who trained a dog to salivate to the sound of a metronome. This procedure is known as *classical* or *Pavlovian conditioning*. You will read about this in chapter 7.

B. F. Skinner (1904–1990) is credited with the development of *operant* or *instrumental conditioning*, which emphasizes the value of the consequences of behaviors. If a child cleans his room and his parents give him $5, the child's positive behavior is likely to happen again. On the other hand, if a child hits his sister and his parents take away television privileges for one week, no positive behaviors have been reinforced, but consequences have been applied to the negative behavior.

Humanistic Perspective

In many ways, the humanistic perspective emerged as a response to the two dominant perspectives of the time: the behavioral and psychodynamic perspectives. Many psychologists believed that the psychodynamic approach overemphasized the unconscious, and they also believed that the behavioral approach was cold and mechanical. Those who adopt the humanistic perspective see the individual as a person with potential who is constantly striving to meet that potential. The emphasis is on an individual's free will and uniqueness. Abraham Maslow and Carl Rogers were pioneers in the humanistic movement. Abraham Maslow (1908–1970) explored the process of *self-actualization*—the journey an individual takes to meet his or her highest potential. Therapist Carl Rogers (1902–1987) developed an approach to therapy that is referred to as *client-centered*, or *person-centered*. The therapist treats his client with warmth, understanding, and respect.

Physiological Perspective

This perspective examines the connection between the body and mental health.

Physiological scientists use tests like computerized axial tomography (CAT) scans, magnetic resonance imaging (MRI), and electroencephalography (EEG) to help them make this important connection. These are all noninvasive tests that study the pathways of the brain and its connection to the body. A scientist who would be considered a pioneer in this psychological orientation is Karl Lashley (1890–1958). Lashley spent many years of his career conducting experiments in an effort to understand how the brain works.

Gestalt Perspective

This perspective focuses on our perceptions of the world. Do we see the world as a whole or as the sum of its parts? The pioneer associated with gestalt psychology is Max Wertheimer (1880–1943). There are many fascinating demonstrations of how our perceptions vary, and how we look at the sum or the parts. Concepts of gestalt are often observable in perception (see chapter 4). For example, when you see a moving arrow or dancing letters on a sign, you are interpreting what you see as movement—you probably do not notice the thousands of small, flashing lights that actually create this illusion. This is called *apparent motion*, and it is covered more fully in chapter 4.

We each have a number of innate tendencies that influence the way we see the world, and although these tendencies are the result of experience and learning, they also tend to have universal qualities.

Cognitive Perspective

The cognitive perspective focuses on the importance of thoughts. The cognitive perspective purports that our perspective or our thoughts about a particular situation influence our behaviors. The scientists associated with this idea are Aaron Beck (1921–) and Martin Seligman (1943–). Aaron Beck has developed an approach to therapy that helps people change their thoughts and therefore change their behavior. The cognitive perspective is not to be confused with cognition, which we cover in chapter 5.

In a classic study by Martin Seligman, Professor of Psychology at the University of Pennsylvania, and his colleague Steven Maier, twenty-four dogs were divided into three groups: the escape group, the no-escape group, and the no-harness control group. The dogs in the escape and no-escape groups were fitted with harnesses and subjected to electric shocks. Dogs in the escape condition had the ability to press a panel on the harness to terminate the shock. The dogs in the control group received no shocks. During the second phase of the experiment, all of the dogs were placed in a box, and ten seconds after the lights were turned out in the box, an electrical current was sent through the floor of the box. All dogs were able to jump over a barrier to escape the shock. After ten trials of the lights–off shock sequence, Seligman and Maier noticed differences in the behaviors of the dogs according to group assignment: dogs in the no-escape condition were less likely to learn to jump over the barrier and escape the shock than were the dogs in the escape and control groups.

Sociocultural Perspective

There is great diversity in our country, and psychology has started to recognize the important role that culture plays in shaping who we are. Culture refers to a whole range of factors. Our culture is determined by our race/ethnicity, our generation or age, where we live, religious affiliation, socioeconomic status, class, and many other factors. Lev Vygotsky (1896–1934) has emphasized the importance of including

the influences from society and culture when trying to understand human behavior.

ENDURING ISSUES IN PSYCHOLOGY

Psychologists don't agree on everything. There are certain issues in the field of psychology that arise repeatedly. Like the chicken and egg debate, these issues may never be resolved. Yet it is important to be aware of these issues and consider your stance. Three of these important issues in psychology are nature versus nurture, person versus situation, and stability versus change.

Nature versus Nurture

We all know a family like the Smith family. There are two parents, Stanley and Sue, and two kids, Adam and Austin. Both children have been raised in a home that is loving and warm, yet these two brothers are very different.

Adam is outgoing and popular with his peers. He is a straight A student and the president of his high school's student council. He volunteers to read to sick children at his local hospital. He is the captain of his school's football team. He was recently accepted to a prestigious college where he plans to major in chemistry. He plans to attend medical school and specialize in pediatrics after college.

Austin is two years older than Adam. He recently returned home after being kicked out of the military. Austin is quiet and spends most of his time alone in his room where he enjoys watching television. He only emerges from his room to grab a bite from the kitchen. Austin's high school career was uneventful, and most other students in his graduating class did not know him. He did not participate in sports or any extracurricular activities. He left for basic training the day after his high school graduation. After a year in the military, he was discharged after an unexplained, unauthorized leave (absent without leave, or AWOL).

The nature/nurture controversy asks: Are we products of our genes (nature)? If that is the case, then Adam and Austin should be the same, since they are both the biological children of Stanley and Sue. Or are we products of our environment (nurture)? What if you discovered that Stanley and Sue were only seventeen when Austin was conceived? They weren't ready for the responsibility of parenthood, but they married and raised Austin together. As a result of her early, unplanned motherhood, Sue resents Austin and all the missed opportunities he represents. Such information might lead you to support the nurture side of the argument. What if, on the other hand, you learned that Austin inherited a rare medical condition that resulted in many childhood hospitalizations and impacted his ability to attend school? Such information might lead you to support the nature side of the argument. Some people strongly believe that we are products of our genes; others believe that we are products of our environment. In actuality, most psychologists agree that we are products of both. It is difficult to tell how much our genetic makeup determines our fate compared with the influence of the environment in which we are raised.

Person versus Situation

We have all been surprised at times by our own behavior or by that of someone else. Maybe you know someone who is described as quiet and withdrawn by classmates, but who goes out to parties on the weekend and becomes outgoing and social. Parents sometimes describe their child in one way, yet the child's teacher describes him in a very different manner. This leads us to wonder whether people change depending on the environment in which they find themselves or whether they stay the same no matter where they go. This is the person versus situation controversy, and again, most believe that the answer is not either/or, but instead falls somewhere in the middle.

Stability versus Change

We've all heard the saying: you can't teach an old dog new tricks. One of the most important questions in psychology is whether or not we have the ability to change. If we can't change, does that mean that the cold and distant person can never express warm or intimate sentiments? Think about self-perceptions that you may have had during adolescence. Do you believe that you are fundamentally the same person now as you were then? The big question is whether or not psychologists are wasting their time developing treatments to help people with problems when, in fact, people are unable to change their basic self-perceptions.

ENDURING ISSUES IN PSYCHOLOGY

- **Nature versus Nurture**—Are we a product of our genetic makeup or our environment?

- **Person versus Situation**—Do we change depending on our environment, or are we the same person wherever we go?

- **Stability versus Change**—Are we fundamentally the same person throughout life, or can different kinds of therapy or self-awareness change our perceptions, and thus our behaviors?

FIELDS AND CAREERS IN PSYCHOLOGY

There are not only numerous perspectives in psychology, but there are also many enduring issues of nature versus nurture, person versus situation, and stability versus change that impact the view of every individual psychologist. As a result, there are many different approaches and fields for a person who decides to pursue psychology as a career.

Who gets to be called a psychologist? And what does a psychologist actually do? First of all, a psychologist has advanced graduate training in one or several different fields. The graduate training takes the form of a master's degree, two years of study beyond a bachelor's degree. A psychologist might also choose to obtain a doctoral degree, which takes approximately four to six years of study following the undergraduate degree.

There are several types of doctoral degrees in psychology. There is the Ph.D., which stands for doctor of philosophy; the Psy.D., doctor of psychology; and the Ed.D., doctor of education. The doctoral degrees differ in the type of coursework undertaken or the school of study. With the Ph.D., there is an emphasis on research (or research and clinical work). The Psy.D. places an emphasis on clinical training, and the Ed.D. is typically offered through a school's department of education rather than the department of psychology.

So, the next time you make an appointment to consult with Alexis Johnson, Ph.D., but are then referred to Jack Cho, Psy.D., who encourages you to contact his associate Shawn MacMurphy, Ed.D., you'll be able to distinguish among the three. If the office door of a counselor reads Madison Tyler, M.A., that person has a master's degree.

What do you think when someone tells you that he is a psychologist? Do you envision Sigmund Freud in an office with a client laying prostrate on the couch? Or do you think of a scientist in a laboratory with a rat in a maze? Either view, or a combination of the two, could be correct. Psychologists may work as clinicians and provide mental health services for those in need. They may also work as researchers who conduct experiments with animals. In addition, psychologists work in corporations where they consult with executives about issues of employee satisfaction. Psychologists also work in college and university settings where they educate and inspire future psychologists. There are many fields in psychology.

Clinical Psychology

Clinical psychologists assess, diagnose, and treat people with disorders. Assessment involves interviewing and/or testing the client and people close to the client, such as the spouse/partner, parents, and children. This assessment allows the clinician to understand the problem and to develop a diagnosis for the client. After the clinician has developed a diagnosis, treatment will begin. Treatment may take the form of individual, couples, family, or group therapy (or a combination of those). Clinical psychologists may specialize in the treatment of a particular mental disorder, such as schizophrenia, phobias, or eating disorders, or they may work with a particular population, such as children, chronically mentally ill individuals, or the elderly.

Counseling Psychology

Counseling psychologists also assess, diagnose, and treat people, but counseling psychologists tend to focus on people with less severe problems than do clinical psychologists. For example, a counseling psychologist may work with a couple with marital problems or a child who has problems interacting with peers.

Community Psychology

Community psychology is all around you. What do you do in case of a fire? Did you answer, "stop, drop, and roll"? Have you ever heard of MADD or SADD? You probably know that MADD stands for Mothers Against Drunk Driving, and SADD stands for Students Against Drunk Driving. Those organizations may have placed a severely damaged car in front of your town's city hall or presented information about the consequences of drunk driving. Those are just a few examples of community psychology at work. Community psychologists focus on changing the behavior of groups rather than individuals and on preventing problem behaviors such as irresponsible driving.

Developmental Psychology

Many think that developmental psychology is synonymous with child psychology, but development does not end with adulthood. You obviously don't look like you did ten or twenty years ago. You are certainly physically different, but you are socially, cognitively, and emotionally different as well. You will also be quite different ten, twenty, or thirty years from now. Some developmental psychologists study the growth and development of infants; others focus on children, and still others on adults.

Educational Psychology

Remember your most rewarding educational experience, and think about what made it so wonderful. Perhaps it was the teacher's approach to teaching the information or your approach to learning new material. Did you study with others? Did you study alone? Did you cram everything into one intense study session the night before the exam? Educational psychologists are interested in how we teach and how we learn. They aspire to develop methods to improve teaching and learning.

Experimental Psychology

There is great variety within the experimental-psychology field of study. Some experimental psychologists focus on animals, and others focus on adults. What the psychologists have in common is the use of scientific procedures to gain a better understanding of some process,

such as memory. For instance, does a rat take longer to run through the maze when a piece of cheese is waiting at the end, or does the rat take longer to run through a maze when another rat, a friend, is waiting at the end of the maze?

Forensic Psychology

Many students are interested in the emerging field of forensic psychology. They've watched *Silence of the Lambs*, *CSI*, *Profiler*, or one of the many other movies or television shows that involve criminal investigation, and now they want to become forensic psychologists. This field of psychology combines psychology and law to gain an understanding of human behavior.

Health Psychology

We all know people who put off going to the dentist or who forget to take their medications. Health psychologists are interested in factors that impact health.

There are a lot of things that can be done to maintain current good health among the healthy population. For example, much work has gone into the prevention of sexually transmitted diseases. For people who are not healthy, much can be done to improve their health or to maintain their current state of health. Health psychologists work on such issues as getting patients to take their medications as prescribed.

Industrial/Organizational Psychology

Industrial/organizational psychologists, or I/O psychologists, focus on the work environment and on what can be done to increase employee satisfaction, which impacts employee productivity and staff turnover. To make a group of employees happier, they might consider a range of ideas, such as offering stock options, flex hours, on-site daycare, or dress-down Fridays.

Physiological Psychology

Simply put, physiological psychologists are interested in the connection between the brain and behavior. They study the structure and function of the brain to understand fully how it influences behavior. An area of psychology that is similar to physiological psychology is behavioral neuroscience, a broader term that encompasses the biological basis of animal behavior. Finally, there is the field of neuropsychology that focuses on the diagnosis and treatment of brain disorders. A wonderful book by neurologist Oliver Sacks, entitled *The Man Who Mistook His Wife for a Hat: And Other Clinical Tales*, chronicles how human behavior can change as a result of brain injury. Neuropsychologists are trained to assess and treat people who have had some damage as a result of a brain injury.

Rehabilitation Psychology

When an accident results in brain damage, a neuropsychologist assesses the damage and designs a course of treatment for the client. A rehabilitation psychologist may also work with this client. Rehabilitation psychologists work with people who have disabilities resulting from epilepsy, mental retardation, or a stroke. The goal of these psychologists is to help their clients adjust socially, physically, and emotionally to daily living.

School Psychology

When you think of the job of a school psychologist, what comes to mind? Most people think of the psychologist who is housed in an office at an elementary, middle, or high school. Although school psychologists do provide mental health services for students and their families, they do even more. School psychologists are responsible for diagnosing and assessing disabilities that impact learning and for developing programs and modifications to curricula designed to make learners successful.

Social Psychology

Humans are all social beings, whether one is a loner who avoids social contact or a social butterfly who thrives on interaction. Social psychologists are interested in how individuals are impacted by their social interactions with others—both with individuals and in groups.

Sports Psychology

Every athlete wants to run faster, hit the ball farther, or jump higher. Obviously, these are issues that an athlete might discuss with his coach, but athletes may pose the same question to a sports psychologist. Sports psychologists work with athletes to help them improve their athletic performance. They may use relaxation training to reduce an athlete's performance anxiety. They may also employ such techniques as self-talk, a strategy with cognitive roots in which the athletes make reaffirming statements about themselves and their abilities, such as "I am strong, and I can do it."

FIELDS IN PSYCHOLOGY

- Clinical psychology
- Counseling psychology
- Community psychology
- Developmental psychology
- Educational psychology
- Experimental psychology
- Forensic psychology
- Health psychology
- Industrial/organizational psychology
- Physiological psychology
- Rehabilitation psychology
- School psychology
- Social psychology
- Sports psychology

FIELDS AND SETTINGS

Obviously, psychology encompasses a variety of fields and careers. It is important to note that there is overlap between fields. For example, some clinical psychologists have an interest in children, so they may receive training in both clinical and developmental psychology. Some social psychologists have an interest in how our behavior is impacted by the legal system, so they may receive training in social and forensic psychology.

One of the perks associated with the field of psychology is that job opportunities can place psychologists in many different settings where they can thrive. Psychologists may be found in educational settings as clinicians, researchers, or educators. Psychologists may be found in clinics or hospitals as clinicians and/or researchers. Psychologists are in corporations, in sports settings, and in the government. Simply put, psychologists are just about everywhere.

CHAPTER SUMMARY

Psychology is a broad field that aims to understand behavior, both human and nonhuman. The history of psychology is a long one, but modern psychology was inspired by the works of Wilhelm Wundt and William James, who attempted to understand behavior.

There are differing viewpoints about the approaches psychologists should use as they attempt to attain this understanding. These approaches include psychodynamic, behavioral, humanistic, physiological, cognitive, gestalt, and sociocultural perspectives.

It is also important to understand the never-ending debates in psychology, the issues that may never be resolved—like the question of which came first, the chicken or the egg. Psychological debates that will continue include nature versus nurture, person versus situation, and stability versus change.

There is also a wide variety of careers in psychology. Psychologists may work in settings that range from hospitals and clinics to universities and athletic fields.

TEST YOUR RECALL AND RECOGNITION

True/False

1. Psychology only focuses on human behavior.

2. A school psychologist may lead workshops for parents and teachers about the effects of exposure to violence.

3. Developmental psychology is the same as child psychology.

4. The campaign against drunk driving is an example of community psychology at work.

5. After a sports injury, an athlete may visit a rehabilitation psychologist.

6. The nature in the nature versus nurture controversy refers to environmental influences.

7. Wilhelm Wundt developed the first psychological laboratory.

8. Sigmund Freud was trained as a clinical psychologist.

9. Behavioral psychologists are most interested in the thoughts of their clients.

10. The role of culture in human behavior has long been addressed by the field of psychology.

Multiple Choice

1. Last night, Mia watched the movie *Silence of the Lambs,* and now she thinks that she would like to become the type of psychologist who helps police officers solve crimes. What field of psychology has piqued Mia's interest?

    a. rehabilitation psychology

    b. developmental psychology

    c. forensic psychology

    d. sports psychology

2. Psychologists might work in which of the following settings?

   a. hospitals

   b. schools

   c. clinics

   d. all of the above

3. Shawn and Marie are having marital problems that seem to stem from Shawn's long work hours and Marie's inability to find a job. They are referred to a psychologist who helps them with their adjustment problems. What type of psychologist would they be most likely to see?

   a. community psychologist

   b. industrial/organizational psychologist

   c. counseling psychologist

   d. neuropsychologist

4. Alexandra noticed a decrease in productivity at her bakery. The bakers and cashiers were calling in sick or showing up late. Alexandra consulted with a psychologist who suggested how Alexandra might improve work conditions. What type of psychologist assisted Alexandra?

   a. industrial/organizational psychologist

   b. developmental psychologist

   c. sports psychologist

   d. school psychologist

5. Which of the following is *not* an orientation/perspective of psychology?

   a. behavioral

   b. sociocultural

   c. responsive

   d. physiological

6. Which perspective emphasizes observable events?

   a. psychodynamic

   b. cognitive

   c. behavioral

   d. humanistic

7. Maslow and Rogers are associated with which perspective of psychology?

   a. gestalt

   b. humanistic

   c. sociocultural

   d. cognitive

8. Sarah's friends describe her as a pessimist. She believes that the world is a dangerous place where few are to be trusted. Her beliefs about the world have had a negative impact on her social life. Her therapist attempts to assist her by helping her to change her view of the world. Sarah's therapist probably has what type of orientation?

   a. physiological

   b. cognitive

   c. psychodynamic

   d. behavioral

9. Psychologists who subscribe to more than one orientation may describe themselves as

   a. multidimensional.

   b. eclectic.

   c. indecisive.

   d. none of the above.

10. Enduring issues in psychology have not yet been resolved, but
   a. solutions are only a matter of years away.
   b. will continue to yield excellent debate.
   c. neither a nor b is correct.
   d. both a and b are correct.

Fill in the Blanks

1. _____ psychologists work with businesses to improve employee satisfaction and productivity.
2. Sharon assesses, diagnoses, and treats individuals with mental disorders. Sharon is a _____ psychologist.
3. Susan works with the women's softball team. Her task is to monitor the mental health of all team members and to assist the coach with the improvement of each team member's athletic performance. Susan is a(n) _____ psychologist.
4. _____ coined the term *behaviorism*.
5. EEG, MRI, and CAT scans are tests that may be used by someone with a(n) _____ approach to psychology.
6. _____developed as a reaction to psychodynamic and behavioral perspectives.
7. According to the cognitive perspective, thoughts may impact _____.
8. Vygotsky is associated with the _____, which considers _____ important features.
9. Nature is to genes, what nurture is to _____.
10. Do we change as we age or are we fundamentally the same throughout life? The _____ controversy would address this statement.

ANSWERS TO QUESTIONS
True/False

1. false	6. false
2. true	7. true
3. false	8. false
4. true	9. false
5. true	10. false

Multiple Choice

1. c	6. c
2. d	7. b
3. c	8. b
4. a	9. b
5. c	10. b

Fill in the Blanks

1. I/O
2. clinical
3. sports
4. John Watson
5. physiological
6. The humanistic perspective
7. behavior
8. sociocultural perspective; society and culture
9. environment
10. stability versus change

ADDITIONAL RESOURCES
Books

Hilgard, E. R. 1987. *Psychology in America: A historical survey.* San Diego: Harcourt Brace Jovanovich.

Sacks, O. W. 1985. *The man who mistook his wife for a hat: And other clinical tales.* New York: Summit Books.

Seligman, M. E. P. and S. F. Maier. 1967. "Failure to escape traumatic shock." *Journal of Experimental Psychology,* 74: 1–9.

Wood, P. J. (1987). *Is psychology the major for you?* Washington, DC: American Psychological Association.

Video

Discovering psychology: Updated edition, video recording, produced by WGBH Boston with the American Psychological Association (2001; S. Burlington, VT: Annenberg/CPB).

Web sites

American Psychological Association, www.apa.org

American Psychological Society, www.psychologicalscience.org

Encyclopedia of Psychology, www.psychology.org

STATISTICS AND RESEARCH METHODS IN PSYCHOLOGY

KEY TERMS

quantitative, qualitative, descriptive statistics, inferential statistics, naturalistic observation, correlational research

It's not always easy to make the connection between statistics and the science of psychology. We wonder how graphs and numbers ever relate to people. But psychologists, just like other scientists, are involved in research, and statistics help them to make sense of the jumble of information that comes from a variety of research methods.

In fact, statistics are something we all deal with on an everyday basis. The radio DJ reports that the median household income has increased; the meteorologist tells us that there is an 85 percent chance of rain; we read that our favorite political candidate leads by a certain amount, with a certain margin of error; and our instructor informs us that on the most recent exam the average score was 75.

We use statistics to help us make sense of data and to organize and understand data. Although this information may sometimes be in the form of numbers and is called *quantitative*, other data may be people's opinions or feelings and is called *qualitative* data. Qualitative data can be equally valuable, although a little harder to "count." Both kinds of research are important in psychology.

Qualitative data can come from surveys, questionnaires, discussions, and a variety of other sources. It tends to be more subjective rather than numerical.

Qualitative and quantitative information obviously has to be organized in different ways. Test scores, ranging from 50 to 100 with an average of 75, are fairly easy to understand. Organizing the information about how the students felt about the test requires a slightly different format.

Learning statistics is like learning a new language. It requires knowledge of symbols, formulas, and new vocabulary terms. But to understand how statistics aid in psychological research, you merely need to understand some basic concepts about statistics and research.

Statistics can be broken down into two categories: descriptive and inferential. Descriptive statistics allow us to describe data. Inferential statistics enable us to use our data to draw conclusions about a research study.

STATISTICS

Descriptive Statistics

Descriptive statistics allow us to take information, known as data, and make sense of that data. There are several types of descriptive statistics, but two of the most frequently used are measures of central tendency and measures of variability. If you were given some numbers and asked to summarize or describe those numbers, descriptive statistics would enable you to do so.

Measures of Central Tendency

When analyzing data, most people usually ask, "What is a typical score?" Measures of central tendency help us answer this query. They give us indications regarding the typical score in a set of data. The three measures of central tendency are *mean*, *median*, and *mode*.

Here's how to apply measures of central tendency. If we use the example of a test with scores ranging from 50 to 100, we might list the results this way:

	X
Daniel	60
Suzanne	50
Craig	85
Allison	100
Hillary	80
Meaghan	80
Erica	95
Thomas	65
Stephen	60
	$675 = \Sigma X$

We have a total of 675 points. In statistics, this sum is known as ΣX; Σ is the Greek letter sigma, and it is used in statistics to represent the sum of whatever follows it. The variable X represents the test scores, which can be measured and are different for each individual. Therefore, ΣX stands for the sum of all of the test scores.

If we take our total of 675 points and divide it by nine, our total number of students, we have an average of 75 points per student. In

statistics the average is also called the *mean*. That is the first measure of central tendency.

The second measure is the *median*, or simply put, the middle number in an array of numbers. If the students' test scores were arranged in numerical order (from lowest grade to highest grade), they would look like this:

50 60 60 65 **80** 80 85 95 100

The median, or the number in the middle, is 80.

The final measure of central tendency is the *mode*. This is the number that appears most often. Take a second look at the scores:

50 **60 60** 65 **80 80** 85 95 100

Both 60 and 80 appear twice, so this distribution is called *bimodal*. Sometimes there is no mode, or one mode, or more than two modes (multimodal). These measures of central tendency allow us to use one number to summarize or describe a group of numbers.

Measures of Variability

Measures of variability are simply different ways to look at the range of numbers presented. Variability allows us to describe the data by looking at whether the numbers are tightly clustered, or whether they are widely spread. Measures of variability include the range and the *standard deviation*.

Our lowest score on the test was 50, and the highest was 100; therefore, the range, or spread, was 50 points. To calculate the range, subtract the lowest score from the highest. We know that some students grasped all the information, and some didn't understand the material. If the highest score was still 100 and the numbers had a very small spread, for instance between 10 and 20, then we would know that all nine students had mastered the material given on the test.

We can also look at the standard deviation, or the distance between a particular score and the mean. It tells us where one person stands compared to the group. For example, Allison received a score of 100, but the average or mean score was 75. She scored 25 points higher than everyone else. Simply put, Allison's score was higher than the mean. We know that our mean on this test was 75, so there was a 25-point gap between both the highest and lowest scores.

Analyzing Qualitative Data

As discussed, data may also take nonnumeric forms. Consider the class of nine students with an average grade of 75 on the test. We have the number of students, the actual grades, the mean, median, and mode. But what if we did a survey of the students asking them about test conditions, preparation for the test, appropriateness of lectures beforehand, or how much sleep they got the night before? This information is not "countable." We can't necessarily graph it, but it is equally valuable.

Researchers take information from interviews or focus groups and use it to gain an understanding about some psychological phenomenon or area of interest. Just as there are methods to help us make sense of quantitative data and methods of data analysis, there are methods of analysis to help us organize qualitative data. Perhaps researchers host a rap session, where a variety of people sit around and talk about particular issues. Responses are recorded, and then the researchers look for patterns in the responses. There might be, for example, topics

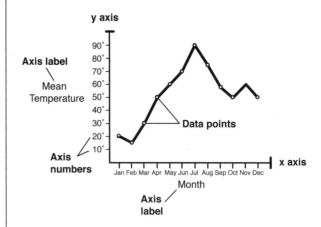

Elements of a Graph

that were frequently mentioned or certain themes in the responses.

Other Issues in Descriptive Statistics

In order to understand descriptive statistics, it is important to have a basic understanding of graphing and the distinction between *sample* and *population*.

- The x-axis, also referred to as the *abscissa*, is the horizontal line on the graph.

- The y-axis, also referred to as the *ordinate*, is the vertical line on the graph.

- Axis labels describe variables for each axis.

- Axis numbers are important so that anyone can read your graph with ease.

- Data points indicate the placement of the data on the graph.

Learning to read a graph can help us to absorb substantial amounts of data. Psychologists may be dealing with groups of thousands of people and many different variables. Using the tools of statistics allows them to group, categorize, and analyze information in a manageable way.

Sample versus Population

When we study a sample of a whole population, the population is the entire group, and the sample is a subset of the population. In our class, with their test scores, our students comprise the whole population. Parameters are used to describe the data from a population. Statistics describe the data from a sample.

Researchers often attempt to make decisions about a population through the use of a sample. For example, is sleep deprivation contributing to some of the lower grades on this test? We can't interview every single college student, but we could take a sample of college students, either from this class or a number of classes, interview them, and make some statements about that population.

Because it is important that the sample is representative of the population, it probably wouldn't be wise to use a subset of this one small class. We would need a greater number of students from a variety of classes. The larger sample should consist of both men and women of varying races/ethnicities, religions, and sexual orientations. To ensure the quality of our sample, we can use a process called *random sampling*. Such sampling means that every member of the population has an equal chance of being selected for the sample.

Inferential Statistics

When we gather data and develop some ideas based on that material, we are making an inference. An inference means making some kind of judgment about a feature of a population based solely on information obtained from a sample of that population.

In our sample class, test scores ranged from 50 to 100. What can we infer from that? We suggested that sleep deprivation might be a factor, but we haven't done the research to support that theory. Perhaps the professor is particularly difficult and not everyone is keeping up. Maybe those students with low scores missed too many lectures.

Inferential statistics provide us with formulas and models for making these kinds of judgments, but in this case, we need more information first. When the results of a study can be generalized to a larger population, it means that the study has good *external validity*. Our sample of nine students might provide the professor with important information about how appropriate his tests are, or whether or not his lectures are comprehended by the students. However, our sample is not adequate (large enough) to make statements about the larger college population.

RESEARCH METHODS

Psychology is a science. People associate certain tools of the trade with certain professionals. A chef uses a blender and measuring cups; a mechanic needs a screwdriver and oil pan; and a painter employs a ladder and paintbrush. One of the most important tools used by psychologists who conduct research are research methods. Although the methods are listed as separate and distinct, in reality, research projects may combine one or more of these methods. The psychologist's tools include naturalistic observation, case study, survey, correlational research, and experimental methods.

Naturalistic Observation

If you were interested in studying children's behavior, you might go to your local playground, plant yourself on a bench, and watch.

If you were interested in the behavior of ducks, you might go to a lake and observe. One way to collect information about behavior is through the process of observation. *Naturalistic observation* allows you to view the subject in his/her natural habitat or setting.

There are some advantages and disadvantages to this research method. The advantage is that the behavior you see is more likely to be an appropriate representation of how the subject typically behaves. The disadvantage is that you may not get a chance to see the behavior you are waiting to see.

For example, if you are interested in the feeding behavior of ducks, and you go to the lake to observe this behavior, you may have to sit and wait until the ducks find a suitable meal. Naturalistic observation does not always guarantee that the behavior of interest will occur.

One solution to the problem in naturalistic observation is observation in a contrived setting where the researcher creates the necessary conditions so that the behavior of interest is certain to occur. For example, the researcher could place the ducks in a laboratory and give them their favorite meal.

Case Study

A case study usually involves one person. Sybil Dorsett, a woman who was diagnosed with dissociative identity disorder (see chapter 12), was the subject of a famous case study.

Case studies often help scientists understand a disorder that is rare or new. The researcher conducts in-depth interviews with the subject and then summarizes the findings. The advan-tage of a case study is that it allows the researcher to learn something about a disorder with which many may be unfamiliar. The disadvantage is that the findings from a case study cannot be generalized to the population and, therefore, have no external validity.

Survey

We've all been called by market researchers who want to know about our favorite fabric softener. Then, in the mall, there are the people with clipboards who want to know what type of toothpaste we use. These are examples of surveys.

Psychologists are interested in understanding human behavior, and one way to collect information about this behavior is by direct observation. Another way is by asking people who know the person whose behavior inter-ests us (indirect observation). A third way is by having that person complete a survey.

A survey may take the form of a questionnaire, and the questions may look much like the questions at the end of each chapter of this book. They may be open-ended, like the fill-in-the-blank questions, or closed-ended, like multiple choice and true/false questions. The advantage of survey research is that it allows the researcher to collect a large amount of data in a short amount of time. The major disadvantage is that the researcher is totally dependent on the accuracy of the subject's report.

Correlational Research

What's the relationship between height and shoe size? If you said the bigger the feet, the taller the person, you are correct. If you said the smaller the feet, the shorter the person, you are also correct. Correlational research allows us to discuss the relationships between variables.

Correlations can be described in three ways: positive, negative, and no correlation. A *positive correlation* means that as one variable increases, so does the other, or as one variable decreases, so does the other. There is a positive correlation between height and shoe size.

A *negative correlation* means that as one variable increases the other decreases. Some may say that there is a negative corre-lation between the number of hours spent watching television and the number of hours spent socializing with friends.

Finally, where there is no relationship, we say there is *no correlation*. For instance, there is no correlation between shoe size and grades.

There is a common and very important saying in correlational research: "Correlation does not imply causation." This statement simply means that we can't say anything about the causes of a phenomenon. We can't say that having big feet causes someone to be tall, or that having small feet causes someone to be short. We can only say there is a relationship between the variables. An advantage of the correlational method is that it allows the researcher to determine the existence of a relationship. A disadvantage of the correlational method is that is says nothing about cause and effect.

Experimental Methods

If you want to know about cause and effect, the experimental method is the one to use. It allows you to make decisions about cause and effect.

EXPERIMENTAL METHOD VOCABULARY

- The independent variable is manipulated by the researcher to test its impact on the dependent variable.

- The dependent variable is measured by the researcher.

- The control group does not receive any treatment.

- The treatment group, or experimental group, receives treatment.

- A placebo is a treatment without any active ingredient. The sugar pill is a classic example.

Sometimes, the expectations of the researcher or the subject may lead to things that might influence the study. Blind studies guard against this. In a type called *single-blind study*, the participant or the experimenter, but not both, is unaware of the condition to which he has been assigned or has assigned subjects. In other words, the individual doesn't know if he is in the control group, which receives a placebo, or in the experimental group, which receives actual treatment. In a *double-blind study*, neither the participants nor the researcher know which group the participants, or subjects, have been assigned to.

If a researcher wants to examine the effect of a new acne medication on the face, she might divide the subjects into two groups. Those who receive a pill that contains the acne medication are in the experimental/ treatment group; the control group receives the placebo, or sugar pill. The amount of acne is the *dependent variable*; after it is measured, the subjects are given either the medication or the placebo.

The subjects are instructed to return two weeks later. When they return, the researcher will measure the amount of acne on their faces. The researcher predicts that those who use the medication will demonstrate a decrease in breakouts as compared to those who do not receive the medication. This last statement refers to the hypothesis, which is the prediction made by the researcher on the outcome of the study. The goal of research is to test the hypothesis.

Hypothesis Testing

There are four steps in hypothesis testing: 1) state the hypothesis, 2) set critical regions which are used in decision making, 3) analyze the data using the necessary statistics, and 4) make the decision. Does the data support the hypothesis?

The decision is stated in one of two ways. If the data shows that there are differences between groups, then the acne medication has been effective. For example, those who received the acne medication had fewer pimples (after two weeks of medication) than those who received the placebo.

Remember, the hypothesis was the prediction, made by the researcher, about the outcome of the study. Actually, this prediction consists of two predictions, the null hypothesis, and the alternative hypothesis. The *null hypothesis* says that there will be no difference between the two groups. The *alternative hypothesis* states that there is some difference between groups.

There are two types of errors one could make, and the concepts of Type I and Type II errors are at the heart of hypothesis testing. In Type I error, the researcher says that the manipulation caused a difference, when in actuality it did not. In Type II error, the researcher says that the manipulation made no difference, when it actually did.

In conclusion, experimental methods allow the researcher to make decisions about cause and effect. The disadvantages include many potential design problems that could impact the research findings. For instance, the subjects may know about condition assignments, and this could impact their behavior and the dependent variable.

Other Research Methods

Longitudinal and Cross-sectional Studies

Researchers may decide to study their subjects using a longitudinal approach or a cross-sectional approach. There are pros and cons to each approach.

Longitudinal studies follow the same subject(s) over a period of time. If we wanted to understand social development in children through longitudinal research, we might interview a child every year throughout her childhood. Such a project would allow us to chronicle the changes that occur and appreciate the child's blossoming social skills and interactions.

A classic example of longitudinal research is a film started by Michael Apted in 1964. He interviewed 14 British seven year olds in an effort to understand the impact of social class on school children. Apted interviewed them again every seven years and captured these interviews on film. The result of the most recent interviews is the film *42 Up* which was released in theaters in 1999 and is available on video. One advantage of longitudinal research is that the researcher obtains a true picture of development over a period of time. The disadvantages are that people may drop out of the project, the research can be expensive, and it is obviously time-consuming.

Cross-sectional studies capture information about changes over time through interviews of several groups at one period in time. If we are trying to understand social development in children using a cross-sectional study, we would interview a group of five year olds, a group of ten year olds, and then a group of fifteen year olds. The advantage of cross-sectional research is that it is less expensive than longitudinal research, and the researcher does not have to wait ten years to understand social development in children.

One major disadvantage of cross-sectional studies involves something called *cohort effects*. Let's say we wanted to test the effectiveness of a new software package that teaches people to type. We want to find out if people of all ages find the software effective. We give this package to a group of fifteen year olds, a group of forty-five year olds, and a group of seventy-five year olds. We measure typing speed before and after use of the typing tutorial.

We may find differences among the groups that have nothing to do with our tutorial; instead, the differences represent generational differences. The youngest group has grown up using software, and so their ability to manipulate the software successfully may differ from the oldest group, who may not be as familiar with computer technology. Some of our findings may be a result of the different experiences and histories of the different groups. These are cohort effects.

WHAT HAPPENS AFTER THE RESEARCH?

Researchers collect data, analyze that data, and ultimately share their findings. Sometimes the end product of research in the field of psychology is a journal article, which may be found in one of the many psychological journals. An excellent text that provides a detailed review of the components of the research article is the *Publication Manual of the American Psychological Association*, 5th ed.

The pieces of a research article are as follows:

- **Abstract**—The abstract is a summary of the article.

- **Introduction**—The introduction includes a literature review, which covers research articles on the topic, a rationale for the current study, and the hypothesis for the current study.

- **Method**—The method explains what the researcher did and includes a section on the subjects, or partcipants (what gender, how old, how many), and a section on equipment (EEG, MRI) or materials, such as a particular questionnaire or test that was used.

- **Results**—The results present the statistical analyses and explain the tests conducted and the findings.

- **Discussion**—The researcher talks about the findings and hypothesis, criticisms of the research, and implications for future research.

- **References**—The researchers acknowledge the work of others. This is very important because it is unethical to take the work of someone else and use it as your own. In addition, if the reader really likes the article and wants more information, the reference section is a good place to look for citations about other articles on the same subject.

• **Appendix**—The appendix can include copies of questionnaires that were used in the study or other supplemental information.

SOFTWARE IN RESEARCH

The examples of research in this chapter have been very simple; obviously there are many times when the sheer quantity of research numbers or elements can be overwhelming to the researcher. Finding the average of nine students' grades can quickly be done on a calculator, but the researcher who has just collected data from one thousand first graders is not going to get too far computing averages in this manner.

Computer software exists that aids the researcher in quick and accurate analysis of data. The most commonly used packages include SPSS, SAS, Microsoft Excel, Statistica and Statview/JMK. These packages are becoming more user friendly and require less training. Data entry may be as straightforward as using a spreadsheet and data analysis or as simple as selecting an appropriate test and entering the appropriate variables.

CHAPTER SUMMARY

In chapter 1, we identified psychology as a science. When psychologists speak of research methods, they are referring to the tools they use in the science of psychology. These include particular methods that guide how research should be conducted and statistics that help us organize and make sense of the data.

There are two types of statistics: descriptive and inferential. Descriptive statistics allow us to describe the data. Examples might be measures of central tendency and measures of variability. Inferential statistics allow us to make statements about the data. For instance, did the subjects who took the acne medication have fewer pimples than those who took the placebo?

Research methods are numerous. Naturalistic observation enables the scientist to learn about behavior by observing a subject in his natural habitat. The case study allows the researcher to gain an in-depth understanding of a topic by collecting data from one subject related to some matter. Surveys provide the researcher with information through the use of interviews or questionnaires. In correlational research, the researcher looks at the relationship between variables. The experimental research method allows the researcher to look at cause and effect. Understanding the experimental methods requires that the researcher understand some new vocabulary, such as independent variable, dependent variable, treatment group, control group, placebo, blind studies, and hypothesis. Longitudinal and cross-sectional studies also allow the researcher to understand developmental processes in psychology.

Computer software helps scientists analyze the data. Although we have focused on quantitative data that takes the form of numbers, there is also qualitative data. The data may be collected through interviews or through focus groups. There are also software packages that help with the analysis of qualitative data.

Finally, when the research is done, the information is shared. Psychologists may publish their studies in many places, but there is a format for the article. All research articles include an abstract, introduction, method section, results section, discussion section, and references.

TEST YOUR RECALL AND RECOGNITION

True/False

1. The data used in statistics only comes in numerical form.

2. Two categories of statistics are descriptive and inferential.

3. There are three measures of central tendency.

4. The correlational research method allows a researcher to look at the relationship between variables.

5. The group that receives the placebo is called the treatment group.

6. Double-blind studies solve the problems of experimenter and subject bias.

7. The median is the middle number in an array of numbers.

8. Two incorrect decisions made by the researcher are called Type Y error and Type Z error.

9. The abstract is a component of the research article.

10. If you want to view the statistical tests that were used in a study, you would refer to the results section of the research article.

Multiple Choice

1. Which of the following is *not* a research method?
   a. case study
   b. survey
   c. study groups
   d. naturalistic observation

2. The x axis is also referred to as the
   a. ordinate.   c. vertical line.
   b. abscissa.   d. none of the above.

3. The mean in a group of numbers is the
   a. total.   c. highest.
   b. average.   d. lowest.

4. Allen has an interest in a psychological disorder that is relatively rare. There are only five reported cases of this disorder. He has decided to create a study to learn more about this disease. Which type of study would be most appropriate?
   a. naturalistic observation
   b. correlational study
   c. experimental study
   d. case study

5. Zoe has designed a study to examine the effects of exercise on mood. She has recruited one hundred subjects for her project. She has assigned subjects to one of two groups: the exercise group or the no-exercise group. Those in the exercise group are instructed to exercise every day for one month. Those in the no-exercise group are instructed to abstain from all forms of exercise for one month. Zoe measured mood at the beginning of the month, assigned participants to one of the groups, and measured mood again at

the end of the month. In this study, mood is the

a. dependent variable.

b. independent variable.

c. placebo.

d. treatment.

6. The control group receives

a. the same treatment as the experimental group.

b. a treatment that differs from the treatment received by the experimental group.

c. no treatment.

d. none of the above.

7. A problem associated with case studies is

a. the availability of naturalistic observation.

b. access to statistical information.

c. inability to generalize to the whole population.

d. the lack of surveys.

8. A problem associated with longitudinal studies is

a. attrition.

b. expense.

c. time.

d. all of the above.

9. The summary of the article can be found in which part of the research article?

a. introduction

b. results

c. method

d. abstract

10. If you read a study, enjoy it, and would like to read other related articles that the researcher refers to throughout the journal article, you should refer to the _____ section.

a. results

b. method

c. references

d. introduction

Fill in the Blanks

1. The _____ is the number in the middle of an array of numbers.

2. Measures of _____ describe the spread of numbers.

3. Statistic is to _____ as parameter is to _____.

4. Case studies and surveys are examples of _____ methods.

5. A person with a clipboard approaches you in the mall and asks about your shopping habits. This person is using a(n) _____ method.

6. Correlation does not imply _____.

7. The researcher manipulates the _____ and measures the _____.

8. The null hypothesis signifies _____. The alternative hypothesis shows a _____.

9. Beverly interviews twenty-five men about their relationships with their children. She plans to summarize comments from these interviews and write an article about parenting. Beverly's data can be described as _____.

10. The section of the research article that contains information about participants and equipment is the _____ section.

ANSWERS TO QUESTIONS

True/False

1. false	6. true
2. true	7. true
3. true	8. false
4. true	9. true
5. false	10. true

Multiple Choice

1. c	6. c
2. b	7. c
3. b	8. d
4. d	9. d
5. a	10. c

Fill in the Blanks

1. median
2. variability
3. sample; population
4. research
5. survey
6. causation
7. independent variable; dependent variable
8. no difference between groups; difference between groups
9. qualitative
10. method

ADDITIONAL RESOURCES

Books

American Psychological Association. *Publication Manual of the American Psychological Association*, 5th ed. Washington, D.C.: American Psychological Association, 2001.

Isaac, S. and W. B. Michael. 1990. *Handbook in research and evaluation*, 2nd ed. San Diego: EdITS publishers.

Kranzler, G. and J. Moursand. 1999. *Statistics for the terrified*, 2nd ed. Upper Saddle River, NJ: Prentice Hall, 1999.

Schrieber, F. R. 1973. *Sybil*. Chicago: Regnery.

Software

JMK,
www.jmk.com

(*Note*: This company also created Statview, which was discontinued at the end of 2002. The company urges all former Statview users to consider this software.)

Microsoft Excel,
www.microsoft.com

Qualpage: resources for qualitative research,
www.ualberta.ca/~jrnorris/qual.html

SAS,
www.sas.com

SPSS,
www.spss.com

Statistica,
www.statsoft.com

Z-Text,
www.cdc.gov/hiv/software/ez-text.htm

Video

42 Up, Motion picture, directed/produced by M. Apted. United Kingdom: First Features, 1999. (Note: *7 Up*, *14 Up*, *21 Up*, and *35 Up* are also available on video.)

BRAIN AND BEHAVIOR

Our behavior is impacted by so many things, chief among them the brain. The physiological psychologist must study the structure and function of the brain to understand fully how the brain influences behavior. What we think, feel, and do, the way we walk and talk: all are directed by various parts of the brain. While different techniques can be used to modify behavior or change a person's feelings about something, the psychologist must have a firm grasp on which parts of the brain trigger certain kinds of behavior in order to fully understand human behavior.

An area of psychology that is similar to physio-logical psychology is behavioral neuroscience. The psychologist who specializes in either physiological psychology or behavioral neuro-science needs to know about the tiniest com-ponent of the nervous system—the neuron—as well as how the central nervous system, the peripheral nervous system, and the endocrine system all work together.

Neuropsychology, a career field mentioned in chapter 1, focuses on the diagnosis and treatment of brain disorders.

BEHAVIORAL NEUROSCIENCE

The central nervous system (CNS), the body's primary control center, consists of the brain and spinal cord. The peripheral nervous system is the network of nerves that reaches throughout the body. The system gathers information and delivers it to and from the CNS. The endocrine system, a group of glands, works with the nervous system to regulate the body's physiology.

Neurons

Approximately two hundred different types of cells make up the fifty trillion cells of the body, and each type serves a different function. Neurons, cells that are the tiniest components of the nervous system, give and receive important information. They carry essential information to organs, muscles, and glands throughout the body at amazing speed—a few thousandths of a second.

The neuron is composed of a cell body, or *soma*, and two structures (*axons* and *dendrites*) extending from it. The axon is the long tail-like structure that carries information away from the cell body. Bundles of axons are called *nerves* or *tracts*. Axons may be covered with a fatty substance that is called *myelin*. Most sensory neurons (which send informa-tion from the sensory receptors to the brain) and motor neurons (which send information from the brain to the muscles and glands) are myelinated. When covered with myelin, axons look like sausages because the myelin

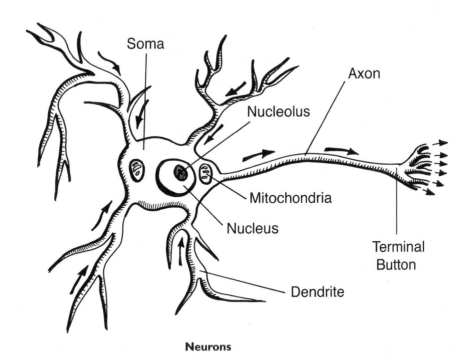

Neurons

covering is interrupted at one-millimeter increments by gaps called the nodes of Ranvier. Axons that are covered by myelin are white, while those axons that are not covered by myelin are gray.

Myelin is like the plastic covering on an electric cord to a kitchen appliance. It protects the axon and speeds the transmission of information. Without the cover, the message to provide electricity might not make it to the appliance.

A serious example of what happens when the myelin cover is damaged is seen in the disorder multiple sclerosis, a disease linked to damage of the myelin sheath. In this disorder, parts of the axons of the nerve, spinal cord, and eye lose myelin. The myelin loss, or demyelination, may result in movement or sensory problems, such as altered vision, numbness, or tingling.

At the other end of the neuron are many fingerlike structures called dendrites. The dendrites, much shorter than axons, receive information from other neurons. Information comes through the dendrite, passes through the axon, leaves via the terminal button, and moves to the next neuron. The terminal button is the portion of the neuron where neurotransmitters are stored until (and sometimes after) they are released into the synapse.

The information transmitted by neurons is carried through a substance called neurotransmitters. The neurotransmitter is released from the terminal buttons into a microscopic space called the synapse, or synaptic space, and then the neurotransmitter activates the dendrite of the receiving neuron.

Sometimes there are problems with this process. The amount of neurotransmitter may not break down, resulting in an excess of neurotransmitter, or there may not be enough neurotransmitter, so important messages are not sent.

Once the neurotransmitter has done its job, it must be removed to allow other messages to come through. There are two ways to clear the synapse so that it may receive new messages: *reuptake* and *breakdown*. In the reuptake process, the neurotransmitter leaves the synapse and returns to the terminal button where it had been stored. In the breakdown process, the neurotransmitter is broken down by enzymes and then removed from the synapse. Both processes leave the synapse clear to receive new messages.

Let's examine the working of four neurotransmitters: acetylcholine, dopamine, serotonin, and norepinephrine.

Acetylcholine

Acetylcholine (ACh) was the first neurotransmitter to be discovered. In 1914, Sir Henry Hallett Dale, an English physiologist, discovered that ACh is released by most nerves that control the central nervous system. Although ACh is also referred to as an excitatory neurotransmitter, for it typically excites the adjoining neuron, it is linked to the parasympathetic nervous system, which helps the body relax. The parasympathetic nervous system is thought to be dominant during periods of quiet or rest. It aids in digestion and maintains bodily functions. This neurotransmitter is also linked to memory and muscle movement. Low levels of ACh are associated with Alzheimer's disease, a degenerative disease that is most often seen in the elderly. The memory of the Alzheimer's patient decreases until he or she is unable to recognize even close friends and family members.

High levels of ACh are found in people with botulism, a disease most often caused by eating severely spoiled foods. Botulism prevents the release of ACh into the muscle, resulting in the inability of muscles to move—including the muscles that control respiration.

Dopamine

Dopamine (DA), unlike ACh, is an inhibitory neurotransmitter. This means that DA makes it less likely that adjoining neurons will fire. DA is linked to emotions and behaviors. Low levels of DA are associated with Parkinson's disease, a generative disorder whose symptoms include tremor and muscle rigidity. High levels of DA are associated with schizophrenia, a disorder associated with a wide range of symptoms that includes hallucinations, delusions, and general lack of connection with reality.

Serotonin

Serotonin (5HT) is also an inhibitory neurotransmitter and is linked to mood, appetite, aggressive behavior, and sleep. Two common foods (turkey and milk) often associated with better sleep contain tryptophan, an amino acid that increases levels of 5HT in the brain. Increased 5HT is connected to feeling good and feeling sleepy. Prozac, one of the most widely advertised antidepressant drugs, is used to treat a variety of anxiety disorders. This drug works by increasing levels of 5HT in the brain.

Norepinephrine

Norepinephrine (NE) is usually described as an excitatory neurotransmitter. Unlike ACh, which is linked to the parasympathetic nervous system, NE is linked to the sympathetic nervous system. The sympathetic nervous system acts as one unit—speeding up the heart, dilating the arteries of the skeletal muscles and heart, constricting the arteries of the skin and digestive tract, and stimulating perspiration. NE impacts mood, memory, and arousal. Amphetamines and cocaine block the reuptake of NE in the brain. As mentioned earlier, reuptake is one way to remove the neurotransmitter from the brain after it has excited the adjoining neuron. Blocking reuptake results in an excess of NE in the synapse, so the adjoining neuron is repeatedly excited. The excessive NE results in the alertness and euphoria associated with the use of these drugs.

Understanding the functions of these four neurotransmitters and how they impact the body is an important part of understanding human behavior.

CENTRAL NERVOUS SYSTEM

The central nervous system (CNS) includes the brain and spinal cord. We know that problems with the brain can result in serious difficulties not only in human behavior but also in human functioning in general. The brain forms the basis of our emotions, memories, behaviors, and moods. This mix is what makes each of us unique.

Brain

The brain is divided into three sections: the forebrain, the midbrain, and the hindbrain.

The brain can also be divided into two parts: the left brain, or left hemisphere, and the right brain, or right hemisphere.

Forebrain

The forebrain contains the corpus callosum, limbic system, hypothalamus, thalamus, and cerebral cortex. The *corpus callosum* connects the right and left hemispheres, allowing for the flow of information from one side to the other.

The *limbic system* is responsible for emotions and motivates such behaviors as aggression, hunger, and thirst.

The next structure, the *hypothalamus*, is also connected to motivation and emotional responses. It also regulates eating, drinking, sexual arousal, and body temperature.

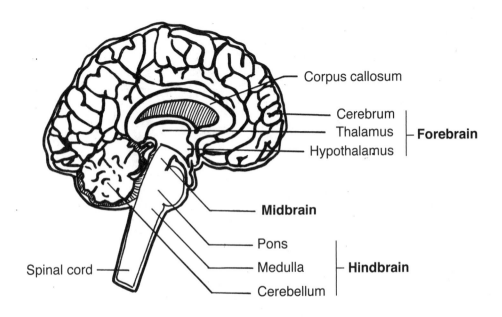

Human Brain

The *thalamus* serves as a messenger or relay system receiving all sensory information except smell, and it sends this information to the cerebral cortex. The *cerebral cortex*, also referred to as the cerebrum, controls complex behavior.

There are four lobes that make up the cerebrum: frontal lobe, temporal lobe, occipital lobe, and parietal lobe.

The *frontal lobe* controls body movement and concentration, and it coordinates information from the other lobes; the *temporal lobe* controls hearing, smell, balance, and some vision; the *occipital lobe* controls vision; the *parietal lobe* controls the sensory area and visual/spatial abilities.

Midbrain

The midbrain is between the forebrain and hindbrain and is a major part of the brainstem. It controls sensory processes, such as vision and movement.

Hindbrain

The hindbrain contains the *medulla*, the *pons*, and the *cerebellum*. The functions of the medulla include the regulation of breathing, heart rate, and blood pressure. The pons connects the cerebrum to the cerebellum. The cerebellum coordinates the body's movement, receiving information from the cerebrum, and directs the position of the arms and legs as well as their degree of muscle tone. It allows the body to move slowly and smoothly.

Left Brain/Right Brain

The two sides of the brain are connected by the corpus callosum, and the two sections seem to have differing areas of concentration. The left side of the brain is associated with verbal abilities, such as speech, language, and writing, as well as science and math. The right side of the brain is associated with visual/spatial skills. Right-brained people are typically stronger in things like music and art appreciation, sculpture, and perception.

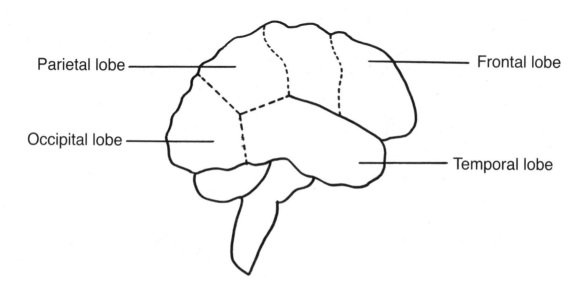

Four Lobes of the Brain

You may hear someone say, "I'm left-brained," or "I'm right-brained." They are probably referring to what they believe are their strengths. Strong with languages? Left brain. Strong with solving three-dimensional puzzles? Right brain.

Another interesting fact about the two sides of the brain has to do with how information is received. More specifically, the left side of the brain receives information from the right side of the body, and the right side of the brain receives information from the left side of the body. So, if I show something to your right eye only (your right visual field) that information will cross the corpus callosum and end up in the left hemisphere.

Spinal Cord

The bundle of axons that connect the brain to the rest of the body make up the spinal cord. These fragile cables are housed inside a string of bones called the spine. The spinal cord is responsible for carrying messages to and from the brain; the spinal cord is also involved in reflex actions. *Reflexes* are very important because they serve protective functions, such as causing you to remove your hand when you accidentally touch the hot grill or causing your eyes to blink when some potentially damaging substance, like a grain of sand, enters one of them.

PERIPHERAL NERVOUS SYSTEM

There are two components in the peripheral nervous system: the somatic nervous system and the autonomic nervous system. The *somatic nervous system* carries information to the central nervous system (brain and spinal cord) and to the senses (sight, smell, taste, hearing, and touch). The ability to enjoy and

appreciate the world through our senses can be attributed to the somatic nervous system.

The *autonomic nervous system* carries information to the body's internal organs, such as the heart and lungs. Within the autonomic system are both the parasympathetic nervous system and the sympathetic nervous system.

The action of the sympathetic nervous system is known as the "fight or flight response" because it helps prepare the body for action. We have all heard stories about the 90-pound mother who lifted the car and pulled her children to safety. The sympathetic nervous system allows our bodies to react in cases of emergency.

Keep in mind that the parasympathetic system, discussed in the section on ACh, is the opposite in that it allows us to relax, causing the body's heart rate to slow.

ENDOCRINE SYSTEM

The endocrine system is a group of organs, often referred to as *glands of internal secretion*, that broadcast hormonal messages to all cells. The nervous system often acts in conjunction with the endocrine system to regulate behavior and mental processes.

The *endocrine system* releases hormones directly into the bloodstream. So, if you skip a few meals, or if your blood concentrations of glucose dip, or if something else changes, the endocrine system reacts and pulls the body back into normal ranges.

The endocrine system is like your own internal thermostat—monitoring the amount of hormones in the blood through a feedback system. Glands affect our behavior and our

GLANDS OF THE ENDOCRINE SYSTEM

Gland: **ADRENAL CORTEX**
Location: one on the top of each kidney
Purpose: responds to stress, the body's water equilibrium, sexual functioning, metabolism, and the immune system; the adrenal medulla produces adrenaline
Problems: adrenal insufficiency leads to symptoms of fatigue, nausea, and deepening skin color
Treatment: pituitary or adrenal gland treatment, depending on the source of the problem; gland removal or treatment with corticosteroids

Gland: **GONADS** (testes in men and ovaries in women)
Location: in the scrotum in males; in the pelvis in women
Purpose: produces androgens, including testosterone (males), estrogen and progesterone (females); promotes sexual development
Problems: difficulties with the secretion of these important hormones can affect growth and reproduction
Treatment: hormone therapy

Gland: **HYPOTHALAMUS**
Location: near the base of the brain
Purpose: controls the pituitary gland by sending messages about stimulating hormone secretions; influences fighting, fear, aggression, and sexual behaviors
Problems: if the hypothalamus isn't working, the pituitary gland doesn't function properly (an example of this is diabetes insipidus); symptoms are excessive thirst, excessive urine production, and dehydration
Treatment: modified forms of antidiuretic hormone

Gland: **PANCREAS**
Location: near the stomach and small intestines
Purpose: secretes two hormones, glucagon and insulin, which are responsible for regulating the body's sugar levels
Problems: people with high sugar (glucose) levels are diabetic (have diabetes mellitus), or have an inability to regulate insulin levels properly; untreated diabetes can lead to blindness, coronary disease, amputation, and death
Treatment: dietary changes and/or insulin

Gland: **PARATHYROID**
Location: attached to the thyroid gland
Purpose: regulates levels of calcium in the blood and affects the nervous system
Problems: too little parathromone, the parathyroid hormone, may result in muscle spasms; too much might cause lethargy
Treatment: calcium supplements, either oral or intravenous

Gland: **PITUITARY**
Location: under the hypothalamus
Purpose: called the master gland; controls many other glands. The posterior lobe controls water equilibrium and the initiation of labor contractions. The anterior lobe controls the thyroid, adrenal glands, and gonads.
Problems: the anterior pituitary controls growth; too much activity results in pituitary giantism, and too little results in pituitary dwarfism
Treatment: radiation therapy or drugs to block or encourage the production of growth hormone

Gland: **THYROID**
Location: in the lower part of the neck below the voice box
Purpose: responsible for metabolism; as thyroid hormone, thyroxin, increases, metabolism increases
Problems: too much thyroid hormone may result in hyperthyroidism and is associated with weight loss, excessive sweating, increased blood pressure, and swelling in neck goiter in adults; too little thyroid hormone may result in hypothyroidism and is associated with slowed growth in children or sluggishness, dry skin, and weight gain in adults
Treatment: thyroid replacement therapy and/or removal of the thyroid gland

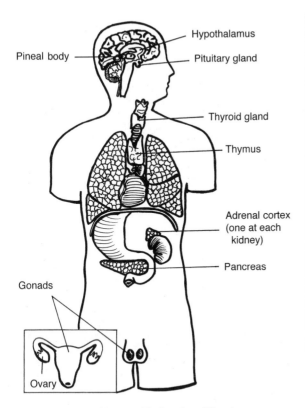

Pineal body — Hypothalamus

Pituitary gland

Thyroid gland

Thymus

Adrenal cortex (one at each kidney)

Pancreas

Gonads

Ovary

Major Human Endocrine Glands

growth, and too much or too little of a hormone can cause serious trouble.

The glands within the endocrine system—hypothalamus, pituitary, thyroid, parathyroid, adrenal, pineal, gonads, and pancreas—each have an important function in the human body.

Mind/Body Connection

Psychologists understand that behavior is controlled by the combination of body and mind. In order to understand the contribution of mind, we need to understand the contribution of the body—or in this case, the brain. We've discussed a variety of disorders that are a result of problems of brain functioning. The behavioral neuroscientist examines problems from this perspective. It's like another orientation, or lens, through which to view a person and begin to understand behavior.

CHAPTER SUMMARY

The psychologist needs to have some understanding of the human body, particularly the brain and endocrine system, to comprehend fully the connection between brain and behavior. Neurons are the foundation of this understanding. They are the cells of the nervous system and are responsible for sending information to the brain and other parts of the body. The neurotransmitters—ACh, DA, 5HT, and NE—are all related to human behavior.

The nervous system consists of the central nervous system (CNS) and the peripheral nervous system. The CNS is composed of the brain and spinal cord. The peripheral nervous system, or the parasympathetic and sympathetic nervous systems, also communicates important messages to the body.

Finally, the endocrine system, which secretes hormones directly into the blood stream, regulates much of the body's functioning. These hormones are as essential as the nervous system to the balance and functioning of the human body. Some neurons even use hormones as a chemical transmitter. The endocrine glands regulate growth, sexual and maternal behavior, the level of energy and mood, and the individual's reaction to stress.

Psychology is not a simple matter of learning or relearning certain behaviors; the complex and miraculous workings of the brain and endocrine system have a distinctive impact on how we function. The job of the physiological psychologist or behavioral neuroscientist is linked to an understanding of these systems.

TEST YOUR RECALL AND RECOGNITION

True/False

1. The axon carries information toward the cell body.

2. Insulin is a neurotransmitter that affects growth.

3. The three sections of the brain are the forebrain, midbrain, and hindbrain.

4. The midbrain is responsible for controlling vision and movement.

5. Reflexes may protect us from hurting ourselves.

6. The two components of the autonomic nervous system are the sympathetic and parasympathetic nervous systems.

7. The pituitary gland is often referred to as the master gland.

8. Males have gonads; females do not.

9. The adrenal gland is associated with responses to stress.

10. Insulin is the hormone associated with the pancreas.

Multiple Choice

1. Two structures carry information to and from the cell body. These structures are

   a. soma and dendrites.

   b. axon and dendrites.

   c. synapse and neuron.

   d. melatonin and insulin.

2. What color are myelinated axons?

   a. gray   c. white

   b. red   d. none of the above

3. The space between neurons is referred to as the

   a. synapse.   c. neuronal opening.

   b. soma.   d. axon.

4. Two disorders or diseases that are associated with an imbalance in dopamine are

   a. Alzheimer's and multiple sclerosis.

   b. schizophrenia and Parkinson's.

   c. schizophrenia and seasonal affective disorder.

   d. diabetes and botulism.

5. Which lobe controls hearing?

   a. occipital   c. temporal

   b. parietal   d. corpus callosum

6. The band that connects the left and right brain is referred to as the

   a. pons.

   b. hypothalamus.

   c. synapse.

   d. corpus callosum.

7. Blinking in response to debris in one's eye is called

   a. reflex.

   b. behavioral compensatory response.

   c. both a and b.

   d. neither a nor b.

8. Which of the following is *not* a component of the peripheral nervous system?

   a. somatic nervous system

   b. central nervous system

   c. autonomic nervous system

   d. parasympathetic nervous system

9. The chemicals that are released by the endocrine system are called

   a. hormones.   c. glands.
   b. neurotransmitters.   d. synaptic fluids.

10. The initiation of labor contractions is associated with which gland?

    a. pancreas   c. thyroid
    b. pituitary gland   d. none of the above

Fill in the Blanks

1. In _____, the myelin sheath is damaged.

2. The cell body in the neuron is also referred to as the _____.

3. Bundles of axons are called _____.

4. The names of four neurotransmitters are _____, _____, _____, and _____.

5. In botulism, the release of _____ into the muscles is prohibited.

6. The fragile cables of the spinal cord are housed in the _____.

7. The _____ nervous system is associated with the phrase, "fight or flight."

8. The gonads in women are called _____, and gonads in men are called _____.

9. People with diabetes may take the hormone _____.

10. There are two _____ glands; each is located on top of a kidney.

ANSWERS TO QUESTIONS
True/False

1. false   6. true
2. false   7. true
3. true   8. false
4. true   9. true
5. true   10. true

Multiple Choice

1. b   6. d
2. c   7. a
3. a   8. b
4. b   9. a
5. c   10. b

Fill in the Blanks

1. multiple sclerosis
2. soma
3. nerves
4. acetylcholine (ACh); dopamine (DA); norepinephrine (NE); serotonin (5HT)
5. acetylcholine
6. spine
7. sympathetic
8. ovaries; testes
9. insulin
10. adrenal

ADDITIONAL RESOURCES
Book

Sapolsky, R. 1998. *Why don't zebras get ulcers: A guide to stress, stress-related disease and coping*, 2nd ed. New York: W. H. Freeman.

Video

The mind (videorecording). New York: WNET in association with the BBC. (1988). (Published by PBS video, 1988.)

Web sites

How Stuff Works,
www.howstuffworks.com

National Institutes of Health,
www.nih.gov

ScienceNet,
www.sciencenet.org.uk

SENSATION AND PERCEPTION

As I sit at the computer writing, I am very aware of the beauty around me, brought to me by my senses. I hear birds chirping outside the window. I smell coffee brewing. I feel the softness of the rug under my feet. I read these words as they appear on the computer screen. I taste the sweetness of a pastry.

How we see, hear, feel, taste, and smell things requires that the mind actively process the information it receives. Our senses process the information without our being totally conscious of it, and our perceptions of that information are key to how we relate to the rest of the world.

Understanding how sensation and perception function helps us recognize those instances in human behavior where sensation and/or perception are faulty. For example, one common symptom of schizophrenia is auditory hallucinations. The schizophrenic hears sounds even though the receptors of the auditory system are not being stimulated.

Both sensation and perception are integral to the understanding of human psychology.

SENSATION

If you were asked to identify the senses, you would probably quickly answer: taste, hearing, sight, smell, and touch. You would probably be just as quick to identify the mouth and tongue, ears, eyes, nose, and skin as the organs responsible for experiencing these sensations.

Everyone's responses to various stimuli differ, making the relationship between what we sense and what is actually there an endless source of discovery. The study of differing reactions to various stimuli is one of the oldest disciplines in psychology. When does the physical reality—the light, sound, and smells around us—become part of our own reality? At what point do you hear, smell, taste, see, or feel something, and why is this different for some people?

As we learned in chapter 3, we know that a large amount of the brain is devoted to the visual and auditory systems. For instance, more than fifty percent of our cerebral cortex is devoted to visual functions, and much of the remainder is devoted to auditory, including speech. Seeing and hearing are by far the most frequently studied senses.

External Stimuli

A sensation is first produced when an external stimulus prompts a *receptor cell*, a specialized portion of the body sensitive to particular kinds of stimuli such as the retina of the eye. This receptor cell then transmits information to the brain, which interprets it, and takes necessary action.

Sensory Thresholds

We don't interpret every sensation, however. For instance, there are some sounds that we, as humans, just do not hear. My mother has a dog that howls. At first, we thought she was howling at nothing, but then we noticed that her howling was always followed by a siren. How was it that this dog could hear sounds long before we heard them? The answer has to do with the sensory threshold. This determines when we will detect sensory stimulation, such as hearing a siren or feeling pressure on the skin. This threshold is different for each of the senses and for different types of animals.

There is a point at which fifty percent of all people would say, "Yes, I see that light," or "Yes, I hear that sound." This is defined as the *absolute threshold*. The absolute threshold may be influenced by other factors. Have you ever noticed that it is easier to appreciate the candles lit on birthday cake in the dark, or that it is more difficult to hear your favorite television program when your neighbor is operating her leaf blower? *Signal detection theory* states that thresholds may differ depending on the presence of background stimuli, such as the leaf blower, and the nature of the signal, such as the brightness of the candle.

Sensory Adaptation

Your interpretation of sensation may also change with time. If you sit still and listen to the sounds around you, you may hear the hum of the air conditioner or heater. Although that sound may be noticeable at first, after a while it becomes barely detectable. This is called sensory adaptation.

VISION

Our ability to see and interpret what we see is complex and fascinating. The perception of color, shape, light and dark, and a multitude of other details allows humans to perceive beauty, to appreciate nature, to create, and to enjoy life more fully.

So, how do we see? The path of vision moves from the cornea, pupil, and lens to the retina. The first thing you notice when you look into someone's eye is the color; this colored portion of the eye is called the *iris*. In the middle of the iris is the *pupil*, an opening that responds to light. The pupil becomes large in a dark room when it dilates to let in more light. It becomes smaller in a bright room as it contracts to restrict the amount of incoming light. Light then passes through the pupil into the *lens* and to the *retina*.

The *sclera* is the white of the eye, and the *cornea* is the bulge in the sclera. It is here, behind the cornea, that you find the lens, which changes shape to help place objects into focus. There are muscles on each side of the lens, *ciliary muscles*, that assist with the job of focusing. The *aqueous humor* is behind the cornea, and it is filled with fluid that provides nutrients to the cornea and lens.

The process of vision begins with some internal or external source of energy, which is picked up by a receptor cell that then passes information to the brain. The receptor cells of the eye are called rods and cones, and they are located in the retina. There are fifteen to twenty times more rods than cones. Cones are responsible for color vision; rods detect light and dark and help us with night vision.

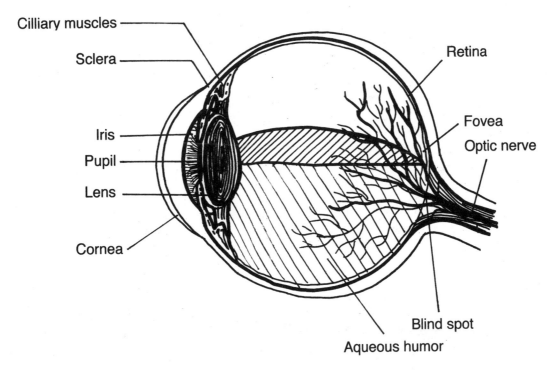

Cilliary muscles

Sclera

Retina

Iris

Fovea

Optic nerve

Pupil

Lens

Cornea

Blind spot

Aqueous humor

Parts of the Eye

Rods and cones connect to a special type of neuron called a *bipolar cell*, which has only one axon and one dendrite. Each cone connects to one bipolar cell, and several rods share one bipolar cell. These cells connect to *ganglion cells*, which link together to form the optic nerve and then send the information to the brain. The portion of the retina where the ganglion cells exit but where no receptor cells reside is called the blind spot. Because receptor cells are necessary for an image to register in the brain, when an image hits the blind spot of the retina, the image cannot be seen.

In the brain, information travels through the optic *chiasm*. The optic chiasm is the area where some fibers from the optic nerve of each eye cross over to the other side of the brain. The optic chiasm can also be referred to as the crossover area. Information goes from the right visual field to the left side of the brain. Other

information travels from the right visual field to the right side of the brain. The occipital lobe receives most of the visual information.

The human ability to see and interpret color is fascinating and has resulted in the development of theories distinct from studies of vision. There are two theories of color vision: the trichromatic theory and the opponent-process theory. The *trichromatic theory* was proposed by Thomas Young in 1802 and revised by Hermann von Helmholtz in 1852. According to this theory, all color is the result of the mixing of three primary colors—red, yellow, and blue. Furthermore, there are three types of cones, the receptor cells responsible for color vision, and each cone responds to one of these primary colors.

The *opponent-process theory* was developed in the 1870s by Ewald Hering in response to the

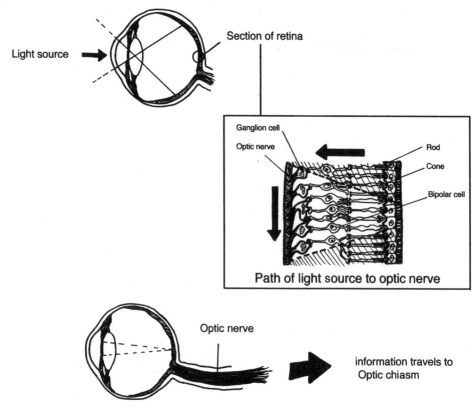

Vision and the Brain

limitations of the trichromatic theory, which does not explain afterimages.

Have you ever looked at an image, then stared at a blank wall or a piece of white paper? You continue to see that image, but it is in a different color. That's an afterimage. If you were to stare at a red strawberry, then look at a white piece of paper, you would see a green strawberry.

According to the opponent-process theory, there are three sets of cones that determine what color is seen. Some cones detect yellow-blue; some, red-green; and others, black-white.

Which theory is correct? Today, most researchers believe that neither theory is incorrect; there is research to support each theory.

HEARING

There are three parts of the ear: outer ear, middle ear, and inner ear. The outer ear consists of the *pinna* and the *auditory canal*. These structures receive sound waves and channel them to the *eardrum*, which vibrates in response to the sound waves. The vibration of the eardrum sets into motion the three bones of the middle ear: *maleus* (hammer), *incus* (anvil), and *stapes* (stirrup). The movement of these bones transmits the vibration to the *oval window*, which connects the middle ear to the inner ear, and to the *cochlea*, which is housed in the inner ear. This snail-shaped structure is filled with fluid and houses the *Organ of Corti*, which contains receptor cells. When these receptor cells vibrate, nerve impulses are sent to the auditory nerve and then relayed to the brain. The ears work like the eyes in that the direction the message takes does vary, so each ear may send information to each hemisphere of the brain, as we just learned in the section about rods and cones.

TASTE

Have you ever noticed that when you have a cold, your sense of taste is dulled? The *olfactory* (smell) and *gustatory* (taste) systems are closely linked. The term *flavor*, for example, is often used synonymously with taste, but flavor is actually brought about through the combination of taste, smell, and touch.

True food connoisseurs will talk about not only the taste of a food, but also the aroma and the feel of the food on the tongue. When you eat a bag of potato chips, isn't part of the enjoyment in the crunch? When you eat a bar of chocolate, you are probably also taking pleasure in the smell of the chocolate. When you discuss taste, you are simply referring to the mouth's contribution to the joy of eating.

Taste Buds

The receptor cells in the mouth are in the taste buds. The taste buds are located on the tip of the tongue, on the insides of your cheeks, at the back of your throat, and on the roof of your mouth.

The taste buds located in the bumps on your tongue are called *papillae*. They are constantly being replaced; you get new taste buds every one or two weeks. In addition, the number of taste buds changes, which impacts your sensitivity to taste. Taste buds increase in number up until the age of forty, at which time they begin to decrease. That is why some elderly people have difficulty tasting food.

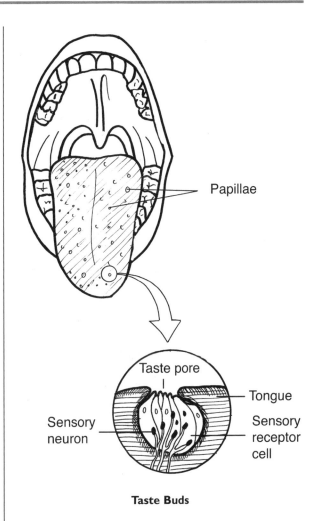

Taste Buds

When food enters the mouth, it combines with saliva. Saliva helps the food to dissolve and leads to the release of chemicals that are called *tastants*. Tastants interact with taste receptors, and these receptors send information to the brain. This information is interpreted as a taste.

Sweet, Sour, Bitter, and Salty

There are four (or five) primary tastes; everything you taste is a combination of these primary tastes. The taste buds located on the tip, sides, and back of your tongue identify things as sweet, sour, bitter, and salty.

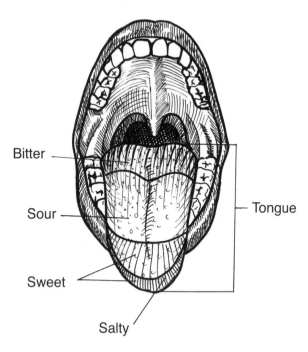

The Mouth and Tongue

Some researchers believe that there is a fifth taste called *umami*. This can be translated to mean savory and is associated with glutamate, an amino acid that is found in monosodium glutamate (MSG).

SMELL

The receptor cells for smell, *olfactory epithelium*, are located in the nasal cavity. The nose collects and filters air, but you may be surprised to learn that it is not responsible for sending messages about smell to the brain. When odor molecules reach this site, they are sent to the *olfactory bulb*, located at the base of the brain, where they are interpreted as smell.

Functions of Smell

The sense of smell has two functions: to detect odors and to communicate aggression, sexual interest, and territory. The second function is

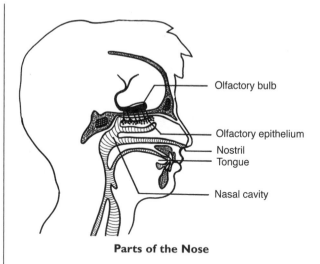

Parts of the Nose

most often associated with animals. We have all seen dogs mark their territory, or male animals flock around a female in heat. They are responding to *pheromones*, the secretion of specific odors that signal specific messages to other animals. Receptors to pheromones are located in the nasal cavity, in what is known as the *vomeronasal organ*.

Although humans have this organ, it is uncertain what role pheromones play in human communication, although there is a variety of research that suggests that we do use our sense of smell to communicate. For instance, researchers have found that through smell, new mothers can identify their newborns after only a few hours of contact; and a newborn can identify its mother in the same way. People recognize the smell of relatives even after they have been separated for extended periods of time.

TOUCH

Our largest organ, skin, is associated with the sense of touch. Skin helps us to detect pressure, temperature, and pain. Our skin is the gatekeeper for our bodies, protecting everything under it from the harsh elements.

The skin has three different types of receptors: thermoreceptors for temperature, mechano-receptors for pressure, and nociceptors for pain. An interesting observation regarding skin has to do with individual differences in pain tolerance.

For example, one person will just fall apart over a small splinter, yet another person can split a board with his hand and show no sign of pain. Although there are no hard and fast explanations for individual differences in tolerance, the *gate control theory*, introduced by Ronald Melzack and Patrick Wall in 1965, proposes that there is a gate in the spinal cord that controls pain messages that go to the brain. When the gate is open, we experience more pain than when the gate is closed. So, one explanation for differences in pain toler-ance is the faulty gate idea. The person who

has a low pain tolerance has a gate that does not close as it should.

PERCEPTION

Sensation relies on physiology. A stimulus is received by a receptor cell, which then communicates with the brain. But how do we make sense of what we have seen, tasted, smelled, touched, and heard? We make sense of our world through perceptions. This can happen through perceptual constancy, distance/depth, and movement.

Our perceptions determine how we interpret our environmental experiences. For instance, at the beginning of this chapter, I wrote about how I felt the rug under my feet, and my per-ception was that it was soft. I heard the birds, and my interpretation was that they were beautiful. I smelled the coffee brewing, and it had a pleasing aroma to me. As humans, our

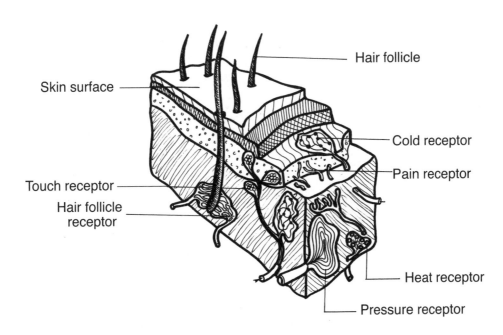

Receptors on Skin

perception of various stimuli is critical to the fullness of our experience.

Constancy

Focus on an object on the other side of the room. Now, stand up, and walk toward that object. As you approach the object, your view will change. The object might become larger, or the shape might change. Maybe, the light will hit the object in a different way. Regardless of the changes you see, the object remains the same. The door did not grow, the chair did not change in shape, and the apple did not become a deeper shade of red. Three ways to measure constancy are size, shape, and brightness. Constancy is important because it allows for stability in our perception of the world.

Distance/Depth

Again, focus on an object that is at a distance. How can you tell what is in front of or behind your target object? Binocular cues and monocular cues influence your perspective. *Binocular cues*, using both eyes, allow us to experience depth and distance. *Monocular cues*, using only one eye, cause some loss of precision, but give us a slightly different perspective. Monocular cues are sufficient for most judgments of distance or depth.

Stereoscopic vision involves the use of both eyes and contributes to our ability to see the world as three-dimensional. To understand stereoscopic vision, close one eye and take in the view; do not move your head. Now, open that eye and close the other one. Each eye gives you a different viewpoint, and together they give you the combined image.

Monocular Cues

Movement

Have you ever made your own moving cartoon? It's simple. Take a notepad and draw some sequence of events, one drawing on each page. Now, flip the pages, and the drawing will appear to move. When a stationary object appears to move, this is referred to as *apparent motion*, as compared to *real movement*, when an object actually moves.

Two interesting examples of perception in movement are the phi phenomenon and stroboscopic motion. The *phi phenomenon* is best described as the way the neon arrow on the sign at the car wash appears to move up and down. *Stroboscopic movement* is apparent when someone stands under a strobe light.

These two phenomena are examples of illusions. They demonstrate how our senses may play tricks on us. We think we see movement—actually we feel quite certain that we do—and our brain processes the illusion as such, but actually there is no movement. An illusion is the act of deceiving. These examples show that there may be some deception between sensation and perception.

CHAPTER SUMMARY

Human beings rely on five senses: vision, hearing, smell, taste, and touch. These senses are important as we try to understand, appreciate, and enjoy the world around us. Each sense is also connected with an organ in our body.

The detection of sensation begins when an external or internal stimulus activates a receptor cell, which then carries information to the brain where the information is interpreted as a visual pattern, a sound, an odor, a taste, or a tactile sensation.

Sensation is primarily a physiological process, and perception is a psychological one. Perception is how the brain interprets the messages that come from the senses. Perceptual constancy, depth/distance, and movement are just some of the concepts important in the field of perception.

TEST YOUR RECALL AND RECOGNITION

True/False

1. Most of the brain is devoted to the gustatory system.

2. Sensory thresholds are the same for all living creatures.

3. The aqueous humor is the fluid-filled structure in the eye.

4. The receptor cells that allow us to hear are located in the Organ of Corti.

5. Flavor and taste are interchangeable terms.

6. Only animals have receptors to pheromones.

7. The gate control theory has been used to explain individual differences in pain tolerance.

8. A "moving" neon sign is not really moving, but it appears to move as a result of shape constancy.

9. Binocular cues are necessary for most depth perception.

10. Shape, size, and brightness constancy provide a sense of stability in our ever-changing visual landscape.

Multiple Choice

1. Which of the following is *not* an example of sensory adaptation?

    a. After waiting for twenty minutes in your doctor's office, you are no longer aware of the hum of the air conditioner.

    b. A dog hears a sound that no one else hears.

    c. Your soup, which initially seemed extremely salty, now seems less so.

    d. When you entered the ocean, the water seemed chilly; but after ten minutes of swimming, you begin to find the water temperature quite comfortable.

2. The white of the eye is called the

    a. iris.   c. sclera.

    b. lens.   d. pupil.

3. The optic disk is also referred to as the

   a. blind spot.

   b. receptor cell.

   c. right visual field.

   d. none of the above.

4. The cones are responsible for

   a. depth perception.

   b. night vision.

   c. peripheral vision.

   d. color vision.

5. What is the name of the snail-shaped structure in the ear?

   a. pupil   c. papillae

   b. pinna   d. cochlea

6. The sense of taste is closely linked to which other sense?

   a. vision   c. smell

   b. hearing   d. none of the above

7. The chemical that allows animals to communicate aggression, sexual interest, and territory is called

   a. pheromone.   c. insulin.

   b. estrogen.   d. testosterone.

8. As Jacquelyn approaches her home, it appears to grow in size. Yet Jacquelyn realizes that her house is not growing. Why?

   a. shape constancy

   b. phi phenomenon

   c. size constancy

   d. binocular cue

9. Which cues are required for most judgments of distance and depth?

   a. binocular

   b. monocular

   c. both a and b

   d. neither a nor b

10. Ned's first visit to the city is overwhelming. He spends most of his day gaping at the tall buildings and the "moving" neon signs. These moving signs illustrate which concept in perception?

    a. binocular cues

    b. apparent motion

    c. shape constancy

    d. both a and b

Fill in the Blanks

1. The point at which fifty percent of people would agree that they smell the same odor is referred to as the _____.

2. The general path of vision moves from _____, to pupil, to lens, to _____.

3. Visual information may cross over from the right hemisphere to the left hemisphere at the _____.

4. The three bones of the middle ear are _____, _____, and _____.

5. Researchers have proposed a fifth primary taste that is called _____.

6. The receptor cells for smell are not located in the nose, but in the _____.

7. _____ is our largest organ and is associated with touch.

8. _____ cues and _____ cues allow us to perceive depth and distance.

9. Real movement is the term used to refer to an object that is actually in motion. _____ is the term used to refer to a stationary object that appears to move.

10. _____ movement is an example of apparent motion.

ANSWERS TO QUESTIONS

True/False

1. false	6. false
2. false	7. true
3. true	8. false
4. true	9. false
5. false	10. true

Multiple Choice

1. b	6. c
2. c	7. a
3. a	8. c
4. d	9. b
5. d	10. b

Fill in the Blanks

1. absolute threshold
2. cornea; retina
3. optic chiasm
4. maleus (hammer); incus (anvil); stapes (stirrup)
5. umami
6. nasal cavity
7. Skin
8. Monocular; binocular
9. Apparent motion
10. Stroboscopic

ADDITIONAL RESOURCES

Books

Cytowic, R. E. 2000. *The man who tasted shapes.* Cambridge, MA: MIT Press.

Gregory, R. L., J. Harris, and D. Rose eds. 1995. *The artful eye.* Oxford: Oxford University Press.

Video

Nature: The nature of sex: A time and place. Television series, directed by R. Godeanu New York: WNET, 1993.

COGNITION

Cognitive psychology examines how we acquire
and use knowledge. Cognition is a part of our
lives. We are presented with problems to solve
and decisions to make, and we use language
constantly to communicate and maneuver
through our days.

Cognitive psychology has come into the picture
in the past fifty years in part because of the
growth in technology. Computers have helped
scientists to study the human mind in depth
and to create cognitive models, tools for understanding how the brain processes information.

The information-processing model, a popular
theory in cognitive psychology, shows us that
thinking comprises many different parts of the
brain. There is overlap with the brain drawing
on one experience or another to help fill in
the missing blanks in a new experience. This
model compares the working of the human
mind to the working of a computer. It is used
to explain the workings of the mind and will
be used again in chapter 7 to explain human
memory. Just as a computer has the ability to
store and retrieve information, so does the
human mind. Understanding cognition means
understanding how we take in various types of
information and use it to our best advantage
in communication, problem solving, and
decision making.

LANGUAGE

In this chapter, when we refer to language,
we are talking about verbal language; but not
all language is verbal. For example, there is
American Sign Language (ASL), which is
described as manual-visual language. This
can be compared to verbal language, which is
described as oral-auditory language. Through
ASL, people communicate with hand signs
and gestures. Just as there are different verbal
languages, which may cause communication
difficulties, there are different sign languages.
For example, a person who uses ASL would
find it difficult to communicate with a person
who uses British Sign Language. Sign language
possesses all the elements of language that we
are about to present.

Language is usually associated with thought.
We often say that we are "thinking out loud"
as we figure things out. Thinking, for humans,
is a type of internal language. We will talk
about language as it pertains to cognition
and how it makes human beings unique.

We know that animals can communicate.
There are lots of examples of dogs barking
at cats, and cats purring in delight, but this
is not language as we are defining it here.
There are elements of language that go beyond
mere communication. First, language involves
displacement, talking about something that
is not physically present. Also, language has
shared meaning or meaningfulness, and it is
productive. A dog may communicate its desire
to go outside by barking and walking in circles

in the kitchen. This behavior may have shared meaning—you understand her wish—but the dog is not able to use the other two elements of language: displacement or productiveness.

Displacement

Displacement, as it is used in reference to cognition, means that someone can talk about something that is not physically present. We use our language to talk about ideas, the past, the future, and other abstract concepts. For example, displacement allows me to talk to a friend about the new dress I bought at the store yesterday while we're having lunch today. Displacement makes our conversation skills distinctly different from the kind of communication tools that an animal might use.

Meaningfulness

If we speak the same language as someone else, and if we each understand what the other is saying, then our interaction has meaningfulness. This shared meaning is the second important characteristic of language. It is important to differentiate between meaning and meaningfulness. All words have meaning, but meaningfulness refers to the presence of shared or similar meaning. For example, consider what happens when you try to communicate with someone who speaks a language you don't understand. Let's say you speak English, and you converse with someone who speaks only French. Each of you will use different words with the same meaning to communicate (you may talk about a book in English; the other person may talk about le livre in French). In this case, you are both using a word that shares the same meaning, but there is no meaningfulness.

Productiveness

Kathryn Boch and Susan Garnsey of the University of Illinois, Urbana Champaign,

estimate that adults know between 30,000 and 80,000 words. We encounter thousands of words in our daily use of language, and we can combine these words to create an untold number of expressions. This flexibility in language gives us an element of productiveness that is not shared by other creatures.

Productiveness does not end with the connection of existing words with their dictionary definitions. New uses for words and new words are being created all the time. I'm referring to slang. *Webster's Dictionary* defines slang as "language peculiar to a particular group, or informal nonstandard vocabulary…" Slang illustrates the productiveness of language and the ways in which language is always changing. Just look at all the new words that have emerged as a result of changes in technology:

SOME COMMONLY USED TERMS IN CYBERSPACE SLANG	
Term	**Definition**
Browser	allows you to find information on the Internet
Crash	a serious computer failure
Cyberspace	the place where humans interact on the Internet
Download	allows you to transfer files from one computer to another
E-mail	allows you to send messages from one computer to another
Home page	the main document on an organization's Web site
Joes	an account where the password and user name are the same
Spam	electronic junk mail
Virus	a program that can infect and damage other programs
Web site	a collection of services that are grouped together; usually developed to provide information about an individual, group, or organization

Language Acquisition

Think about a young child learning to talk. At what age does he learn to speak? How long does it take before he can use the three characteristics of language: displacement, meaningfulness, and productiveness? Language is complex, and it takes years before a child has mastered language skills.

Yet there appears to be a period during which children are most receptive to learning a new language, usually during the preschool/kindergarten years. As we grow older, learning another language becomes more difficult. This may be because children are born with a skill called *language acquisition device (LAD)*, a theory developed by Noam Chomsky in 1972, in his book *Language and Mind*.

Chomsky—who was trained as a linguist, not a psychologist—proposed that children are born with an internal device that allows them to understand and produce language. According to Chomsky, this device explains why all children, regardless of culture, follow the same sequence for language development. Simply put, children begin by cooing, then babbling, then uttering one-word phrases, two-word phrases, multiple sentences, and then more complex phrases. We will explore this sequence in chapter 8.

Another theory of language development, which has been supported by behaviorists such as B. F. Skinner (we will talk more about the behavioral orientation in learning in chapter 7), suggests that language acquisition is learned, and that it is acquired as a result of interactions with the environment, rather than being present at birth. The language development issue, then, is another example of our enduring nature versus nurture debate. According to behavioral theories, we learn language because we are rewarded or reinforced when we use it. Think about how parents respond to a child's first word. The hugs, smiles, and kisses all reinforce the behavior of speaking. But this does not explain how we create new words. If we know that we are going to receive reinforcement for particular utterances, why not just stick with those? Why try something new?

Chomsky argues that we are born with some skill; it's biological (our nature). The behavioral perspective says that this skill is developed through our interactions with the environment (namely, nurture).

Recently, researchers have looked at the merit of both theories—language acquisition device and the behavioral theories—and use a combination of them in their explanations of language acquisition. Today, most psychologists believe language acquisition occurs through some innate device that allows us to learn language, and this process is strengthened through the positive feedback we receive from caregivers when we speak.

PROBLEM SOLVING

You are certainly aware of the fact that you solve problems every day, but you are probably not aware of the types of approaches that you use to solve them. Psychologists are interested in understanding and labeling these approaches in an effort to determine which strategies are most effective in obtaining a solution.

Methods for Problem Solving

We will discuss five problem-solving strategies: retrieval from memory, trial and error, brainstorming, algorithms, and heuristics. At the end of the section, you will find a variety of problems that have been used by psychologists to understand problem-solving behavior. As you solve these problems, make note of the strategies that you use.

Retrieval from Memory

One way to solve a problem is simply to pull the solution from memory. If I were to ask you how to boil water, you would retrieve the information from memory—tell me to pour water into a pot and then place the pot on a hot surface. This method taps into the information-processing model that focuses on the storage and retrieval of information. We will talk about this in more detail in chapter 7. If only all problems were this easy to solve! Unfortunately, we don't have the solutions to every problem stored in memory.

Trial and Error

We all use trial and error to solve problems. This approach involves trying different strategies until we obtain the solution. For example, I have two seemingly identical keys. One opens the door to my office, and the other opens the door to my office suite. I always use trial and error to open these doors. I know that if one key does not work, I should try the other. This would not be the best strategy if I had to fumble among ten keys rather than two. That leads us to criticisms of this approach: it is not efficient, it can be time-consuming, and it is random. This approach works best when the number of choices is limited.

Brainstorming

This is a commonly used problem-solving strategy where many solutions are produced. Solutions are not evaluated until all possible solutions have been proposed. So, given the problem of how to get to work tomorrow, what would you do? Possible solutions may include taking the bus, hailing a cab, hitchhiking, rollerskating, walking, or asking a friend for a ride. As you can see, some of these solutions are good; others aren't so good. But the goal of brainstorming is to come up with as many solutions as possible. Brainstorming is a strategy that does not result in a correct solution, but it elicits many possible solutions. Brainstorming is useful in that it forces us to consider a wide range of options. Thus we avoid a road block to problem solving called *set*, which is defined as our inclination to use a narrow scope in finding solutions.

Algorithm

How do we calculate the mean? If you recall from chapter 2, we take the sum and divide that by the number of items. Another method in problem solving is the *algorithm*, which provides us with a systematic procedure for problem solving. If used correctly, the algorithm always yields the correct solution; unfortunately not every problem has an algorithm.

Heuristics

There are groups of problem-solving strategies that are called *heuristics*. Heuristics are rules that are used to help simplify problem solving, but unlike the algorithm, they don't guarantee a solution. We will discuss four strategies that fall into this category: working backward, hill climbing, subgoals, and means-end approach.

- *Working backward*: I spent a good amount of my childhood in my mother and father's grocery store, where I worked as a cashier. This provided me with an opportunity to witness many examples of this heuristic. In this approach, you work backward from the goal to your desired condition. In my case, a child would enter the store with the goal of purchasing candy and would have a quarter to reach this goal. In working backward, the child purchases pieces of candy, and after each purchase inquires, "How much is left?" This process continues until the child has spent all his money. Working backward can be compared to working forward (as in the algorithm), where the child might inquire about the price of each piece of candy, calculate how many pieces he could obtain for a quarter, and then purchase his candy.

• *Hill climbing*: Another technique for solving problems is called hill climbing. In this approach, the person takes small steps to solve the problem. There is only forward motion toward the goal; the person is not allowed to move backward or to digress from the goal. The classic example of the hill climbing approach is the strategy that we use to solve multiple choice questions when we are not certain of the answer. Given a multiple choice question, we could immediately select the correct response using retrieval from memory, or we can eliminate incorrect choices until only one answer is left. After we have decided that d is not the answer, we do not go back to reconsider that answer. Once we decide that a is not the answer, we do not go back to reconsider that answer, and so on until we only have one answer left.

• *Subgoals*: With subgoals, the problem is broken down into small steps, and then each of the smaller steps is approached in an effort to solve the bigger problem. Subgoals are especially helpful when the problem seems overwhelming. One overwhelming problem that may be approached in this manner is the task of relocating to another city. Relocation could be broken down into finding a new home, locating a new job, and obtaining information about schools in the area. As you can see, each of these responsibilities is fairly arduous, so we could further break each into subgoals.

When all these subgoals have been addressed, we will have solved our big problem.

• *Means-end analysis*: This approach combines components of subgoals and hill climbing. Means-end analysis is also known as subgroup analysis. As with the subgoal approach, the problem is broken into smaller steps that are referred to as partial solutions. As with the hill climbing approach, the means-end analysis approach involves evaluating where you are and where you want to be and taking actions to move toward your goal. Unlike hill climbing, the subgoals that are used in the means-end approach may involve moving backward, or digressing, which is not permissible in hill climbing. The difference between means-end and subgoal is subtle. Unlike the subgoal approach, in means-end analysis, there is constant evaluation of the difference between current state and desired goal.

Road Blocks in Problem Solving

Problem solving can be hampered by a variety of such factors as mood (emotion), motivation, and set. Set occurs when we solve problems based on previous experiences with problem solving, and we demonstrate an inability to look beyond routine solutions.

One of the issues in set is that we all have schemas—things that we expect to happen given a certain situation, a type of person, or some experience. If we can take the information learned from previous encounters and relate it to a new situation, without confining ourselves to one schema, then we are more likely to be able to handle whatever curve balls come our way. In the same sense, we follow certain scripts in life. For instance, we know just how to act if we walk into a room where our boss and coworkers are enjoying an after-hours cocktail party. But if a usually

CULTURE AND PROBLEM SOLVING: COPING STRATEGIES

An important concept in psychology is that of coping. Coping is a strategy used to decrease the effects of stress. Although not explicitly stated, the presentation of a problem may result in stress, defined as an environmental demand that results in an unpleasant physiological experience such as headache or muscle tension. A recent study by Erica Frydenberg and her colleagues at the University of Melbourne examined the types of strategies adolescents use to deal with stress. Frydenberg's study is a cross-cultural one in that the adolescents in the study represent Palestine, Colombia, Germany, and Australia. She discovered that there were differences in the types of strategies used by the Palestinian (mean age 15) and Colombian youths (mean age 16). They were more likely to use strategies that focused on seeking spiritual support and social action, using a positive outlook, engaging in active problem solving, and using worry strategies (concerns about the future). The German (mean age 14) and Australian (mean age 17) adolescents were more likely to use strategies that focused on physical recreation.

Such a study is important to help us understand the different strategies that are used to deal with problems. For example, we may find that a person does not use certain strategies because he is unaware of them. We can then use education to provide him with knowledge of effective problem-solving strategies.

prim, straight-laced worker becomes inebriated and picks a fight with the boss, the script is ruined. Most of us will feel uncomfortable, and no one will know exactly how to act.

One commonly seen type of set is *functional fixedness*, where we see an object as only being useful in one way, and we are unable to view other uses for that object. A popular phrase that refers to a way around this problem is "thinking outside the box." Instead of viewing problems in one way, a more creative person will look for solutions that are more versatile or unusual.

Problem Solving versus Reasoning

Psychologists differ on whether reasoning is the same as problem solving. Although there is overlap between the concepts, psychologists tend to use the term *problem solving* when referring to a specific topic (for example, math). Whatever your stance, it is inarguable that our ability to solve problems is related to our ability to reason. We will present two important elements in reasoning: deductive and inductive.

Deductive reasoning usually begins with someone looking at the whole scenario and then breaking things down to see if an idea applies to the present situation. He then goes on to develop a hypothesis about the situation, which shows if he is right or wrong when it is tested. Let's use an example to illustrate the concept. Before the parents of a newborn leave her with the babysitter, they give the babysitter the following instructions: "Comfort the baby if she is in distress." Later that evening, the babysitter runs into the nursery when she hears the baby crying. She picks the baby up. Why? What reasoning led her to this behavior? The words of the parents were "Comfort the baby if she is in distress." So the babysitter breaks this into the following segments: crying is a form of distress; holding the baby provides comfort; therefore, I will pick up the baby.

Inductive reasoning, also referred to as non-deductive reasoning, begins with very specific ideas or hints. As someone begins to notice patterns that are repeated, he develops a hypothesis based on those observations, and this leads to a larger conclusion that can be tested. Using our babysitter example, let's say that the babysitter has noticed the following situations: babies cry when distressed, and holding a baby is a form of comfort. The sitter then combines these two specific ideas to come to the larger conclusion: If the baby cries, holding her will ease her distress.

TRY THESE PROBLEMS

Now that you're familiar with the approaches, try your hand at problem solving. The solutions appear at the end of the chapter.

1. *The candle*
   Using two candles, a box of matches, and a box of thumbtacks, how would you mount the candles to the wall?
2. *The hourglasses*
   You have a nine-minute and a five-minute hourglass. Given only these two hourglasses, how can you time a thirteen-minute swim?
3. *The six-match problem*
   Arrange six kitchen matches so that they form four equilateral triangles.

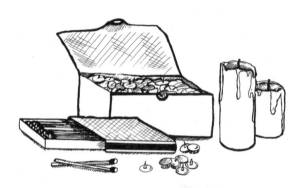

Two Candles, a Box of Thumbtacks and a Box of Matches

DECISION MAKING

We must make a variety of decisions every day, such as what to wear, what to eat, which route to take to a restaurant, and which movie to see. We also make many larger decisions, and these choices may impact our family life, career, and health. Psychologists are interested in discovering and understanding strategies that can improve our ability to engage in effective decision making.

Decision making is similar to problem solving, except we already know all our possible choices. Given these options, we select the one that we think will yield the best outcome. And how do we know what the best outcome might be? Here is the major difference between decision making and problem solving: decision making is subjective. What might yield the best outcome for me may not yield the best outcome for you.

Two common approaches to making decisions are the compensatory and noncompensatory models.

Compensatory Model

The compensatory model is a logical approach to decision making. The individual lists all the options and creates criteria for each option. Next, she analyzes each option and gives it a score based on various criteria. The option with the highest score is probably her choice. Let us say the decision involves a new or previously owned car purchase. Her criteria are attractiveness, new features, and price. The maximum score for each criterion is ten.

	Attractiveness	New features	Price	Score
New car	9	10	1	20
Previously owned	7	6	10	23

Given these criteria and the final score, her decision should be to go with the previously owned car. The advantage of this approach is that it allows a weak area in one criterion to be balanced out by a strong area in another criterion. The disadvantage is that decision making is not so rational. Although the numbers point to the purchase of a previously owned car, what if she just can't get over her desire for that new car smell? We will discuss the power of emotions in the next chapter, but it's important to notice here how those strong feelings might sway an otherwise logical decision.

Noncompensatory Model

Most people do not opt for such a systematic approach when faced with a decision. Think of the new car/used car decision just mentioned. Additionally, some actions may require quick decision making, and the opportunity of sitting, listing, and evaluating options—as in the case of the compensatory model—is not always possible. In this case, a person may use the noncompensatory model of decision making, where the weakness of one criterion in an option is not balanced by the strength of another criterion in that same option. One example of a noncompensatory approach is common: someone lists all his options and then eliminates some. There isn't any consideration for balancing the weak and strong areas of an option. In the case of the person purchasing a car, she may totally eliminate the option of purchasing a previously owned car because she cannot find one with a DVD player. Psychologists agree that this type of decision making is short-sighted and may result in not making the best decision about a dilemma.

CHAPTER SUMMARY

The area of cognition or cognitive psychology examines how we acquire and use information. In this chapter, we covered three areas in the field of cognition: language, problem solving, and decision making. These areas are of great interest because they are an integral part of our everyday lives.

Language allows us to share information, thoughts, ideas, and feelings with others. Language has the qualities of displacement, meaningfulness, and productiveness. One theory in language acquisition proposes that the ability to acquire language is innate; another theory suggests that our environment reinforces language acquisition.

Approaches to problem solving include retrieval from memory, trial and error, brainstorming, algorithms, and heuristics. Each has advantages and disadvantages. Decision making may be involved in trivial or life-altering dilemmas. Approaches to decision making include the systematic compensatory model or the nonsystematic noncompensatory model.

Solutions to Problems

1. *The candle problem*
   This problem illustrates functional fixedness; that is, you have set ideas about what you would do with these materials. The solution to the problem: dump out the contents of one of the boxes, either the matches or the thumbtacks. Use the thumbtacks to attach the box to the wall. Place one of the candles on top of the box. Attach the candle to the box with a thumbtack. The box can be used as a candleholder.

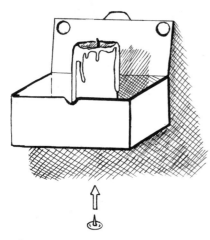

Candle Mounted on Wall

2. *The hourglasses*
   The solution to the problem: start both hourglasses. When the five-minute hourglass runs out (five minutes have elapsed), turn it over to start it again. When the nine-minute hourglass runs out, turn over the five-minute hourglass. At this point, there will only be one minute left in the five-minute hourglass; therefore, when you turn the hourglass over, it will only run for four minutes. Consequently, when it again runs out, you will have been swimming thirteen minutes.

3. *The six-match problem*
   Join the six matches to form a pyramid. This solution taps into set, because when you think four equilateral triangles, you probably think of the triangles as being separate rather than joined.

Arranged Matches

TEST YOUR RECALL AND RECOGNITION

True/False

1. Cognition focuses on our expressions of feelings and behaviors.

2. Language must be verbal.

3. Language has the following characteristics: displacement, meaningfulness, and productiveness.

4. According to Noam Chomsky, language acquisition is innate.

5. A child speaks, and her parents hug and kiss her; this pattern illustrates the behavioral theory of language acquisition.

6. In an effort to work his way through a maze, a rat tries different pathways until he finds the exit. This pattern illustrates an approach to problem solving.

7. "Coffee filters are only for making coffee." This statement illustrates functional fixedness.

8. Decisions are subjective and influenced by emotions.

9. When attempting to make a decision, we typically rely on complementary and non-complementary models of decision making.

10. Topics in cognition are difficult to apply to human experiences in daily living.

Multiple Choice

1. Cognitive psychology emphasizes
   a. thinking.
   b. language.
   c. problem solving.
   d. all of the above.

2. You describe your plans for summer vacation to your coworkers. This illustrates which characteristic of language?

    a. displacement

    b. meaningfulness

    c. productiveness

    d. none of the above

3. Although two-year-old Sara only knows a hundred words, she can use them to make thousands of sentences. This ability illustrates which characteristic of language?

    a. displacement

    b. meaningfulness

    c. productiveness

    d. none of the above

4. When your supervisor explains the use of the new copier, although you are unfamiliar with the equipment, you understand his words and can grasp his instructions. This illustrates which characteristic of language?

    a. displacement

    b. meaningfulness

    c. productiveness

    d. none of the above

5. What does LAD stand for?

    a. learning and describing

    b. learning acquisition device

    c. language acquisition device

    d. language aversion device

6. As Lily approaches her office building, she begins to search through her purse for her employee identification card, which is required for entry into her building. As she walks down the street, she randomly pulls items out of her purse and places them in her pockets. She extracts her house keys, her address book, a credit card, and then, finally, her ID. What approach to problem solving is Lily using?

    a. means-end analysis

    b. hill climbing

    c. compensatory model

    d. trial and error

7. Cynthia must decide what color to paint her living room. She begins by listing every color that might complement the furniture in the room. Which problem-solving strategy is she using?

    a. brainstorming

    b. working backward

    c. retrieval from memory

    d. trial and error

8. Although it will break his budget for the month, Wayne purchases a new tennis racket. When asked why, Wayne replies, "Because I love it, and now I will be the envy of all my friends." Wayne's decision making illustrates which idea?

    a. Decision making is subjective.

    b. Emotions are involved in decision making.

    c. What might be the best decision for one person may not be the best decision for another.

    d. All of the above.

9. In an effort to decide which school to attend, Fern makes a list of her school options and then her criteria for schools. She then examines each school and rates each school on each criterion. When finished, one school has a higher overall score than the other schools. Fern decides that this is the school she will attend.

Which model of decision making did Fern utilize?

a. trial and error

b. noncompensatory

c. hill climbing

d. compensatory

10. Which of the following is *not* related to cognition?

a. thoughts

b. mental images

c. internal language

d. all of the above

Fill in the Blanks

1. Cognition examines the _____ and _____ of knowledge.

2. Two people are engaged in discussion; both nod in response to the other. This nonverbal behavior communicates, "I understand what you are saying." This interaction illustrates the characteristic of language known as _____.

3. Computer slang illustrates the _____ of language.

4. Adults find it difficult to learn a new language, but young children don't seem to have such difficulty with language _____.

5. Behavioral theories do not account for the acquisition of _____ language.

6. _____ _____ allows a person to estimate his proximity to a goal.

7. Our approach to problem solving is based on previous experiences with problem solving. This sometimes results in a narrow scope in our approach and is referred to as _____.

8. The problem in which subjects are given candles, a box of matches, and a box of thumbtacks and then asked to mount the candle on the wall is used to illustrate _____ _____.

9. Jasmine has been assigned a term paper for her history class. She decides to tackle this problem by breaking the project into smaller projects. She is using _____ as her problem solving strategy.

10. Two approaches to decision making are the _____ model and the _____ model.

ANSWERS TO QUESTIONS
True/False

1. false	6. true
2. false	7. true
3. true	8. true
4. true	9. false
5. true	10. false

Multiple Choice

1. d	6. d
2. a	7. a
3. c	8. d
4. b	9. d
5. c	10. d

Fill in the Blanks

1. acquisition; use
2. meaningfulness
3. productiveness
4. acquisition
5. new
6. Hill climbing
7. set
8. functional fixedness
9. subgoals
10. compensatory; noncompensatory

ADDITIONAL RESOURCES

Books

Baars, B. J. 1986. *The cognitive revolution in psychology*. New York: Guilford Press.

Baron, J. 1988. *Thinking and deciding*. Cambridge: Cambridge University Press.

Davis, G. A. 1973. *The psychology of problem solving*. New York: Basic Books.

Duncker, K. 1945. "On problem solving." *Psychological monographs*. 58, no. 5: 113.

Gardner, H. 1985. *The mind's new science*. New York: Basic Book.

Kahnerman, D., P. Slovic, and A. Tversky, eds. 1982. *A judgment under uncertainty*. New York: Cambridge University Press.

MOTIVATION AND EMOTION

biological motivator, psychological motivator, social motivator, stimulus, nonverbal expression, verbal expression, emotion, homeostasis

One of the mysteries of life is why people act the way they do. We've all been puzzled by other people's behavior, the words they have spoken, or their unwarranted emotional responses. One of the challenges of modern psychology is to understand what motivates people to act and speak as they do, and what is really meant by their emotional responses.

Consider the following examples. An apparently well-balanced, well-prepared college student studies through the night in preparation for an exam. A young child, who has no indications of being troubled, suddenly steals a loaf of bread from the local grocery store. A depressed woman tells her doctor how much better she is feeling now that she's in therapy, but a few days later, she attempts suicide.

What makes these people behave in ways that ultimately cause them harm? Unfortunately, it is impossible to answer such questions because the answer is different for every individual and for every situation. Psychologists have struggled for years to find answers to why people behave in particular ways.

We do know that our motivations are closely linked to emotions. We can classify motivation in three categories—biological, psychological, and social—and study theories and expressions of emotion. We cannot, however, always

predict human behavior, because even the simplest-seeming motivations and emotions are complex and intertwined.

MOTIVATION

Motivation directs our behavior. Motivation can be defined as an urge or a need that leads to a goal-oriented behavior. A simple example of motivation occurs when you are thirsty, and you get a drink. Thirst is the motivator, and the goal-oriented behavior is the action that helps you quench your thirst.

To find examples of negative motivators, you only need to open a newspaper. Why did a mother murder her children? Why did a group of teens in New York City beat a homeless man to death?

For any motivation, there are many different goal-oriented behaviors. To satisfy your thirst, maybe you went to the refrigerator and selected a bottle of juice, went to the store and bought

MOTIVATORS OF HUMAN BEHAVIOR

Biological:	instinctive actions necessary for survival
Psychological:	actions that bring about a sense of well-being
Social:	actions that are learned and help a person achieve or feel successful

a bottle of water, or reached across your desk and grabbed a can of soda. The urge is triggered by a stimulus. Your thirst could be the result of a recent long-distance run, the sweltering temperature, or the bag of salty peanuts that you recently consumed.

Simply put, stimulus initiates need, and the need results in a behavior. Probably the motivators of which we are least aware, or which aren't frequently questioned, are those that are driven by biological needs.

Biological Motivators

We don't learn biological motivators or primary drives; we are born with them. Necessary for the survival of the individual, biological needs take priority over any other type of drive.

You may study all night because you feel the need to achieve (social drive), but if you need to use the restroom, that biological need will probably take priority over the social drive.

Primary needs are also key in homeostasis, the body's need to return to a previous balance. In other words, engaging in a certain behavior returns you to a previous state of being. For example, after you consume a tall glass of water, you are no longer thirsty. You feel as you did before. Examples of primary drives include— but are not limited to—hunger, thirst, the excretion of waste (urine and feces), and sleep.

Psychological Motivations

Psychological drives are linked to mental well-being. Answering the call of a psychological drive does not impact life or death, but it will make you feel better. Has your curiosity ever spurred you to take apart an electrical appliance so that you could see how it works? If so,

HUNGER: A WELL-RESEARCHED BIOLOGICAL MOTIVATION

The biological drive that seems to have elicited the most research is hunger. Why do people get hungry? The answer to this question is not simple. In an effort to understand what triggers hunger, researchers have looked at various areas of the body including the brain, the bloodstream, and the receptors of the stomach.

In the hypothalamus, located at the base of the brain, there are centers that signal hunger or satiation. Rats with a lesioned hypothalamus will overeat or starve to death. Hunger appears to be signaled by low glucose levels in the blood and low fat levels in the stomach.

Hunger is also signaled by nonbiological factors. People rarely start or finish a meal based solely on bodily cues. Research has shown that rats overeat when they are in groups and when the food is varied and attractive. What does this mean for humans? You probably should decline all offers from friends to attend the all-you-can-eat Sunday brunch!

then you understand the strong urge or drive associated with curiosity.

According to George Lowenstein in his study "The Psychology of Curiosity: A Review and Reinterpretation," published in the *Psychological Bulletin* in 1994, the psychological drive may come from a desire to obtain a missing piece of information, and once we have that, we have satisfied the urge. In essence, information is the food for curiosity.

Sex

One psychological drive that constitutes a popular area of study is sex. Although some believe sex to be a biological drive, most psychologists agree that it is not, for two reasons. First, sex is important for the survival of the species, but it is not necessary for the survival of the individual. It is impossible to live for long without food or water (we can live for about three days without water and a little over a week without food), but people can live without sex.

Second, even though sex creates a sense of well-being, that sense comes from arousal, not homeostasis. Other motivations initiate behaviors that return us to the state we were in to begin with; they do not fuel behaviors that change that state.

Aggression

Another psychological drive that receives a lot of attention is aggression. If you have ever honked your horn and gestured to the motorist who almost caused you to hit a light pole, you are familiar with road rage. If you have ever felt like kicking the person who sat in the airline seat next to you for encroaching on your personal space with her laptop, cell phone, palm pilot, and briefcase, you have experienced air rage. If you have ever considered shredding all the newspapers, magazines, catalogs, and other personal papers of your office mate because his belongings always seem to end up in your workspace, you have experienced the latest rage: desk rage.

In an article in a publication of the American Psychological Association, *Monitor on Psychology*, dated July/August, 2001, author Jennifer Daw discusses the implications of these types of aggression. We've all heard stories of people who were injured or killed in road rage disputes. Recently in the news, we heard stories of airline employees who have been beaten by disgruntled passengers. Now, such aggression has become the focus of research in the work-

place. Two industrial psychologists, Michael McIntyre and Lawrence James at the University of Tennessee, discovered that aggression in the workplace is not always observed as being physical or direct. These researchers found a preponderance of indirect aggression, such as the employee who tries to hurt others through gossip, who arrives late for work or meetings, or who communicates his feelings in a passive-aggressive manner.

In an effort to prevent the violence that such rage may elicit, Eric Shaw of the Storz Association in New York is developing software to detect e-mail aggression. This software will look for certain negative words (for example, kill) in messages. Information about patterns of aggression in e-mail messages will be passed on to the employer who will then make decisions about whether or not to intervene.

Social Motivators

Social motives are learned. We are not born with these motives. We must not underestimate the power of social motives, however, as they drive behavior. Think about the student who overcomes the need for sleep and rest in order to study all night. The social motivation to earn an A in that class is quite strong.

David McClelland, one of the authors of *The Achievement Motive*, published in 1953, is noted for developing a sketch of a person who has a high level of achievement motivation, and for developing a method to assess the need for achievement. In his sketch, people described as hard workers are confident, energetic, and quick to accept challenges. However, high achievers may also suffer from physical problems like ulcers because they push themselves too hard, sometimes at the expense of their health.

Some people are driven by other learned motivators, such as money and power. You've seen the person for whom life is fast paced. He works long hours in a stressful, competitive environment. He is constantly trying to make more money and get a promotion, and both must occur now! This person would be described as a type A personality. The health complications most often associated with type A personality are cardiac related.

This pattern of behavior was first identified in the 1950s by two cardiologists, Meyer Friedman and Ray Rosenman. The opposing personality is the easygoing type B personality.

A final social motivator is belongingness. People engage in behaviors because they feel a need to belong to a group. In a volume of the *Psychological Bulletin* published in 2003, Roy Baumeister of Case Western Reserve University and Mark Leary of Wake Forest University compared the need for belonging to the need for food. The need to belong may have evolutionary ties, since being a part of a group often meant receiving protection and food; therefore, belonging meant survival. An understanding of the importance of belonging sheds light on why some people remain in belonging situations that aren't healthy. For example, why a woman remains with an abusive spouse or an adolescent becomes affiliated with a gang.

EMOTION

Emotions are even more complex than motivations. They drive behavior, yet one emotion can elicit many different behaviors.

If you ever want to explore the range of behaviors linked to one emotion, just watch a game show on television. What do the winning contestants do? Some jump, some laugh, some grab the host, and others cry. The contestants might describe themselves as happy, but their behaviors vary widely.

Similarly, one behavior may be linked to a variety of emotions. For example, many emotions are associated with crying. People cry when they are sad, fearful, or happy.

Emotions are important to understand. The ability to read emotions may lead to an improved understanding of a person's behavior. However, the complexity of emotions cannot be overstated. Two very important theories of emotions are the James-Lange Theory and the Cannon-Bard Theory.

Theories of Emotion

The earliest theory of emotion, the *James-Lange Theory*, developed by two researchers, Carl Lange and William James in the 1880s, maintains that physiological change precedes emotion. Interestingly, these two men worked independently of each other, James in the United States and Lange in Denmark. They developed the theory at the same time, and so it carries both their names. According to the theory, some stimulus in the environment (for example, you are home alone and you hear a loud sound outside your window) results in a physiological change (for example, your heart begins to race, your breathing becomes more rapid), which is then interpreted as an emotion (for example, I'm afraid). This process is instantaneous, and you are unaware that it is happening.

IN THE ENVIRONMENT		
Stimulus	Physiological Change	Emotion
Game show host: "You've just won a trip to Hawaii!"	increased heart rate	"I'm so happy!"

Criticisms of the James-Lange theory led to the development of the *Cannon-Bard Theory* of emotion by Walter Cannon and Philip Bard in 1927. The James-Lange theory was criticized because there were instances when people felt some physiological arousal, but no emotion was appropriate to label that arousal. For example, when you exercise and your heart rate increases, you don't associate an emotion with the change in heart rate. You just say, "Oh, my heart is racing because I'm exercising."

Another criticism is that the James-Lange theory makes it sound as if some time elapses between the stimulus, the physiological change, and the emotion, even though we know that these events appear to happen all at the same time. Conversely, according to the Cannon-Bard Theory, emotions and physiological changes occur simultaneously, not one after another. If we return to the example of the game show host, instead of feeling first the physiological change followed by happiness, you would experience the increased heart rate and feeling of happiness at the same time.

So what causes us to feel emotions? Do our bodies tell us through some physiological change? Or do our emotional responses happen in tandem with our physiological responses? These two theories were the first to attempt to answer those questions. Since the development of the theories, researchers have explored other avenues to understand what causes us to feel emotions. Recent research by Paul Ekman points to the possibility that facial expression, not just internal physiology, has an influence on emotions.

Expressions of Emotion

Expressions of emotion provide insight into the feelings of another. This expression may come in the form of nonverbal communications: a smile, a wave, increasing or decreasing personal space. This expression may also come in the form of verbal communication: a word or many words.

The human face has forty-four facial muscles, and only four are used for chewing; the remaining forty are used to create facial expressions. That number says a lot about the importance of facial expressions.

A glare can lead to physical confrontation. A smile will probably lead to something much more pleasant. The interesting thing is that in spite of all the different languages spoken in this world, the interpretation of facial expressions is universal. When Paul Ekman, a researcher affiliated with the University of California at San Francisco's Department of Psychiatry, asked people from a variety of countries (Estonia, Greece, Hong Kong, Indonesia, Italy, Japan, Scotland, Turkey, United States of America, and West Germany) to identify the meaning of facial expressions, they were mostly in agreement. As a result of his studies, Ekman proposed that there are seven emotions: happiness, surprise, sadness, fear, disgust, anger, and contempt.

Other examples of nonverbal expressions of emotion in our everyday lives include body language—our posture and the way we sit, stand, or move. When children are angry and they pout, what do they often do with their arms? They fold them. In 1987, Shunya Sogon conducted a study in which college students were asked to identify emotions based on body movements. Although students found positive emotions more difficult to identify than the negative emotions, overall, the students were quite successful at decoding body language.

We also express our feelings through the use of personal space. Ever notice a young couple intertwined on a bench or an angry parent who walks far ahead of a brooding child? Typically, we stand closest to those for whom we have positive feelings (like the young lovers), and keep our distance from those who have upset us (like the feuding parent and child).

Understanding personal space also requires an understanding of cultural differences. The normal conversation distance between people differs across cultures. In 1982, Sussman and Rosenfeld conducted a study with subjects from three countries: the United States, Japan, and Venezuela. They found that subjects from Japan had the greatest conversational distance, and those from Venezuela had the least conversational distance. The amount of conversational distance expressed by those from the United States fell in between that of the other two countries.

For the psychologist, the correct interpretation of nonverbal expressions of emotion is key. For the client who is reluctant to share emotions or is uncertain of the many emotions swirling within, a therapist who is able to decode nonverbal expressions can make the difference between successful diagnosis and treatment and an incorrect approach to therapy.

Verbal Expression

Although it may seem obvious for people to say what they mean, we know that is not always the case. A person says she is happy while scowling, or grins as she tells us that she is going to hurt herself. The chapter on abnormal behavior (chapter 12) discusses some disorders associated with this inconsistency (the difference between what is said verbally and what is said nonverbally).

Finally, a relatively new area of research focuses not on what is said but on how something is said. This new area of interest, called *paralanguage*, focuses on vocal expression—such as tone, rate of speech, pauses, and vocal inflections—and what these characteristics of language communicate about emotions.

Clinicians look for characteristics of speech and use them diagnostically. For example, depressed patients are known to speak with a low voice and flat tone. Because of the slow motor responses seen in depressed people, the depressed person may also exhibit long pauses between words or phrases. The person exhibiting a manic phase will speak quickly and may even have to pause to catch his breath.

CHAPTER SUMMARY

People have long wondered what motivates behavior, what elicits certain emotions, and why there are so many individual differences in the expression of emotions.

Motivations can be divided into three categories: biological, psychological, and social. Biological motivations are necessary for the survival of the individual. They are not learned. They include hunger, thirst, sleep, and the need to excrete waste.

Psychological motivations are not necessary for the survival of the individual. The goal of psychological drives is to bring about a sense of well-being. Sex and curiosity are two examples of behaviors that are associated with psychological drives.

Social drives are learned. Refer to chapter 7 for a more detailed description of learning. The need for achievement is an example of a social drive.

Emotions are feelings, and they may be expressed verbally or nonverbally through facial expressions and body language. Based on the work of Paul Ekman, seven emotions have been identified: happiness, surprise, sadness, fear, disgust, anger, and contempt.

For the psychologist, understanding the categories of motivations and the behaviors they result in and being able to interpret human emotion are integral to the study of human psychology.

So, why did that child steal that loaf of bread? Was it to satisfy the primary, or biological, need of hunger? Why did that woman kill her offspring? Was this aggression out of control? Why did those teens murder that man? Did this occur because of their need to feel a sense of belonging to a group? Of course, it is not that simple. There are more factors that drive behaviors than motivations alone, and some behaviors may even be driven by a combination of motivators. For example, looters who destroy their neighbors' property out of a sense of belonging and a necessity to meet biological needs are operating under the influence of multiple motivators.

It is the task of the psychologist to couple an understanding of what motivates a person to act and what emotions are communicated, because both factors precede a behavior. Both motivations and emotions can help us understand behavior.

TEST YOUR RECALL AND RECOGNITION

True/False

1. For each need, there is one corresponding behavior.

2. The behaviors brought about through primary drives are necessary for the survival of the individual.

3. People eat only when hungry.

4. Curiosity and sex are two examples of behaviors that are controlled by psychological drives.

5. People who are high in need of achievement may work to satisfy achievement goals at the expense of their physical health.

6. Most of the muscles in the face are devoted to chewing.

7. Two of the earliest theorists of emotion are James-Lange and Smith-Wesson.

8. According to Paul Ekman, facial expressions are universal.

9. There is always consistency between verbal and nonverbal communication.

10. Paralanguage refers to vocal tone and inflections.

Multiple Choice

1. The term *primary drive* is often substituted for which of the following terms?

    a. psychological drive

    b. social drive

    c. biological drive

    d. secondary drive

2. Rebecca loves bird watching. While vacationing in the rainforest, she spies a rare and beautiful bird. She is thrilled! She begins to follow the bird, and he leads her to a river. Upon reaching the banks of the river, she realizes that she is thirsty. She returns to her campsite for a drink. This example illustrates the power of

   a. social drives.

   b. psychological drives.

   c. developmental drives.

   d. biological drives.

3. Which behavior is *not* motivated by a psychological drive?

   a. thirst

   b. curiosity

   c. sleep

   d. both a and c

4. Ursula will graduate first in her law school class, but this comes as no surprise to those who know her. She has always been an excellent student. She sets high standards for herself and studies all the time. Which type of drive motivates Ursula's need for academic excellence?

   a. biological

   b. psychological

   c. social

   d. none of the above

5. Jennifer has just received news that she has been accepted to her favorite college. After reading the letter, she begins to sob. Jennifer's behavior speaks to the complexity of

   a. motivations.

   b. emotions.

   c. both a and b.

   d. neither a nor b.

6. Physiological changes occur at the same time as the emotion. Which theory of emotion is associated with this reasoning?

   a. Cannon-Bard

   b. Johnson-Johnson

   c. James-Lange

   d. Freud-Skinner

7. Which of the following is *not* an emotion defined by Ekman?

   a. embarrassment   c. contempt

   b. sadness   d. surprise

8. Joshua is not thrilled about today's job interview. He has worked hard to become a great pastry chef. Because he is in desperate need of money, he has agreed to interview for a job at a local diner. As he waits for the interview to begin, he sits with arms and legs crossed. Joshua is communicating his disgust with his situation through

   a. verbal language.

   b. paralanguage.

   c. nonverbal language.

   d. facial expressions.

9. Ruby is underconfident and she communicates this lack of confidence in many ways, including the way she speaks. Every phrase uttered by Ruby sounds like a question. Ruby recently went on a first date, and most of the conversation that evening sounded like this:

   Cody: "How old are you?"

   Ruby: "I'm twenty-four?"

   Cody: "I'm twenty-five. So hey, that means you graduated with Pete Williams. Do you know him?"

   Ruby: "Yes, I know Pete Williams?"

Ruby's pattern of speech may be of interest to someone who studies

   a. paralanguage.

   b. sign language.

   c. nonverbal language.

   d. facial expressions.

10. Which of the following person(s) is/are interested in interpreting emotions?

   a. therapists

   b. researchers

   c. the general public

   d. all of the above

Fill in the Blanks

1. _____ leads to need, which leads to behavior.

2. A lesion in a rat's hypothalamus led to _____ or starvation.

3. Hunger and thirst are associated with _____ or _____ drives.

4. _____ means to return the body to a previous state of being.

5. Sex is most often characterized as a(n) _____ drive, not a(n) _____ or _____ drive.

6. McClelland developed tools to help assess a person's need for _____.

7. James-Lange theory states that stimulus leads to _____, which in turn leads to emotion.

8. According to Ekman, there are seven emotions: _____, _____, _____, _____, _____, _____, and _____.

9. Therapists may interpret inconsistencies between _____ language and _____ language as a problematic signal.

10. Paralanguage examines not what you say, but _____ you say it.

ANSWERS TO QUESTIONS

True/False

1. false	6. false
2. true	7. false
3. false	8. true
4. true	9. false
5. true	10. true

Multiple Choice

1. c	6. a
2. d	7. a
3. d	8. c
4. c	9. a
5. b	10. d

Fill in the Blanks

1. Stimulus

2. overeating

3. primary; biological

4. Homeostasis

5. psychological; primary; biological

6. achievement

7. physiological change

8. happiness; surprise; sadness; fear; disgust; anger; contempt

9. verbal; nonverbal

10. how

ADDITIONAL RESOURCES

Books

Ekman, P. 2003. *Emotions revealed: Recognizing faces and feelings to improve communication and emotional life.* New York: Henry Holt & Company, Inc.

Ledoux, J. 1996. *The emotional brain: The mysterious underpinnings of emotional life.* New York: Simon & Schuster.

LEARNING AND MEMORY

classical conditioning, operant conditioning, neutral stimulus, chunking, reinforcement, punishment, shaping, rehearsal, proactive and retroactive interference, startle reflex, recall, recognition

How much does biology, or genetics, influence the kind of person each of us becomes, and how much does our environment influence us? The nature versus nurture debate examines the influence of both factors. Up to this point, through our discussion of physiological psychology, sensation and perception, cognition, and motivation and emotion, we have focused primarily on nature. Now, it's time to explore the impact of environment on our behavior.

Psychologists who view behavior as a consequence of prior experiences are called behavioral psychologists. It is through learning that we develop certain behaviors, and that learning is made possible by memory.

LEARNING

According to behavioral psychologists, we are a result of our environmental experiences. If we can understand a person's environmental background and how he learns, then we can understand his current behavior and predict future behaviors as well.

We will focus on classical conditioning—when we learn to react to a stimulus in the environment—and on operant conditioning—when we react to a reward or punishment.

Classical Conditioning

Classical conditioning is often referred to as Pavlovian, or respondent conditioning. In 1927, Ivan Pavlov, a Russian physiologist and pioneer in this area, conducted a study that has become synonymous with the term *classical conditioning*.

Pavlov's initial research focused on digestion; he received a Nobel Prize in 1904 for his work. During the course of his research, Pavlov noticed that the dogs in his laboratory salivated in response to food.

Salivation is automatic, reflexive, and quite functional. The production of saliva is important in the digestive process. Pavlov, however, took things one step further and added something that would not elicit a response in a dog. He used the sound of a metronome, referred to as a tone or bell. He presented the tone, then food. After repeated pairings of tone and food, Pavlov noticed that the dog would salivate just in response to the tone.

In Pavlov's study, the food is referred to as the unconditioned stimulus (US). The unconditioned stimulus is a feature of the environment and leads to an unconditioned response (UR). The unconditioned response in this case is salivation.

Think of reflexes as examples of unconditioned responses. If someone blows air into your eye, what is your automatic reaction? You blink. The air is the unconditioned stimulus; the blink the unconditioned response.

Pavlov paired the unconditioned stimulus (food) with a neutral stimulus (tone). A neutral stimulus is one that elicits no response. Before conditioning, the tone did not elicit a response in the dog. After conditioning, salivation was no longer an automatic unconditioned response. It became a conditioned response (CR), which was elicited by the conditioned stimulus (CS). The tone was no longer a neutral stimulus; now that it elicits the salivation, it is referred to as a conditioned stimulus. Whenever the dog heard the tone, he salivated.

The pairing of two stimuli (neutral stimulus and the unconditioned stimulus) is most effective when three factors are evident: 1) the conditioned stimulus precedes the unconditioned stimulus, 2) the subject has not had any previous exposure to the conditioned stimulus, and 3) the pairing occurs more than once. In Pavlov's experiment, all three conditions were met.

Classical Conditioning

Before conditioning:

Food → salivation
(US)   (UR)

During conditioning:

Tone   +   food →   salivation
(Neutral Stimulus)   (US)   (UR)

After conditioning:

tone → salivation
(CS)   (CR)

In psychology, other studies illustrate how classical conditioning works. In one famous study by John Watson and Rosalie Rayner in 1920, a toddler named Little Albert was conditioned to fear a white rat. This study is important because it illustrates that conditioning can occur in humans, not just dogs.

It is important to note that Little Albert had not responded to white rats before conditioning. The rat was a neutral stimulus. In the beginning, one researcher made a loud noise that caused Little Albert to cry. His response was a startle reflex, just as you might jump at the sound of a car backfiring.

Because Little Albert was only eleven months old, he was startled by the loud noise, and he began to cry. His response was labeled as fear. During conditioning, one researcher placed a white rat in front of the toddler while the other researcher made the loud noise (US); the response was that the baby cried (UR).

After repeated pairings of rat and noise, the researchers noticed that Little Albert would cry in response to just seeing the rat.

This study applied the principles of classical conditioning to a human subject and demonstrated how a fear may develop. In the same way, classical conditioning can be used by psychologists to unlearn a fear. We'll examine this further, later in this chapter. For now, understand that although the Little Albert study contributed to our knowledge of conditioning, such a study would not be permissible today given the strict guidelines regarding the use of children in psychological research.

The Conditioning of Little Albert

Before conditioning:

$$\text{Loud noise} \rightarrow \text{fear}$$
$$\text{(US)} \qquad \text{(UR)}$$

During conditioning:

$$\text{White rat} \ + \ \text{loud noise} \rightarrow \text{fear}$$
$$\text{(Neutral Stimulus)} \qquad \text{(US)} \qquad \text{(UR)}$$

After conditioning:

$$\text{White rat} \rightarrow \text{fear}$$
$$\text{(CS)} \qquad \text{(CR)}$$

Exception to the Rule of Classical Conditioning

There is a concept in classical conditioning that violates the rule that *repeated* pairings of US and CS are necessary for conditioning to occur: taste aversions. In the classroom, I usually begin my lecture on taste aversions by asking if anyone has a taste aversion. Some of the stories are priceless. I've heard about a variety of foods, (bad seafood, sour milk, corn on the cob, too much chocolate), which have all led to the same end result: illness, usually in the form of nausea and vomiting. You only need *one* pairing of the food and the nausea to set the dislike of the food for the rest of your life.

Recent researchers have looked at the development of taste aversions in cancer patients undergoing chemotherapy. If you understand the classical conditioning paradigm, you can anticipate how taste aversions develop in cancer patients. A patient eats, undergoes some procedure that results in nausea, and links the nausea to the food that was eaten before the procedure. Paul Jacobsen and his colleagues at Memorial Sloan-Kettering Cancer Center in New York City have documented the existence of these taste aversions in women undergoing treatment for breast cancer. For a cancer patient for whom food is vital for maintaining health and strength, the development of unpleasant associations with varying foods is a problem. This is where the health or clinical psychologist can intervene and work with the physician and patient to eliminate the patient's negative associations with food.

Operant Conditioning

Operant conditioning is often referred to as instrumental conditioning. Pioneers in this field include Edward Lee Thorndike (1874–1949) and B. F. Skinner (1904–1990). Thorndike was an American psychologist who worked from a laboratory at Columbia University. Skinner was also an American psychologist, and one of the biggest proponents of behaviorism. He wrote many books about behaviorism, including *Walden II* and *Beyond Freedom and Dignity*. Skinner received his degree from Harvard and then spent some time there doing research, but he was pretty much a free agent in that he went on lecture tours to discuss his stance on behaviorism.

Like Pavlov's dogs, Thorndike's subjects were nonhuman. In 1911, in one of Thorndike's most famous studies, a cat was placed in a wooden box that contained a latch. The door of the crate opened in response to being touched by the cat. When food was placed within the cat's view near the crate, Thorndike observed that the cat quickly learned to open the door of the crate. The food served as a positive reinforcer for the cat's behavior.

Operant conditioning examines the influence that reinforcement and punishment, also called consequences, have on behavior. A reinforcer strengthens behavior. The use of reinforcement makes it more likely that the behavior will occur in the future. There are two types of reinforcement: positive and negative.

Let us look at a typical example of positive reinforcement. James cuts the grass. For this behavior, his father buys him a CD. The behavior is cutting the grass; the reinforcer is the CD. As a result of this experience, James will be more likely to cut the grass in the future.

Negative reinforcement can also be used to strengthen behavior through the removal of an aversive stimulus or punisher, which is something the subject finds unpleasant. For instance, Helen steps outside, and it begins to rain. She opens her umbrella so that she can remain dry. The behavior is opening the umbrella. The aversive stimulus is the rain. As a result of this experience, Helen will be more likely to open her umbrella in the future when she is caught outside in the rain.

Notice that the end result of both positive and negative reinforcement is that the behavior will be more likely to occur in the future under similar circumstances.

Punishment

Operant conditioning also examines the influence that punishment, also called consequences, has on behavior. When we say punishment, most of us think of something negative. It's a reprimand, a fine, some kind of deprivation, but the original intention is that it will weaken a negative behavior. Ideally, punishment is used in combination with reinforcement to strengthen a desirable behavior. For example, if you are caught driving your car beyond the legal speed limit, you will be punished by getting a speeding ticket, and the ticket might help to keep you from driving too fast in the future. The consequence of punishment is that the behavior is less likely to occur in the future under similar circumstances.

Punishment can be both positive and negative. Positive punishment weakens a behavior through the application of some aversive stimulus or event. For instance, Karin arrives at soccer practice ten minutes late; her coach makes her run ten laps around the track. The behavior is being late for practice. The punishment is the exercise. As a result of this experience, Karin will be less likely to be tardy for soccer practice in the future.

Negative punishment weakens a behavior through the removal of a reinforcer. Lyle parks his car in a tow-away zone while he makes a quick trip into the bank. When he returns to the parking lot, his car is gone. His behavior is illegal parking. The reinforcer that has been removed is his car. As a result of this experience, Lyle will be less likely to park illegally in the future.

Reinforcement and Punishment

As you can see, there are some key similarities and differences between both positive and negative reinforcement and positive and negative punishment.

What Happens to the Behavior?

	Behavior is strengthened	Behavior is weakened
Application of stimulus	positive reinforcement	positive punishment
Removal of stimulus	negative reinforcement	negative punishment

Corporal Punishment

Recent research on the effects of corporal punishment is still not entirely clear. For example, researchers, such as Diana Baumrind at the University of California at Berkeley, argue that mild to moderate corporal punishment can be used effectively by parents. In a 2002 review of the literature on corporal punishment, Elizabeth Thompson Gershoff at the National Center for Children in Poverty at Columbia University links it to negative outcomes, such as increased antisocial behavior and aggression. There were certain factors that seemed to buffer the negative effects of corporal punishment, such as the quality of the parent-child relationship, how often parents use the punishment, how forcefully they use it, and how emotional they are when they use it.

One of the problems with corporal punishment is that it leads to immediate compliance in the child. This compliance in essence reinforces the parent's use of corporal punishment. Therefore, it is likely that the parent will use the technique again. This may ultimately result in the overuse of corporal punishment by the parent. Behaviorists have long suggested that the best approach for strengthening desirable behaviors is reinforcement. Rewarding children when they are doing well will emphasize the positive behavior. Undesirable behaviors are best removed through benign approaches like negative punishment. Positive punishment is to be used as a last resort when other approaches have been tried, yet have proven unsuccessful.

Shaping

Reinforcement and punishment may be used to strengthen or weaken an existing behavior, but how can you bring about a behavior that is not in existence? If you ever visit a water park or aquarium, you will see advertisements for various shows. One animal who often stars in these shows is a seal who can play the horn, or dunk a ball, or clap on command. Of course, you realize that this talented seal was not born with these skills. They were created through an operant process that is known as *shaping*.

Shaping is used to create and strengthen nonexistent behavior and does so through the teaching of small steps called *successive approximations*, which build up to the target behavior. A list of successive approximations for teaching a seal to dunk a ball may look like this: touch ball, roll ball, pick ball up with nose, approach basket, place ball in the basket. The training process would begin by reinforcing the seal's actions when the seal touches the ball. (Fish seem to be a popular reinforcer.) After the seal shows that he can consistently touch the ball, the trainer would move to the next step: rolling the ball. Now, the trainer does not reinforce the seal for touching the ball, the seal only receives a fish when he rolls the ball. After he has mastered rolling, the trainer moves to the next step and so on until the seal is, finally, able to place the ball in the basket.

Shaping is the most appropriate approach for teaching behaviors that are nonexistent and complex or consist of many components. Think about a complex task that you have mastered, such as a dance combination or a piece of music on an instrument. It is likely that you learned the skill in small steps and slowly worked your way to your ultimate goal. For example, your dance or music teacher provided positive reinforcement each time you mastered the new material as opposed to capably performing the old.

Applications of Classical Conditioning

So, in what other ways does classical conditioning work in our everyday lives? We've discussed common experiences with classical conditioning, in addition to recent research in health psychology and classical conditioning. In this section, we will discuss how classical conditioning can be used as treatment for undesirable behaviors. The 1971 movie *A Clockwork Orange* illustrates classical conditioning. In this legendary film by Stanley Kubrick, the main character, a young man named Alex, engages in a variety of heinous behaviors, among them the murder of a woman, for which he is sent to prison. While in prison, he is selected to participate in a special program that promises to change him from a rogue to a respectable young man. While in this program, Alex is classically conditioned to become physically ill when exposed to scenes of violence or sex. This movie provides an extreme but memorable example of classical conditioning.

Just as behaviors can be learned through classical conditioning, they may be unlearned through similar methods. This was discovered as far back as 1924 by Mary Cover Jones, a pre-eminent behavioral psychologist at the University of California, who died in 1987 at the age of ninety-one. In her groundbreaking study, Jones taught three-year-old Peter to unlearn his fear of rabbits. First, she allowed Peter to watch other children playing happily with rabbits. Next, he was allowed to eat a favorite food, candy, when he saw the rabbit. Finally, he had a positive response to both the rabbit and the food.

Unlearning a Phobia: The Case of Peter

Before conditioning:
$$\text{Candy} \rightarrow \text{smile (pleasant response)}$$
$$\text{(US)} \qquad \text{(UR)}$$

During conditioning:
$$\text{Rabbit} \;+\; \text{candy} \rightarrow \text{smile}$$
$$\text{(Neutral Stimulus)} \quad \text{(US)} \qquad \text{(UR)}$$

After conditioning:
$$\text{Rabbit} \rightarrow \text{smile}$$
$$\text{(CS)} \qquad \text{(CR)}$$

Behavioral therapists use techniques developed by researchers like Jones to help people unlearn undesirable behaviors, such as phobias. These techniques will be discussed in detail in chapter 13.

Applications of Operant Conditioning

So far we have focused on continuous schedules of reinforcement. Continuous schedules means that every time John cleans his room, he receives $1. But some behaviors operate on an intermittent schedule of reinforcement, which means that the reinforcer is not delivered after each and every instance of the behavior.

The four intermittent schedules of reinforcement are fixed ratio, fixed interval, variable ratio, and variable interval. In a *fixed ratio* (FR) schedule, the reinforcer is delivered after a set number of responses. For example, an employee on an assembly line gets $20 for every ten bicycles assembled. The abbreviation for this type of schedule is FR10. In other words, ten responses are required for reinforcement. In a *fixed interval* (FI) schedule, the reinforcer is delivered after a set amount of time has passed, for example, a paycheck that comes every Friday. This schedule is abbreviated as FI7 because reinforcement occurs after seven days have passed. The schedule could also be abbreviated in a number of other ways such as FI40. Reinforcement occurs after one full work week, which is forty hours long. In a *variable ratio* (VR) schedule, the reinforcer is delivered after a set number of responses occur, on the average. For example, instead of getting $20 for every ten bikes assembled—as with a fixed ratio schedule—

the reinforcement may come after five bikes, or after fifteen, but averaging out to every ten bikes. This schedule of reinforcement is abbreviated as a VR10. In a *variable interval* (VI) schedule of reinforcement, the reinforcer is delivered after a set amount of time has passed, on the average.

Returning to our example of the person on the bicycle assembly line, reinforcement could occur at various times, not necessarily after every four hours, but perhaps after six hours, then after two, but averaging out to every four hours. This schedule of reinforcement would be abbreviated as VI4. The distinguishing factor for the variable schedules is that the time of reinforcement is uncertain. This may result in greater productivity. For example, if you know that you are going to receive $20 after you complete the tenth bike, you may decide to take a break. It has taken you all morning to assemble ten bikes, you are tired, and you decide to rest before you begin working on the next ten bikes. This break is referred to as a postreinforcement pause.

If, on the other hand, you have no idea when reinforcement will occur—after fifteen bikes, after ten, after five—you are less likely to break after receiving reinforcement. The variable schedule of reinforcement explains why you find it so hard to tear yourself away from slot machines. Although you have used your entire roll of quarters, you scrape the bottoms of your pockets looking for one more quarter because you truly believe that the next quarter will give you the big win and will result in reinforcement.

We've all experienced a variety of types of operant and classical conditioning throughout our lives. We continue to engage in some behaviors because they result in reinforcers—praise, paychecks, or awards—and we refrain from other behaviors because they result in punishment, such as tickets, fines, or criticism.

These experiences guide our current and future behaviors. Both operant and classical conditioning are influenced by our ability to remember things and are impacted by forgetfulness.

INTERMITTENT SCHEDULES OF REINFORCEMENT

Type	Definition	Example
fixed ratio	reinforcement occurs after a set number of responses	you receive $20 after making ten bikes
fixed interval	reinforcement occurs after a set amount of time has passed	you receive a paycheck every Friday
variable ratio	reinforcement occurs after a set number of responses, on the average	you receive $20 after making ten bikes, on the average
variable interval	reinforcement occurs after a set amount of time has passed, on the average	you receive a paycheck after one week has passed, on the average

MEMORY

Our ability to remember impacts our behavior. In fact, without memory we would hardly know how to act at all. Recent research has developed into a straightforward explanation of how various types of memory work.

The most widely accepted model of memory is the Information Processing Model that is based on the work of R. C. Atkinson and R. M. Shiffrin in 1968. Their study, "The Psychology of Learning and Motivation: Advances in Research and Theory, vol. 2," proposed three distinct types of memory: sensory memory, short-term memory, and long-term memory.

Information Processing Model/ Atkinson-Shiffrin Model

Sensory memory	→	Short-term memory	→	Long-term memory
↓		↓		↓
lost almost immediately		lasts a few seconds		retrieval difficulties (interference, decay)
↓		↓		↓
limitless capacity		limited capacity (7 ± 2 items)		limitless capacity

Sensory Memory

At any given time, a multitude of stimuli surrounds you. As you read these words, notice other things in your environment like the sounds, the sights, and the smells. When you stop to focus, you are aware that other stimuli exist, but you are not always paying attention to them. If you were, you would find it difficult to read these words.

A study conducted by George Sperling in 1960, "The Information Available in Brief Visual Presentations," clearly illustrates the fleeting nature of sensory memory. Subjects were presented with twelve objects arranged on a 4 × 3 grid (three rows, four objects per row). The experimenter presented the grid for a brief period of time, then asked subjects to identify objects either from the top, middle, or bottom row.

The longer the researchers waited before asking subjects to identify by memory objects from either the top, middle, or bottom row, the poorer the subjects' recall. If they were quizzed immediately, they could name nine to twelve objects; after only a few seconds, the amount recalled decreased to one or three out of twelve.

Short-Term Memory

Once we notice a stimulus, it leaves sensory memory and becomes a part of short-term memory. Unlike sensory memory, we are aware of information in short-term memory. Short-term memory is limited in that only a certain number of items may be stored in short-term memory at any given time. George Miller set the range for this limit at 7 ± 2, or between five and nine items, in his 1956 study "The Magical Number, Seven Plus or Minus Two: Some Limits on Our Capacity for Processing Information." A strategy called *chunking* may be used to expand the capacity of short-term memory.

We can use a list of household chores as an example of chunking. You have ten things to remember: wash the dishes, clean the shower, make the bed, clean the refrigerator, clean the oven, vacuum the bedroom carpet, scrub the toilet, empty the bathroom garbage can, dust the bedroom furniture, and wash the bedroom curtains.

As you can see, this list clearly exceeds our limit of five to nine items, but that limit does not mean that we should give up on completing the household chores. Instead, we should try grouping these items by room.

Bedroom: Make the bed, vacuum the carpet, dust the furniture, and wash the curtains.

Kitchen: Wash the dishes, clean the refrigerator, and clean the oven.

Bathroom: Clean the shower, scrub the toilet, and empty the garbage can.

With the use of chunking, we have successfully reduced our list of items from ten to three. This makes it much more likely that we will remember everything.

Short-term memory is also limited in duration. Items remain in short-term memory for seconds. After this, the items are either lost, or they pass on to long-term memory. One strategy to facilitate the transfer of information from short-term to long-term memory is called *rehearsal*.

Have you ever received a telephone number, only to realize that you have neither pen nor paper? What did you do next? You probably ran for the nearest notepad while mumbling, "123-555-1212 . . . 123-555-1212 . . . 123-555-1212." If this scenario sounds familiar, then you understand rehearsal, a strategy that is used to hold memory and facilitate transfer.

We've talked about short-term memory and how to improve it, and how to move information from short-term to long-term memory, but how do things get into short-term memory in the first place? Initial explanations developed by Donald Broadbent in his 1958 study, "Perception and Communication," revolved around filtering. The idea is that we use selective attention to decide what we will and will not notice. In other words, we shut off unimportant stimuli while attending to important stimuli.

Something called "the cocktail party phenomenon" easily illustrates this idea. Imagine the following scenario: the DJ is playing music, the partygoers are laughing, the smell of food fills the room, and you are engrossed in conversation with an old friend. Although there are many stimuli competing for your attention, you are able to focus on your friend's description of her new car. As you are listening, someone across the room mentions your name. How is it possible for you to identify your name if you are paying attention to only one stimulus at a time and shutting off all other incoming information? Well, the cocktail party phenomenon, expounded by E. Colin Cherry and J. A. Bowles in 1960, demonstrates that filtering is variable—like a dimmer switch as opposed to a traditional light switch. You can turn it up and down, not just on and off, as Anne Treisman discovered in her studies in 1960 and 1964. While socializing at the party, you turned down the volume on the extraneous sounds of the party and turned up the volume on your friend's new car conversation. Because the extraneous sounds were just turned down and not off, you were able to recognize your name being spoken by someone across the room.

Long-Term Memory

Unlike short-term memory, there are no limits on the capacity of long-term memory. The types of information stored in long-term memory may be autobiographical—such as your address, your middle name, the color of your first car—or episodic, as in factual information such as the name of the president, today's date, the number of items in a dozen. Once information enters long-term memory, it remains there until it is needed by short-term memory. Movement between long-and short-term memory is two-way. When we need to remember that number 123-555-1212, we retrieve it from long-term memory and place it in short-term memory, where it is utilized.

Measuring Memory

We all know how important it is to be able to retrieve or pull something from long-term memory and place it into short-term memory. For example, your address and your social security number often need to be retrieved. Experimental psychologists use the ability to retrieve information from long-term memory to assess whether or not information has been remembered or learned. Two techniques to assess learning are the ability to recall information and the ability to recognize information.

Recall involves retrieving information from long-term memory when the information is not in front of you. *Recognition*, on the other hand, involves retrieving information from long-term memory when the information is in front of you but is hidden among other information. At the end of each chapter in this book, you will find examples of tests of recall and recognition. The fill-in-the-blank questions test recall of the information because you are expected to pull the information from within, without any cues. The multi-ple-choice questions test recognition of the information because the information (the answer to the question) is in front of you; it is just hidden in a list with other possible answers.

Forgetting

Information may leave long-term memory as a result of interference. This interference may be proactive or retroactive. In *proactive interference*, old information blocks the retrieval of new information. In *retroactive interference*, new information blocks the retrieval of old information.

EXAMPLES OF PROACTIVE AND RETROACTIVE INTERFERENCE

Problem:
You can't remember your aunt's telephone number.

Reason:
Proactive interference—your aunt recently moved and the only number that comes to mind is her old number; the old information blocks the new.

Retroactive interference—your aunt's son recently moved out of her home, and the only number that comes to mind is the number at his new apartment; new information blocks the old.

How Reliable Is Human Memory? The Issue of False Memories

The star witness sits on the witness stand and testifies that she saw the defendant at the scene of the crime. During examination, she provides great detail about the defendant's actions on the night of the crime. Based on the testimony of the witness, the defendant is sent to prison. Years later, DNA evidence shows that the defendant was not responsible for the crime. False memories can have serious consequences. We all like to think that we accurately remember events and experiences, but research has shown that we are all susceptible to false memories. Forensic psychologists are especially interested in the truthfulness of eyewitness testimonies.

In one of the many cleverly designed studies to assess eyewitness memory, Roy Malpass and Patricia Devine at the State University of New York at Plattsburgh staged a crime in the classroom. During a lecture, college students watched as an unidentified male (who was actually an actor in the study—a confederate) entered their classroom, argued with their instructor, knocked over some classroom equipment, and then left the class. The students were then asked to identify the assailant in a lineup. One hundred students participated in this study, and the researchers discovered that accuracy in identification of the assailant depended on the instructions for lineup identification. Students who were told that they must choose a suspect from the lineup were less accurate in their identifications than those who were told that they did not have to make a choice from a given lineup.

The most prolific researcher in the area of eyewitness testimony, Elizabeth Loftus at the University of California at Irvine, has conducted countless studies on the accuracy of eyewitness testimony. In one of her most recent studies, Loftus, along with Daniel Wright (from the University of Sussex, United Kingdom) and Melanie Hall (also at the University of Sussex), showed subjects an event, either a scene from a restaurant or a drunk driving scene. They were later shown the same event again, but a portion of the event had been removed. When asked to recount

what they had seen, many left out the missing event from their descriptions of the scene.

In response to research on false memories, Janet Reno ordered the creation of "Eyewitness Evidence: A Guide for Law Enforcement." This document was published in 1999 by the United States Department of Justice and may be obtained through the Web at www.ncjrs.org/pdffiles1/178240.pdf. This guide provides concrete examples of steps that law enforcement officials can take to protect the accuracy of eyewitness testimony. The steps include suggestions for the layout of mug books, for interviewing witnesses, and for providing instructions for lineups. It is an excellent example of how psychological research can be used to address the problems of everyday life.

CHAPTER SUMMARY

Environment shapes behavior. According to learning theories, behavior is influenced by experiences. Learning may be referred to as either classical or operant conditioning.

In classical conditioning, an unconditioned stimulus (US) is paired with a neutral stimulus. This pairing results in an unconditioned response (UR). After repeated pairings, the neutral stimulus becomes a conditioned stimulus (CS) as it elicits a conditioned response (CR).

In operant conditioning, the focus is on the consequences of the behavior. Consequences may strengthen behavior (reinforcement), or consequences may weaken behavior (punishment).

The connection between learning and memory is extremely important. Without memory, learning is meaningless. If we are not able to recall the consequences of a particular behavior, we are at great risk. If I can't remember that the last time I touched a hot pan with my bare hand I received a painful burn (positive punishment), then I am at risk of burning my hand again in the future.

According to the information processing model, there are three components to memory: sensory memory, short-term memory, and long-term memory. Information remains in sensory memory for a very brief period of time. Most information is lost from sensory memory, but some is filtered out and sent to short-term memory. Although the capacity for short-term memory is limited and information remains in short-term memory for a brief period of time, there are strategies to increase capacity and to ensure that information is transferred to long-term memory.

Once in long-term memory, information may remain indefinitely. When needed, information is retrieved from long-term memory and placed in short-term memory. Problems with this retrieval may be due to proactive or retroactive interference. In addition, memory is not flawless; we are all susceptible to false memories.

TEST YOUR RECALL AND RECOGNITION

True/False

1. Behaviorists are concerned with the influence of environment on behavior.

2. An eye blink in response to a puff of air is an example of a CS.

3. Little Albert was conditioned to fear a white rat.

4. Reinforcement is a term associated with Pavlovian conditioning.

5. Punishment weakens behavior; reinforcement strengthens behavior.

6. Although many of the subjects of early conditioning studies were nonhuman, the tenets of learning theories apply to human behavior, too.

7. Little Peter was unconditioned to fear a white dog.

8. There are no limits to the capacity for short-term memory.

9. Chunking items will decrease the likelihood of forgetting.

10. Information may be forgotten as a result of interference.

Multiple Choice

1. At the age of five, Stanley was attacked by the neighborhood dog. Although more than forty years have passed since that attack, Stanley cannot pass a dog without shuddering. Stanley's fear of dogs developed through

   a. operant conditioning.
   b. instrumental conditioning.
   c. classical conditioning.
   d. Thorndike conditioning.

2. Classical conditioning may also be referred to as

   a. Thorndike conditioning.
   b. Watson and Rayner conditioning.
   c. Pavlovian conditioning.
   d. Cover Jones conditioning.

3. During dinner, Trevor used an offensive term. As a result of his behavior, his parents removed his telephone privileges for one week. This example illustrates the use of
   a. positive reinforcement.
   b. positive punishment.
   c. negative reinforcement.
   d. negative punishment.

4. Thorndike observed that when the cats in his laboratory opened the door of the crate, they walked out of the crate, approached the food dish, and ate the food in the dish. The food served as
   a. reinforcer.
   b. aversive stimulus.
   c. punisher.
   d. conditioned response.

5. In a fixed-ratio schedule, the reinforcer is delivered
   a. after X number of responses, on the average.
   b. after X number of responses.
   c. after X amount of time, on the average.
   d. after X amount of time.

6. Classical conditioning is most effective when
   a. the CS is presented before the US.
   b. the subject has no previous experience with the CS.
   c. both a and b.
   d. neither a nor b.

7. Which schedule of reinforcement is associated with a postreinforcement pause?
   a. continuous schedule
   b. variable interval
   c. variable ratio
   d. none of the above

8. Your middle name is stored in
   a. sensory memory.
   b. short-term memory.
   c. long-term memory.
   d. momentary memory.

9. You have just received the new PIN for your ATM card. As you drive from the bank, you repeat, "9876, 9876, 9876." What are you doing?
   a. chunking
   b. rehearsing
   c. forgetting
   d. none of the above

10. Items remain in sensory memory for
   a. years.
   b. weeks.
   c. days.
   d. none of the above.

Fill in the Blanks

1. Pavlov's subjects were _____, while Thorndike's subjects were _____.

2. Fido receives a treat whenever he sits on command. Fido is on a(n) _____ schedule of reinforcement.

3. Mary Cover Jones' work with _____ demonstrated that fears can be _____ as well as learned.

4. In negative reinforcement, a(n) _____ is removed.

5. Vivian works for a new company where she is paid, on the average, every thirty days. Vivian is on a(n) _____ schedule.

6. In positive reinforcement, a(n) _____ is applied.

7. You cannot remember your new PIN because your old PIN is stuck in your head. This is an example of _____.

8. To ensure that you do not forget the twenty people who you must call, you might engage in _____.

9. _____ might study the accuracy of eyewitness testimony.

10. Items are permanent once they enter _____.

ANSWERS TO QUESTIONS

True/False

1. true	6. true
2. false	7. false
3. true	8. false
4. false	9. true
5. true	10. true

Multiple Choice

1. c	6. c
2. c	7. d
3. d	8. c
4. a	9. b
5. b	10. d

Fill in the Blanks

1. dogs; cats
2. continuous
3. Peter; unlearned
4. punisher (aversive stimulus)
5. variable interval (VI)
6. reinforcer
7. proactive interference
8. chunking
9. Forensic psychologists
10. long-term memory

ADDITIONAL RESOURCES

Books

Hock, R. 2001. *Forty studies that changed psychology*. Upper Saddle River, NJ: Prentice Hall.

Skinner, B. F. 1971. *Beyond freedom and dignity*. New York: Bantam/Vintage.

Skinner, B. F. 1974. *About behaviorism*. New York: Random House.

Video

A clockwork orange, motion picture, directed by S. Kubrick. United Kingdom: Warner Bros., Swank/16. 1971.

Web site

Association for Behavior Analysis, www.abainternational.org

LIFESPAN PSYCHOLOGY: CONCEPTION, INFANCY, AND CHILDHOOD

KEY TERMS

germinal period, embryonic period, fetal period, zygote, embryo, fetus, teratogens, enzyme-linked immunosorbent assay test, human chorionic gonadotropin, gestational period

Does your genetic make-up determine the kind of person you will be? Can you benefit from or overcome the influences of environment after your birth? We must return to the nature versus nurture debate as we begin to discuss child development. This is one of the topics that receives the most air time. We are always learning about infant bonding and parenting and child development, and probably all of us spend some time wondering exactly what makes us the way we are.

To understand basic issues of human psychology, we need to take a look at issues of conception, infancy, and childhood. The developmental journey into adulthood is complex and filled with choices that are made for each child. The study of changes throughout the lifespan is the focus of the developmental psychologist. We will cover the journey from conception to old age in two chapters: first here, and then in chapter 9, which covers adolescence and adulthood.

Why do we begin our study with conception, infancy, and childhood? Regardless of orientation, researchers agree that what we are today is the result of years of living. Understanding human behavior means understanding an individual's journey on the road of developmental progression.

Two running themes will prevail throughout these chapters: the nature versus nurture debate and the stability versus change debate. If you have ever wondered how a socially outgoing mother could produce a socially withdrawn child, or how identical twins can look the same but have such different dispositions, you have already considered the role of nature and nurture on development. If you have ever attended a high school reunion, you have experienced the stability versus change debate. When I attended my fifteenth high school reunion, I was struck by all the physical changes in my classmates. The captain of the football team is now bald, the most popular girl has crow's feet at her eyes, and both are carrying extra pounds. However, when I interacted with these old friends, I was amazed at how little they had changed. The football captain has maintained his sense of humor, the popular girl her exuberance and love of life. Although there are great changes in development over your life span, other things change very little.

In this discussion, we will talk about development in terms of the average child, but there really is no such individual. There are common milestones in human development, but it is important to realize that no two children develop exactly alike. Each child is unique and is a product of his culture (race/ethnicity, religion, socioeconomic status) and many other environmental factors.

CONCEPTION AND PREGNANCY

Conception

Pregnancy begins with conception: the union of the male's sperm and the female's egg. Embryologists talk of pregnancy in terms of three periods that vary in length. The first is the germinal period (from fertilization to two weeks). This is followed by the embryonic period (weeks two through eight), and finally, there's the fetal period (eight through thirty-eight weeks). Our discussion of prenatal development will follow the embryologist's time frame.

The germinal period begins with fertilization, which typically occurs in the fallopian tubes. The fertilized egg then moves down to the uterus. The organism is referred to as a *zygote*, and its size is microscopic. At the end of this stage, the zygote has firmly planted itself into the uterine wall.

During the embryonic period, the organism is referred to as an *embryo*, and major structures begin to develop. These include the central nervous system, heart, arms, legs, teeth, palate, ears, and external genitalia. At the end of this period, the embryo is only two inches long and weighs less than an ounce.

During the fetal period, the organism is referred to as a *fetus*. Most of the development of the nervous system occurs during this period. Quickening, the movement of the baby in the uterus, is felt by the mother in the fourth or fifth month. After the fifth month, the fetal heartbeat becomes clearer. After the seventh month, the baby is well developed, and its primary job is to grow to an appropriate size. The average baby weighs seven and a half pounds and measures twenty inches.

1 - 2 weeks: zygote to formation of embryonic disc

Zygote   embryonic disc

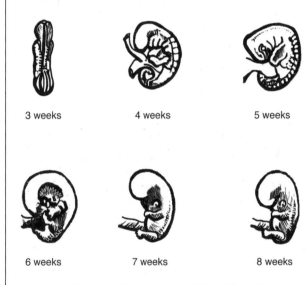

2 - 8 weeks - Embryonic maturation

3 weeks   4 weeks   5 weeks

6 weeks   7 weeks   8 weeks

Embryonic, Germinal, and Fetal Periods

When a woman becomes pregnant, there are certain telltale signs, such as nausea, fatigue, a missed period, increased breast size, and weight gain. Each of these symptoms might be attributed to other conditions, so the only way to determine whether a woman has conceived is through a pregnancy test.

The enzyme-linked immunosorbent assay (ELISA) test can detect even low levels of human chorionic gonadotropin, a sure sign of pregnancy, in the urine. Some very sensitive tests can detect pregnancy within days, even before the first period is missed. A pregnant woman with one fetus will double her levels of human chorionic gonadotropin levels every two days for the first 60 days of a pregnancy. Pregnancy tests can be done either at home or in the physician's office and are very accurate and quick.

The gestational period of pregnancy in humans is forty weeks from the date of the last period, or thirty-eight weeks from conception. The fetus remains in the uterus where the mother's body provides it with everything necessary for growth and development.

Because the fetus totally depends on the mother for nourishment, pregnant women are advised to avoid ingesting anything that might harm the fetus. Teratogens are agents that can cause abnormal growth or development in a developing fetus. These include alcohol, nicotine, illegal/street drugs (such as cocaine), over-the-counter drugs such as aspirin, and many prescription drugs. The period of greatest vulnerability is the embryonic stage (two to eight weeks after fertilization). Exposure to any harmful substances during that time can impact the development of vital structures.

Research has provided some information on the effects of teratogens on prenatal development. It is important to note that before accepting the results of these findings, you should consider the contributions of the environment after birth (nurture), and the genetic contributions of the mother (nature). You must also consider issues in the research methods of these studies.

For instance, because it is unethical to give a pregnant woman drugs and to study the effects of exposure on the newborn, the first studies in this area used animal models. Are the results from these models applicable to humans? Studies since then that have used humans as subjects have relied on women who are battling not only substance use, but also financial and psychological issues. Are the results of these studies applicable to most women? These are questions that drive further exploration into factors that affect development.

Alcohol

Research has long supported the dangers associated with alcohol use during pregnancy. It is the leading cause of birth defects and is most often associated with Fetal Alcohol Syndrome (FAS). The characteristics of this syndrome are facial defects, mental retardation, and slowed growth. Fetal Alcohol Effects (FAE) is the term used to refer to the effects associated with small amounts of alcohol consumption during pregnancy. We are using the term "small," but the research has not yet determined what constitutes small. Since the effects of minimal consumption are controversial, there is currently no safe level of maternal alcohol consumption.

But the research has consistently found that there *are* consequences. A 1990 study by Helen Barr and colleagues looked at prenatal exposure to alcohol as well as other substances and their effects on fine and gross motor performance in four-year-old children. These researchers discovered that the children exhibited problems with fine and gross motor skills, balance, and slowed motor responses that were attributed to their exposure to alcohol before birth.

A review of the literature by Joanne Brady and colleagues in 1990 on the effects of alcohol on prenatal growth outlined the increased risk of miscarriage, stillbirth, premature birth, and low birth weight. The policy of the American Medical Association is that physicians inform their patients of the risks and encourage them to abstain from alcohol while pregnant.

Illegal Street Drugs

Illegal, or street, drugs include heroin, marijuana, PCP, and cocaine, as well as its most popular variation, crack. There are a variety of negative outcomes for the children of drug-using mothers. Some of these effects are compounded by the child's postnatal environment, which may be impoverished and lacking in basic requirements of life, such as food, shelter, clothing, and a sense of safety.

The growing popularity of crack during the 1980s led to the now popular term "crack babies." Joanne Brady and her colleagues list seven conditions for which these babies are at increased risk: premature birth, premature detachment of the placenta, small head size, low birth weight, low Apgar scores (discussed later in this chapter), behavioral problems during the first weeks of life, and meconium staining, which can lead to respiratory complications. Meconium staining occurs when the green intestinal substance, usually passed at birth, is passed before birth and is inhaled by the fetus. Any of these conditions can lead to damage of the central nervous system.

Besides the implications of the physical disabilities, these conditions may result in psychological conditions as well. Marilyn Stern of the University of Albany and Katherine Karraker at West Virginia University found that people tend to hold different expectations for premature infants (babies born before thirty-seven weeks of pregnancy). These expectations impact the adults' perceptions of the infants, something called *prematurity stereotyping.* When subjects were told that babies were born early, they were more likely to label the babies as weak, less social, smaller, less cognitively competent, and less behaviorally appealing than full-term babies. The danger here is that these perceptions may become a self-fulfilling

prophecy where the mother's expectations result in a child who is less competent, feels less loved, and is less secure.

With all the attention on crack, fewer recent studies have looked at the effects of exposure to heroin. Some of its effects appear to be the same as those for cocaine: premature birth, small head size, low birth weight, meconium staining, and miscarriage. After birth, these babies will experience withdrawal symptoms, also referred to as Neonatal Abstinence Syndrome (NAS) as well. The symptoms of this syndrome include irritability and tremors.

Although we will discuss heroin dependence in adults in chapter 11, the implications are significant for the unborn child as well. A common treatment for heroin use is methadone. This drug prevents users from feeling withdrawal symptoms. Pregnant women who are dependent on heroin may connect with a methadone program that will also provide prenatal and postnatal education and care.

Marijuana is the most commonly used illegal drug during pregnancy. The effects are based on heavy usage, and they will appear familiar: low birth weight, meconium staining, premature delivery, and neurological abnormalities.

Polydrug use is another concern. Polydrug use refers to people who use more than one drug, and this makes the researcher's ability to observe the effects of any one drug even more difficult. For example, a pregnant woman may smoke a "blunt," which is a cigar stuffed with marijuana. Here, we have the combination of nicotine and marijuana. Another example is a "squirrel," a combination of PCP, marijuana, and crack or cocaine, which is smoked. In instances of polydrug use, how do we tease apart the effects of the marijuana from the PCP or from the crack/cocaine?

The research on phencyclidine hydrochloride, more commonly referred to as PCP, is nowhere near as extensive as the research on the other illegal drugs. But the existing research points to problems associated with the use of PCP during pregnancy. These include premature delivery and meconium staining, and these babies are characterized as difficult to soothe, which can make parenting such a child incredibly stressful.

So, overall, we know that there are many negative consequences associated with the use of illegal drugs during pregnancy, and these manifest themselves in the form of problems with the newborn. What might be the solution? A controversial approach is to incarcerate pregnant women who are known to take drugs until they deliver. Proponents of this approach say that they are protecting both mother and child. Critics say that drug use is a problem that requires treatment, and incarceration does not provide treatment. In addition, the pregnant woman is made to feel like a criminal, when she is actually a victim dependent on drugs. Another criticism is that such an approach forces women who are actively using drugs while pregnant to hide during their pregnancies. Such a situation makes it less likely that they will receive prenatal care.

Over-the-Counter Drugs

There are many symptoms of pregnancy, and some, which develop as the pregnancy advances, can cause much discomfort. In addition to nausea and fatigue, women commonly suffer from hemorrhoids and back pain. In an effort to cope with painful conditions, some women may reach for over-the-counter drugs. But even these drugs can be harmful. For example, the use of aspirin in pregnant women has been linked to bleeding problems in both mother and child.

Another seemingly benign group of drugs that are used during pregnancy are herbal supplements. I have several friends who swear by the pregnancy teas, which can be found in any supermarket or health food store. But according to a 2003 report by the March of Dimes, these supplements are not regulated by the Food and Drug Administration; therefore, the contents of these supplements can vary greatly by brand or even batch. Some herbal teas, like raspberry or peppermint, when taken in large amounts, may be linked to contractions of the uterus, which could lead to preterm labor or miscarriage. Therefore, it is important that pregnant women avoid all medication, traditional or alternative, until they have consulted their physician.

Prescription Drugs

Some prescription drugs may also be considered teratogens. Therefore, the moment that a woman suspects she is pregnant, she must be made aware of their potential harm. Medications used to treat acne, epilepsy, diabetes, anxiety disorders, cancer, and infections can all have harmful effects on the fetus. Interestingly, some of these drugs can also harm the fetus if the mother took them prior to becoming pregnant. For example, the drug Etretinate, which is used to treat skin problems, can be stored in fat and slowly released in the body. Women who take this drug are encouraged to stop taking it for one year before they become pregnant. It is also important that all medical personnel—dentists, physicians, x-ray technicians, and others—know that a patient might be pregnant.

Pregnant women make a lot of decisions that impact the health of the fetus. Avoiding drugs and alcohol are critical, but a healthy diet and exercise also benefit the baby. Recommendations on diet, exercise, prenatal vitamins, avoiding exposure to harmful substances, caring for existing medical conditions, and getting proper prenatal care come from years of research.

Recently, the popular media has touted the link between prenatal and postnatal exposure to classical music and intelligence. "The Mozart Effect" espouses that prenatal exposure to classical music will improve intelligence. This belief was based on the findings of a 1993 study by Frances Rauscher, Gordon Shaw, and Katherine Ky, who reported that listening to Mozart increased the IQ scores of college students.

What do the experts say? Recent research has overwhelmingly shown that listening to Mozart or any classical music does not result in a significant change in intelligence. Researchers, including Kenneth Steele at Appalachin State University, Christopher Chabris at Harvard Medical School, and Pippa McKelvie and Jason Low at the University of Wellington at Victoria, have all conducted research that fails to replicate the original findings of Rauscher, Shaw, and Ky. This does not mean that all the CDs, DVDs, and videos that promise to boost your child's IQ should be discarded. Stanley Greenspan, one of the country's leading experts on child development, emphasizes that the music still has enhancing properties that contribute to a child's development. Even more important, listening to music can provide many enjoyable experiences, even if it doesn't increase intelligence scores.

The fetus that is protected from harmful substances and receives proper nutrition is at an advantage when it comes to beginning life on his own. Healthy, normal development after birth depends on proper care and nutrition during prenatal development. We will now begin our discussion of postnatal development with a description of the delivery environment.

Delivery Environment

After the mother-to-be has navigated the stages of pregnancy, labor and delivery await. Even babies born under the most arduous circumstances can be happy, well-adjusted infants, but a safe, comfortable delivery improves the odds for all.

Babies may be born at home, in hospitals, or in birthing centers. A hospital or birthing center provides a pleasant, comfortable room with quilts, pictures, and rocking chairs. Additionally, hospitals provide medical equipment that may be necessary in case of a medical emergency. A home birth allows for the delivery to occur in a comfortable and familiar setting. Although the comfort of the mother and baby may not have been uppermost in the minds of medical professionals fifty years ago, today most young couples can deliver their babies in ways that suit their needs and temperaments.

After the Baby's Delivery

There is so much to wonder about in those first moments after a baby is born. Everyone wants to know if it's a girl or boy, does he have any hair, and whom does he look like? Questions abound, but before we look at the first moments of infant development, we should return briefly to the parents.

Adjusting to the birth of a child is both physically and psychologically demanding. The physical demands are evident. There is sleep deprivation, along with the physical recovery that occurs in the mother after delivery, including the many hormonal changes as the mother's body returns to its pre-pregnancy state. The psychological demands are not as obvious.

About seventy percent of new mothers will experience what we call the "baby blues," but these feelings of sadness are fleeting and do not impact the mother's ability to care for her newborn. A smaller number of women will go on to develop postpartum depression, according to a 1999 article by Carolyn Cowan and Philip Cowan, "Interventions to Ease the Transition to Parenthood: Why They Are Needed and What They Can Do." This disorder is characterized by depressed mood, thoughts of harming self or the baby, and hallucinations.

Postpartum depression has been a topic of particular interest in light of a famous case that involved a woman from Texas named Andrea Yates. Yates admitted to drowning her five children on a summer day in June 2001. Her defense was that she was suffering from postpartum depression at the time of the crime, and, therefore, could qualify for an insanity plea. Nevertheless, on March 13, 2002, a jury found Andrea Yates guilty of murder in the drowning deaths of her children. She was sentenced to life in prison and will be eligible for parole in the year 2042.

Although postpartum depression is considered a difficult defense in the United States, this is not the case elsewhere. Other countries, including Italy, Canada, and Great Britain, currently recognize postpartum depression

as a legal defense. Women who have had a history of mental illness before pregnancy are especially vulnerable to postpartum depression. It has been reported that this was true for Yates, who says that she has battled mental illness for many years.

Bonding

The baby's first social contacts are with his caretaker. How that person responds to him, with warmth and kindness, or maybe brusquely and nervously, begins to shape how that infant will respond to others.

The study that introduced the general public to the concept of emotional bonding between mothers and babies was conducted by Marshall Klaus, John Kennell, and colleagues in 1970. They assigned mothers to one of two groups. The mothers of one group visited with their newborns briefly after delivery, and then, after six to twelve hours of separation, interacted with their babies every four hours during feeding.

The mothers in the other group had one hour of skin-to-skin contact with their newborn soon after birth, and then, in addition to the regular feeding schedule, were permitted to spend an additional five hours per day with their newborns.

The mothers in the second group, who received the extra time with their newborns, appeared to be more involved with their babies at one month and one year after birth. In addition, these babies performed better on tests of mental and physical abilities than their peers who did not receive the extra time with mother soon after birth.

Based on this study, it was believed that there was a critical period during which bonding needed to occur, typically as soon after birth as possible. But what then were the implications for emotional bonding when the mother was unable to engage in immediate contact with the newborn? What about mothers who, because of a complicated delivery, are unable to hold their babies? What about adoptive mothers who are not present during the birth of their babies? Are these babies and mothers doomed not to bond? Fortunately, the research says no. Later reviews of bonding by Diane Eyer at the University of Pennsylvania and Rachel Levy-Shiff and colleagues at Bar-Han University will serve as a comfort to those parents who are concerned that they have missed their one opportunity to bond.

Although men are now active participants before, during, and after the birth of a child, little research discusses the effects of pregnancy, childbirth, and new parenthood on the father. In general, what research has been done points to the importance of the father's involvement in a child's development. Men who are interested in being present at the birth of their child are more willing to be involved in the care of the newborn, which serves as a source of support for the mother. Additional discussions of the father tend to focus on the changes in the marital relationship that come with the birth of a child.

It would seem logical that having a child would bring a couple closer together, but the birth can also be a stressful time. The reality of dealing with a newborn usually impacts the quality of a couple's relationship. In their research, Carolyn Cowan and Philip Cowan of the University of California–Berkeley, evaluated intervention programs that are designed to ease the transition into parenthood. These programs varied in their approach. Some provided parent education, some focused on the marital relationship, and others were support groups that provided new parents with exposure to other new parents. They found that the most successful programs were the ones connecting parents to nurturing and supportive counselors.

INFANCY (0 to 2 years of age)

The infant has come through the gestational period, hopefully with the right care and nutrients, and is delivered into the hands of the parents. It has been a miraculous period of growth in a short period of time, but from the moment of birth, the infant begins physical, cognitive, and social/emotional development at a pace that can be both astonishing and bewildering to new parents.

Apgar Test

At one minute after birth, five minutes after birth, and sometimes ten minutes after birth, the infant receives the Apgar test, which bears the name of its creator, Virginia Apgar. This test, based on a range of zero to ten, looks for appearance, pulse, grimace, activity, and respiration. In a hospital setting, the physician looks at each of these five categories and gives a score that ranges from zero to two for each category, resulting in a minimum of zero and a maximum of ten. A score of four or lower is cause for concern, and scores between seven to ten indicate that the baby is healthy.

Reflexes and Motor Skills

Reflexes: It was once believed that infants had few abilities, but the newborns' motor skills are evident through their reflexes. Reflexes are unlearned reactions to stimuli, and the newborn has quite a repertoire. These include the following:

Rooting reflex—when the newborn's cheek is stroked, he turns his head toward the source of food.

Stepping reflex—when pressure is applied to the feet, the baby responds with a stepping motion.

Moro reflex—a loud sound causes the baby to stretch out his arms and legs.

Grasping reflex—when a pressure is applied to the baby's palm, he attempts to grasp it.

Most of these reflexes disappear before the end of the first year.

Motor Skills: A multitude of milestones in terms of motor skills occur during the first two years. By the end of the first three months, the average infant can hold his head up. By the end of the seventh month, he can sit without support. By the end of the twelfth month, he can stand without support, and by the end of the eighteenth month, he can probably walk.

Developmental psychologists describe motor development as proximodistal and cephalocaudal. *Proximodistal development* is development that occurs from the trunk outward. So, for example, babies gain control of their arms before their fingers. In fact, activities that require fine motor skills, or use of the fingers, like holding a pencil or tying a shoe, are not mastered until early childhood. *Cephalocaudal development* is development that occurs from the head downward. For example, babies can hold their heads up before they can sit without support.

Cognitive Development

The theorist most often associated with cognitive development in children is Jean Piaget. His theory of cognitive development defines the period between birth and two years as the *sensorimotor period*. Children in this stage of development learn from interacting with the world around them, and they learn through their senses.

Have you ever given a baby an object to hold? One of the first things a baby will do is place the object in her mouth. This is one way that babies learn about their world. This period ends at twenty-four months with a milestone that Piaget calls *mental representation*. What he means by this is that they are now able to create mental images.

JEAN PIAGET'S THEORY OF COGNITIVE DEVELOPMENT

Stage	Approximate Ages	Description
Sensorimotor	birth to 2 years	Learning through the senses; object permanence
Preoperational	2 to 7 years	Decisions are ruled by perceptions; egocentric thinking
Concrete operations	7 to 11 years	More logical thinking; conservation
Formal operations	11 to 15 years	Hypothetical thinking

Background: While working with Alfred Binet and Theodore Simon (of the Stanford-Binet intelligence test fame), Jean Piaget became interested in children's cognitive development. His theory is based on observations of children (including his own) and suggests that development occurs in orderly, predictable stages.

Up until that point, babies have lived life on the assumption that if they can't see something, it no longer exists. If an object is taken from a young baby and hidden, the baby won't bother looking for it. Babies lack the concept of *object permanence*. Toward the end of the sensorimotor period, babies develop the ability to hold images mentally. If you take an object away from a baby who is almost two years old, he will begin to search for it, knowing that just because he no longer sees it, doesn't mean it no longer exists.

Language

Language development begins immediately upon birth. Infants communicate through crying, cooing, and babbling. Initially, crying is a baby's primary mode of communication. Caregivers become very good at decoding the message behind the cry. Peter Wolff in his study "The Natural History of Crying and Other Vocalizations in Early Infancy," published in 1969, determined that there are different types of cries—each to communicate messages such as anger, pain, or hunger. The anger cry is very loud, and each cry is prolonged. This is possible because lots of air is being pushed through the vocal cords. The pain cry consists of a high-pitched, loud wail that is followed by silence, which is the result of breath-holding. This is followed by another wail and more silence. This pattern is then repeated. The hunger cry is a brief, low-pitched cry that is followed by silence, so the pattern is cry-silence-cry-silence. Finger or fist nibbling or placing objects into the mouth may accompany the hunger cry. Finally, the rhythmic cry is a transitional cry that comes after one of the other types of crying.

Language development continues with babbling, around four to six months, like "mamamama." The first word usually occurs around twelve months and is called a *holophrase* because one word may be used to communicate a phrase. About eighteen months there may be two-word phrases like "bottle bad," which could indicate a variety of things. Perhaps the milk in the bottle tastes bad; it is not good to drink out of a bottle; or the bottle is too hot or cold. The end of infancy is associated with two- and three-word sentences.

Another occurrence during the end of infancy is the naming explosion. During this time, vocabulary increases dramatically, with about twenty new words a week. This is the period in development when a child will walk from object to object pointing and asking, "What's this?" Throughout the development of language, it is important to remember that babies can understand much more than they can express. Developmental psychologists use the phrase "comprehension exceeds expression" when discussing this phenomenon.

Social/Emotional Development

Within a few weeks, the average baby can recognize his mother's voice. By seven weeks, a baby can make eye contact and smile. This simple gesture on the part of the infant goes a long way to cement the bond between mother and child. Mothers respond with great satisfaction when their child begins to recognize them. Mothers often become more affectionate and stimulating in response, encouraging the infant to respond even more. In essence, both mom and baby are providing and receiving positive reinforcement.

The interesting thing about this first social response is that infants all over the world begin to respond at about the same time. Even blind babies will start to smile at this age, although in response to the mother's voice rather than her facial expressions. However, babies raised in orphanages where they are given little social interaction gradually decrease their frequency of smiling.

In the earliest months, infants will smile at anything resembling a human face; gradually, they become more discriminating. They also begin to form attachments. Attachment is defined as a close emotional relationship between child and caregiver.

Mary Ainsworth, a pioneer in attachment research, developed a groundbreaking research design called the Strange Situation Procedure to understand different types of infant attachment. In her study, Ainsworth recruited mother-infant pairs as subjects. Mother and baby were placed in a room; then a stranger entered the room and spoke with the mother, who then left the room for a first separation. The mother then returned to the room, and the stranger left. The mother then left the room again, leaving the baby alone in the room for a second separation. When the stranger returned to the room, the mother also returned, and the stranger left. Ainsworth studied the reaction of infants when their mothers left the room, and the reaction of the infants when their mothers returned to the room.

As a result of this research, four types of attachment were defined: secure attachment, insecure-avoidant attachment, insecure-resistant attachment, and disorganized attachment. Most infants were securely attached. These babies were upset upon separation but were happy to see their mother when they returned. These babies use their mothers as a secure base from which to explore.

Secure attachment describes those children who, upon entering a new environment, cling to mom but gradually move away from her to explore. Children with an *insecure-avoidant attachment* rarely cry when mother leaves and then express anger with her when she returns. Children with an *insecure-resistant attachment* are upset when mother leaves and express anger toward mother when she returns. Children whose attachment is described as *disorganized* exhibit less clear, disoriented behavior in response to the mom's departure and return. In the original Ainsworth study, this category was referred to as unclassified.

About Day Care

This research has implications for working mothers who must leave their children in the care of another on a regular basis. The concern is whether or not creating a close connection with another caregiver negatively impacts the mother-child attachment. Cross-cultural research by Melvin Konner, an anthropologist at Emory University, where he is affiliated with the anthropology department and the psychiatry and neurology departments, has explored mother-infant attachment in cultures where the amount of time spent with the infant varied. For example, babies on a Kibbutz in Israel have a variety of caregivers and do not spend as much time with their mothers as babies in the !Kung society. Members of this population are located in isolated areas of Botswana, Angola, and Nambia, and babies are with mother twenty-four hours a day.

The encouraging discovery is that in both situations, babies form healthy attachments to their mothers. Researchers now believe that children may form healthy attachments to a variety of caregivers, and not just to one. Therefore, an infant may find comfort and security not only in mom or dad, but also in grandparents, aunts, uncles, and other relatives who are involved in the care of the child.

What about an individual babysitter who cares for the child in the child's home or a larger child-care center? A checklist for parents who are evaluating day care options was developed by the American Academy of Pediatrics. Caregivers should enjoy working with children, respect parents' beliefs regarding child rearing, know first aid, and provide activities to promote cognitive and social growth. The center should have enough indoor and outdoor space for children to move freely, an open-door policy regarding parent visitations, and enough caregivers to adequately care for the children. It should also be clean and have age-appropriate toys.

The overall view is that quality day care will not negatively impact attachment and can have positive effects on cognitive and social development.

At this stage, babies rely on their caregivers for food, comfort, and love, and they are not particularly interested in playing with other children. They tend to engage in solitary play or parallel play where they play alongside another baby but don't interact with her.

Temperament

Research has indicated that babies have three distinct temperaments: easy, difficult, and slow to warm. The *easy child* adjusts to changes in the environment without difficulty. He has has a positive mood and regular eating and sleeping habits. The *difficult child* has difficulty with change, demonstrates a relatively negative mood, and has irregular eating and sleeping habits. The *slow to warm child* adapts to change, but does so slowly, and he is relatively negative in mood.

This research was conducted by Alexander Thomas and Stella Chess in a major longitudi-nal study called "The New York Longitudinal Study" that began in 1956. Thomas and Chess also found that a baby's temperament was a fair predictor of an older child's temperament. Although it may instinctively seem easier to raise an easy child than a difficult child, researchers point to the importance of "fit," also referred to as "goodness of fit," between parent and child.

To illustrate this point, let's consider twelve-month-old Yolanda who is a picky eater, fusses when put to bed, and refuses to interact with anyone outside of her immediate family. Some would feel sorry for her mother and father who must contend with her difficult nature, but her parents aren't disappointed. On the contrary, they value her spunk, strong opinions, and independent nature. So the ideal parenting situation is one in which there is harmony between the parents' perceptions and expectations of the child and her temperament.

CHILDHOOD (2 to 12 years)

Because childhood covers a wide range of ages and there are vast developmental differ-ences between a child at two and one at twelve, the phase has been divided into two subcategories: early and middle childhood.

Early Childhood (2 to 6 years)

The infant's growth between birth and two years is nothing short of miraculous. The infant becomes attached to caregivers, devel-ops language and cognitive skills, conquers highly challenging motor skills, and estab-lishes himself as a little person. In the period between two and six years, caregivers may not witness growth on a weekly basis, but these years are a magical period as the child develops relationships with others, explores the world, develops sophisticated language skills, and makes significant progress in terms of cognitive development.

Physical Development

Physical development may not be as dramatic as it was from birth to two years, but during this time, remarkable physical changes occur. To illustrate, look at the physical appearance of a child at the beginning of this period (two years), and compare this to the physical appearance of a child at the end of this stage (six years). During early childhood, the amount of fatty tissue, or baby fat, decreases and children experience rapid growth of bone and muscle. During this period, children learn to climb, to ride tricycles and then bikes, to run, to balance themselves, and to handle a multitude of other gross motor skills.

As fine motor skills develop, children begin to dress themselves, tie their own shoes, handle small toys, clay, crayons, scissors, and they learn to complete an assortment of tasks involving self-care and play.

A clear hand preference emerges. Estimates of left-handedness in the general population range from ten to thirty percent. Although children were once discouraged from using their left hand, attitudes about left-handedness have changed. I've heard many stories of parents and teachers who made attempts to discourage left-handedness because it was once believed that being a "lefty" put a person at a disadvantage. Today, parents are encouraged by health-care providers to allow each child to use the hand of choice.

Cognitive Development

Piaget called this stage of cognitive development the preoperational stage. At this point, children make decisions about their world based on their perceptions. This is when children may say things like "why is the moon following me?" This type of thinking associated with this period is called *egocentric thinking*.

Contrary to belief, this does not mean that the child is selfish or self-centered. Egocentrism simply means that the child believes everyone sees the world as she sees it. David goes to the toy store to purchase a birthday present for his friend, Sheila. He selects a train set. David thinks that what he likes is exactly what Sheila will like as well.

For some children, this is the period when they are introduced to formal education. Today, in the United States, many children attend nursery school, and almost all children attend kindergarten. This is in contrast to thirty years ago when about twenty percent of three and four year olds attended nursery school, and kindergarten was viewed as an optional pre-school program for wealthy families.

Some critics have expressed concern that formal education forces children to grow up too quickly, including David Elkind, who has published numerous books on child development. He believes that parents should allow their children to slow down, enjoy childhood, and avoid creating a stressed and overscheduled child.

Social Development

During this stage children are becoming much more social. One of the most important social activities seen during this period is play. Play is universal, and it is seen not only in humans but also in animals. Play allows children to develop physical skills, cognitive skills through imaginative play, and social skills through an improved understanding of the wants and needs of others.

The parallel play seen in infancy fades as children begin to interact. The magic of this period can be seen in play in which children create and act out elaborate and creative scenes. Role-play is evident during this time. "You are the baby, and I'm the mommy," a form of cooperative play, is common.

Another common type of play seen during early childhood involves an imaginary playmate. Imaginary playmates are not only acceptable during early childhood, but a recent article in the *APA Monitor* highlights research by Sandra Russ and colleagues at Case Western Reserve University that suggests children who engage in imaginative play during early childhood are better problem solvers and creative thinkers at the ages of ten and eleven.

Gender differences are also evident in play. In spite of societal changes regarding gender roles, visit any preschool, and you are likely to find most of the boys in the building block area and the girls in the housekeeping area.

In 1998, researcher Susan Albers of the College of Wooster discovered that after the age of four, children begin to prefer playmates of their own sex. This preference lasts until adolescence. In general, boys' play is characterized as rough and tumble play, such as wrestling and running, and girls' play is characterized by more nurturing activities.

Emotional Development

Children at this age are learning to control their emotions, but they are not masters at it yet. Have you ever shopped and selected what you thought would be the perfect gift for a preschooler, only to watch him break into tears because it's not an action figure?

Preschoolers are learning emotional display rules that tell them when it is appropriate to say "I hate that," and when it's appropriate to smile and accept the gift graciously. This leads to the ability to fake emotions and to interpret fake emotions in others.

It is during the preschool years that children begin to understand that people may pretend to be happy or sad, or they are, in other words, hiding their true feelings. It is through this understanding of the feelings of others and self—as well as learning to control the feelings of self—that children develop emotional intelligence.

Middle Childhood (7 to 12 years)

Physical Development

It is during this period that we see the growth spurt. Such rapid growth was last seen during infancy. During the preschool years, boys and girls are similar in size. By the end of this period, the girls are about three pounds heavier than boys and are also slightly taller.

The difference in size will continue until the end of adolescence and makes for awkward interactions between the sexes at a time when children are starting to become more concerned with physical appearance. As in early childhood, there is a continued decrease in fat and an increase in muscle and bone tissue.

Cognitive Development

The Piagetian stage associated with this period is referred to as *concrete operations*. Children are no longer dependent on perceptions for decision making and now engage in activities that demonstrate this.

Piaget would say that a child's thinking becomes more logical during this period. One experiment, called conservation tests, checks to see if a child realizes that changes in the physical appearance do not mean that the object is changed. For instance, take two glasses of the same size and fill them with equal amounts of liquid. Ask the child if the glasses contain equal amounts of liquid. Children in both the preoperational and concrete operations stages would answer, "Yes, both glasses contain the same amount of liquid."

Now, take a third glass that looks different. It may be taller and narrower. Pour the contents of one glass into this container. Ask the child if the glasses still contain the same amount of liquid. Preoperational children will respond, "No." Remember, children at this age rely on appearances, and the glasses are not the same; neither are the liquid levels.

Children in the concrete operations stage will respond, "Yes, both containers have the same amount of liquid." They realize that liquid was not added, not taken away, so even though the amount of liquid looks different in the taller container, it has not changed.

Social Development

Friends take on greater importance during this stage of childhood. Unlike the preschooler, children during this period perceive friendships as enduring relationships that are based on mutual respect, reciprocity, and shared interests. The importance of friendship will continue to grow during adolescence.

In addition, the views of peer acceptance or rejection begin to take on added importance. This emphasis on the importance of being liked and accepted by peers continues through adolescence.

John Gottman, in his 1977 article, "Toward a Definition of Social Isolation in Children," developed five categories of social status that describe a child's social standing. The *sociometric stars* are the popular children who are liked by most. *Mixers* interact with everyone and are liked by some, but not by others. The *teacher negatives* are liked by some, but not by others, and are often liked by teachers. *Tuned-out* kids don't interact much, and they are not disliked by peers, but rather they are ignored. The *sociometric rejectees* are actively disliked, rather than ignored.

These categories are not set in stone. Actually, children may tend to have differing standings in differing settings. So, let's say that at school Todd is quiet and does not have many friends, but when he goes to chess group, where he is regarded as the best player, he shines. He interacts with all the other chess players and is liked by all. In school, Todd would be described as tuned out, but in chess group, Todd is a sociometric star. Although it may appear that the future for the rejected child is bleak, research suggests that even children who are rejected by most find close and satisfying friendships.

Emotional Development

During middle childhood, children also develop empathy, the ability to understand the state of mind and feelings of another. This is quite a departure from the egocentric thinking of early childhood.

Empathy emerges and has been described by Robert Selman in *The Growth of Interpersonal Understanding*. The stages he describes emerged from a study in which Selman told children a story about a little girl who falls from a tree. After her accident, she promises her father that she will not climb trees again. Then, one day, her friend's cat gets caught in a tree, and she is

STAGES OF SOCIAL COGNITION	
Stage (ages)	**Description**
Egocentric (3 to 7 years of age)	The only perspective is the child's.
Social-informational (4 to 9 years of age)	The child begins to understand that others have an opinion but feels that others would feel the way she does if they were given the same information she possesses.
Self-reflective (6 to 12 years of age)	The child begins to recognize and express differing points of view.
Mutual (9 to 15 years of age)	The child can now consider his point of view and the point of view of another at the same time.
Social and conventional (12 to adulthood)	The child can integrate the views of society into his perspective and his discussion of an issue.

the only one who can save the cat. The children who heard the story were asked about the main characters, such as their opinions about the feelings of the father, the feelings of the friend, and then what they would do in a similar situation. As a result of these interviews, Selman developed five stages of social cognition or perspective taking. These stages are not tied to specific ages, so you'll see that the age ranges overlap.

CHAPTER SUMMARY

The union of sperm and egg results in a fertilized egg. In a typical pregnancy, this is the beginning of prenatal development. The zygote becomes an embryo, then a fetus, and then a newborn. The prenatal stage is a time when great care needs to be exercised for the sake of the fetus. It must be protected from teratogens and provided with proper nutrition and care so that the infant is born with the best possible physical and neurological makeup. The newborn starts life with certain reflexes, the ability to communicate through

crying, and, within hours, the ability to bond with a caretaker.

Development is not just about physical changes that occur, but also cognitive, social, and emotional changes. During the first two years of life, an infant undergoes rapid physical development. Cognitive development is evident in an infant's growing vocabulary and his ability to hold objects in mental representation.

Socially, the infant is still very interested in the company of her caregivers. Early childhood is characterized by increasing independence, egocentric thinking, and creative play.

During middle childhood, children experience a growth spurt and an increasing interest in social relationships outside the family. The ability to complete conservation tasks successfully, like analyzing the glasses of water, illustrates the logical thinking of the child in middle childhood.

Emotional development involves the development of empathy and perspective taking.

Social development during middle childhood involves the ever-growing importance of peer acceptance and rejection.

TEST YOUR RECALL AND RECOGNITION

True/False

1. The embryonic period encompasses weeks one to ten after fertilization.

2. Fertilization occurs in the ovaries.

3. The fertilized egg is called a zygote.

4. The embryo is most vulnerable to teratogens during the last two weeks of prenatal development.

5. The theorist most often associated with cognitive development is Jean Piaget.

6. The Apgar test is given to newborns at one, five, and, sometimes, ten minutes after birth.

7. Postpartum depression is the same as "baby blues."

8. During early childhood, children master control of their emotions.

9. At the end of middle childhood, the average girl is heavier and taller than the average boy.

10. By the age of ten, most children have mastered Piaget's conservation tasks.

Multiple Choice

1. A pregnancy test can accurately determine if a woman has conceived
   a. only after the first period has been missed.
   b. within days.
   c. about one month after conception.
   d. none of the above.

2. Which of the following does *not* occur during the fetal period?
   a. implantation into the uterus
   b. growth
   c. fetal movement
   d. development of the nervous system

3. The fetus is housed in the
   a. fallopian tubes.
   b. placenta.
   c. uterus.
   d. ovaries.

4. Consumption of alcohol during pregnancy has been linked to
   a. fetal alcohol syndrome.
   b. birth defects.
   c. both a and b.
   d. neither a nor b.

5. What are some issues faced by researchers who study the effects of prenatal exposure to street drugs on later development of a child?
   a. Mothers who use street drugs often use other drugs as well.
   b. Mothers who use drugs may not receive adequate prenatal care.
   c. Mothers who use drugs may not eat properly, and, therefore, are more likely to suffer from malnourishment.
   d. All of the above are correct.

6. During the fetal period, the baby is
   a. fully grown.
   b. moving so that the mother can feel it.
   c. microscopic in size.
   d. considered a zygote.

7. Which of the following is an example of social development during infancy?

    a. comparison of weight at birth to weight at twelve months

    b. the relationship between baby and caregiver

    c. the use of one-word phrases

    d. none of the above

8. Which of the following is an example of cognitive development during early childhood?

    a. the ability to tie a shoe or ride a bike

    b. cooperative play

    c. egocentric thinking

    d. none of the above

9. Which of the following is an example of physical development during middle childhood?

    a. the growth spurt

    b. concrete operations

    c. evaluations of self-competence

    d. none of the above

10. Which of the following stages of cognitive development are *not* covered during infancy or early and middle childhood?

    a. sensorimotor period

    b. preoperational period

    c. concrete operations

    d. formal operations

Fill in the Blanks

1. The germinal period occurs anywhere from _____ to _____ weeks.

2. The average newborn must score _____ to _____ on the Apgar to be considered healthy.

3. The gestational period for humans is _____ weeks.

4. The four types of infant cries are _____, _____, _____, and _____.

5. If pressure is applied to a baby's feet, he will move them as if he were walking. This response is called the _____ reflex.

6. Talia's parents describe her as a happy baby who eats anything and adjusts well to change. Talia's temperament can be described as _____.

7. Piaget describes the thinking of preschoolers as _____.

8. "You are the conductor and I am a passenger." This statement is typical of _____ play.

9. The growth spurt occurs during _____ childhood.

10. Middle childhood is defined as the period between _____ years and _____ years.

ANSWERS TO QUESTIONS

True/False

1. false	6. true
2. false	7. false
3. true	8. false
4. false	9. true
5. true	10. true

Multiple Choice

1. b	6. b
2. a	7. b
3. c	8. c
4. c	9. a
5. d	10. d

Fill in the Blanks

1. fertilization; two weeks
2. seven; ten
3. forty weeks from last period or thirty-eight weeks from fertilization
4. angry; hungry; pain; rhythmic
5. stepping
6. easy
7. egocentric
8. cooperative
9. middle
10. seven; twelve

ADDITIONAL RESOURCES

Books

Brazelton, T. B. and S. Greenspan. 2001. *The irreducible needs of children: What every child must have to grow, learn, and flourish.* Cambridge, MA: Perseus.

Nilsson, L. 1990. *A child is born.* NY: Delacorte Press.

Videos

Miracle of life, produced by L. Nilsson. Boston: WBGH, 1983.

Nova: Life's greatest miracle, produced by B. G. Erikson and L. Nilsson. Boston: WBGH, 2001.

Web sites

The American Academy of Pediatrics, www.aap.org

Society for Research in Child Development, www.srcd.org

CHAPTER 9

LIFESPAN PSYCHOLOGY: ADOLESCENCE AND ADULTHOOD

KEY TERMS

lifespan theory, puberty, menarche, semenarche peer group, menopause, empty nest syndrome, death gene, metamemory, metacognition, self-esteem, fluid intelligence, crystallized intelligence, Alzheimer's disease

It is unfortunate that some people only associate development with childhood. Are you the same person physically that you were twenty years ago? Have you become taller, heavier, balder, or grayer? What about changes that may have occurred cognitively and socially? If you think for a moment about the development of a person, you will understand that we will continue to change until the day we die.

The previous chapter discussed how children develop from birth through age twelve. In psychology, it's important to understand the course of development in adults as well as children. Unlike the other developmental theories (for example, those of Jean Piaget and Sigmund Freud, which we touched on in chapter 8 and will cover more in chapter 10), Eric Erikson's theory covers development from birth to death. Therefore, as we enter our discussion of the second part of development, adolescence and adulthood, for the most part, we will consider Erikson's theory of psychosocial development.

Erikson was a student of Freud; therefore, his approach has a psychoanalytic foundation. Yet, unlike Freudian theory, which we will cover in detail in the next chapter and which

emphasizes sexual urges, Erikson's approach emphasizes the role of social influences in development. We will use Erikson's theory to guide us through most of the stages in this chapter.

Again, it is important to remember that development does not occur in a vacuum; a great number of factors influence development. These include biological changes, cultural issues, and even social factors. It is the nature versus nurture debate again.

The ages that are indicated in this chapter are general guidelines; each person is unique, and therefore unpredictable, and we don't always enter the appropriate stages of development at the time that is predicted.

ADOLESCENCE (13 to 20 years)

Ask someone about adolescence, and you will probably hear some of the following phrases: rebellious teenager, adolescent angst, growing pains, and the second toddlerhood. Actually, adolescence is not always as tumultuous as the general public believes, but it is a time of great change, socially, physically, and cognitively. And it is also the period when the physical changes associated with the onset of puberty can upset the equilibrium of even the most mild-mannered child.

We will discuss two types of physical development: those related to primary sex characteristics and those related to secondary sex characteristics.

Physical Development

In chapter 8, when we last discussed physical development of children, the girls had outgrown the boys physically. These gender differences in development continue during adolescence. This period is also referred to as *puberty*.

Gender differences fall into two types: primary and secondary characteristics. Primary sex characteristics are directly related to reproduction, and secondary sex characteristics are other physical changes that indicate sexual maturity has occurred.

During puberty, the hypothalamus tells the pituitary gland to secrete hormones. In boys, this hormone is testosterone, and it is responsible for the production of mature male sperm, around fourteen years of age. Secondary sex characteristics include the development of body hair and deepening of voice.

In girls, secretion of estrogen is linked to *menarche*, the first period, around twelve years of age. Secondary sex characteristics are the development of body hair and breast development.

The boys finally catch up to the girls' advantageous growth in middle childhood; by the time adolescents have reached age eighteen, most boys are taller and heavier than most girls once again.

There are psychological considerations associated with these many significant changes in physical development during adolescence. During fifth grade, I had a female classmate,

Audra, who had always been taller and heavier than everyone else. Every year, the fifth-grade class embarked upon an overnight field trip where we would stay in a cabin and enjoy a summer camp type of atmosphere. Soon after we arrived, we found Audra sitting in the cabin crying. As we all rushed to comfort her, she was approached by one of our teachers who also tried to offer support and assess the situation. We watched as Audra and our teacher talked in hushed tones, and then as Audra was rushed away from our cabin and sent home. When we returned to school, we all were curious: why did Audra leave camp? Audra eventually explained that her period had started, and now her life would be different. Our teachers never spoke of the incident. The entire event was shrouded in secrecy and shame.

For many women, this is the typical experience of menarche. In a 2002 study by Daryl Costos, Ruthie Ackerman, and Lisa Paradis from Boston University, adult women were asked about the messages they had received about menstruation from their mothers. Most responded that they had received negative messages. Carol Beausang and Anita Razor at Indiana University conducted a similar study in 2000. In that study, adult women were asked to recall their early experiences with mothers and teachers regarding menstruation. Most recounted experiences that were off-putting. Teachers were embarrassed and uncomfortable discussing the subject in an open classroom, and this discomfort led them to impart information that was unclear and misleading.

The first period is an important milestone. The manner in which parents and teachers prepare a girl for menarche can have powerful psychological implications. In a 1995 study by Elissa

Koff and Jill Rierdan, recommendations are made to prepare girls for menstruation. The authors emphasize that lack of preparation may result in feelings of inadequacy, shame, and disgust. Koff and Rierdan interviewed fifth-grade girls who had already experienced menarche and asked them for recommendations. The girls said that it was important to provide a calm, reassuring environment, give information about hygiene, and emphasize that it is just a normal and healthy part of growing up. Recommendations, specifically for mothers, were to provide support and education about hygiene—and for fathers to provide support and to understand that it's difficult to discuss menstruation with fathers.

The male counterpart to menarche, the first ejaculation, is an even more taboo topic in our society. This is not surprising because *semenarche* is more often associated with sexual desire than reproduction, although semenarche signifies the existence of mature sperm. Loren Frankel at Cornell conducted a study to understand communication between parents and sons about semenarche. Interestingly, Frankel found that parents rarely talked to their sons about first ejaculation, and when asked if they planned to, most replied, "I've never thought about it."

Cognitive Development

This is the one stage where we will focus on Jean Piaget's theory of cognitive development rather than Erikson's. This is because our discussion of lifespan psychology is synonymous with cognitive development through the lens of Jean Piaget's theory. It is the last stage in Piaget's theory, suggesting that Piaget believed that cognitive development ended with adolescence. Piaget calls this stage *formal operations*.

The formal operations stage begins somewhere around the age of eleven or twelve and is characterized by the ability to think hypothetically. Now children can think in terms of "what if?" Adolescent thought is characterized by this ability to think in hypothetical terms along with less concrete, more abstract thinking. This comes in handy with science and math concepts that may involve abstract ideas.

Thought also involves the ability to think about thinking (*metacognition*) and to think about memory (*metamemory*). Being able to think about your own thoughts and the working of your mind has many implications for school achievement. A 1998 study by Jeffrey Landine and John Stewart discovered that there is a strong correlation between metacognition/metamemory and academic achievement. This is not surprising, because the ability to assess your own strengths and weaknesses in thought and memory is essential to good academic performance. In other words, if I know that my memory for historical dates is poor, then I will create some unique strategies to help me prepare for my upcoming history test.

Famous researcher David Elkind suggests another type of thinking during adolescence. Elkind uses the term *adolescent egocentrism* to describe thought patterns. This is quite different from Piaget's egocentrism, which is seen during early childhood. In adolescent egocentrism, the teen views herself as different from others. Two examples of this thinking are the imaginary audience and the personal fable. The teenager who thinks in terms of her *imaginary audience* believes that others are watching her at all times. Consider the girl who stumbles into the school cafeteria and drops her tray. There is no doubt in her mind that all eyes were on her at the time of the mishap.

There are lots of examples of adolescents who think in terms of *personal fables*. There is the young man who believes that he is different from everyone else. This teen will say things like, "I'm invulnerable," or "It won't happen to me." This type of thinking may result in risky adolescent behaviors such as unsafe driving, alcohol and drug consumption, and unprotected sex. Again, the belief is, "I can exceed the speed limit; nothing will happen to me. Accidents happen to people who don't know how to drive."

Erik Erikson's Psychosocial Stages of Development

Erik Erikson's theory of development focuses on lifespan development, rather than on child development. His theory has a psychoanalytic orientation. (He was trained by Anna Freud, Sigmund Freud's daughter.) You will see many parallels between Erikson's theory and Freud's "Theory of Psychosexual Development" (which we will cover in chapter 10), but unlike Freud's theory, which emphasizes sexual urges, Erikson's

STAGE	APPROXIMATE AGES	ADAPTIVE WAYS OF COPING
Trust vs. mistrust	Birth to 18 months	If caregiver is responsive to needs of infant, the baby will develop a sense trust.
Autonomy vs. shame and doubt	18 months to 3 years	If the caregiver allows the child to explore and be an independent being, the child will develop a sense of autonomy.
Initiative vs. guilt	3 to 6 years	If caregiver encourages child's self-initiated activities, the child will develop a sense of initiative.
Industry vs. inferiority	6 to 12 years	If parents and teachers provide positive feedback as children master new skills, children will develop a sense of industriousness,
Identity vs. identity diffusion	12 to 18 years	If the adolescent is able to begin to answer the questions, "Who am I?" (identifying values, beliefs, aspirations), the adolescent will develop a sense of identity.
Intimacy vs. isolation	Early adulthood	If the adult is able to establish close committed relationships with others, the adult will develop a sense of intimacy.
Generativity vs. stagnation	Middle adulthood	If the adult is able to reach out and guide members from the next generation, the adult will develop a sense of generativity.
Integrity vs. despair	Late adulthood	If the adult is able to reflect on life and feel a sense of satisfaction, the adult will develop a sense of integrity.

emphasizes the role of society and culture on development. Each stage is marked by a crisis, which will be resolved in one of two ways, an adaptive or maladaptive way of coping, thus the title for each stage. Here is an example—trust vs. mistrust—to illustrate this point. A responsive caregiver will instill a sense of trust in the baby, but an unresponsive caregiver (one who does not respond to cries, for example) will instill a sense of mistrust in the child. In the table on page 108, we provide definitions of adaptive ways of coping for each stage.

Social Development

Erikson's theory of psychosocial development calls the adolescent stage *identity versus identity diffusion*. During this period, the adolescent struggles to develop a sense of self. Therefore, it is not uncommon to see a teen "try on" or experiment with different identities. Erikson refers to this period as a transition from childhood to adulthood; he describes this period as a break during which teens are free to ponder who they are and who they will become. Erikson's official term for this break is an *adolescent moratorium*. Friends and peers are key in this struggle. Ideally, an adolescent will leave this stage with a strong sense of self and identity. Sometimes, teens don't develop a sense of self and simply adopt beliefs that are vague or lack definition. This undesirable situation is identity diffusion.

Definitions of self include establishing educational and occupational aspirations, religious affiliations, political viewpoints, ethnic identity, and sexual orientations. We will briefly discuss the development of the last two because these are often overlooked areas in lifespan development.

Ethnic Identity

Children from ethnic minorities need to develop a strong, positive sense of connection to their ethnic group. A positive connection with one's ethnicity is linked to a positive sense of self. This sense of connection is commonly called racial pride. There are several theories about how this comes into being. We will refer to the options of identity formation that were developed by Jean Phinney and Mona Devich-Navarro at California State University in 1997, but the classic theories of William Cross on the Stages of Becoming Black are also helpful. According to the Phinney and Devich-Navarro model, teens adopt one of the following four paths on their search for ethnic identity: assimilation, marginalization, separation, and biculturalism.

Assimilation occurs when the teen rejects the norms of the minority group in favor of those of the majority group. This may be seen in the Asian-American teen who discards his ethnic first or last name and adopts an American name because his friends and teachers have repeatedly told him that his name is too difficult to pronounce. This adolescent has surrendered something from his culture in an effort to fit in with mainstream culture.

In *marginalization*, the teen lives with the majority culture but exists on the edge of society; this teen is viewed as an outcast and is rejected by both the majority culture and his culture of origin. Youths who are gang members experience this sense of not being accepted by either the majority or the minority societies.

In *separation*, the teen rejects the mainstream culture and adopts the values of the minority culture. In 1966, a group of young black adolescents who were fed up with the challenges of being black in America formed the separatist group called the Black Panthers. This group illustrates separation.

The final path is *biculturalism*. In this path, the teen opts for an identity that reflects both the majority culture and the minority culture of which he is a part. There are those who oppose biculturalism and those who favor it. The analogy often used to illustrate this point is the idea of the United States being a "melting pot." Those opposed to biculturalism compare the melting pot to a bowl of soup, wherein each ingredient loses its original flavor and tastes like every other ingredient in the bowl. Those who favor biculturalism liken it to a bowl of stew, wherein each ingredient maintains its shape, texture, and flavor while complementing the other ingredients in the bowl.

Sexual Identity

Establishing a sexual identity means establishing a sexual orientation, which is a preference for a sexual partner of the same sex (homosexual orientation), the opposite sex (heterosexual orientation), or either sex (bisexual orientation). This can be especially challenging in our society, because openly acknowledging one's homosexual orientation may result in ostracism (at the least) and violent reactions (at the worst).

The brutal beating and murder of Matthew Sheppard in Laramie, Wyoming, in 1998 illustrates the dangers of being openly gay in our society. Although adolescents report an awareness of their sexual preferences early in adolescence, many gay teens do not "come out," that is, voice their sexual preference to others, until late in high school or early in college.

Differing psychological perspectives offer different theories about sexual orientation. Behaviorists think it is a choice predicated by learning. Those with a biological orientation think that some biological component predisposes one to a certain orientation. The analytic perspective looks at parental relationships. The variety of approaches is certainly more open-minded than it was in the days when homosexuality was listed as a disorder in the *Diagnostic and Statistical Manual of Mental Disorders*. Such theories provoke strong reaction because they suggest, respectively, that sexual orientation can be unlearned (behavioral theory), that people lack the ability to control their sexual orientations (biological theory), or that parents are somehow culpable (analytic theory).

Peers and Friends

We've talked about the influence of peer rejection and acceptance during middle childhood. Let us return to this discussion of friends and peers and their influence. It is important to distinguish between the different types of social relationships encountered by the adolescent. There are peer relationships, friendships, and romantic relationships, or dates.

Peers, who are defined as equals, may consist of classmates, teammates, or neighbors. Peers might influence choices in music, clothes, and hairdos. Ask the average thirteen year old why his hair is spiked or dyed red, why he is dressed in black, why he is listening to certain music, and he will probably tell you that everyone else is doing it. You have only to think back to your own adolescence to remember how you dressed and the music you selected to comprehend the powerful influence of peers. These were not necessarily your friends, but the people who surrounded you at school, in the neighborhood, at camp, and so forth. It is very important, especially for young teens, to feel that they fit in with their peers.

Friends, on the other hand, constitute a different relationship, and they change as the adolescent develops. Thomas Berndt at Perdue University has written extensively on friendships during childhood and adolescence. It is through his work that we have learned much of what we know about the quality of children's friendships. During the first three years of adolescence, children define their friends as people who have the same likes and dislikes. Friendships are centered on shared activities.

During middle adolescence, friendships become more emotionally intense. Instead of being all the people with whom a teen spends time, friendships may begin to be limited to one best friend or a small group of friends. Teenagers' friends are most likely to be similar to them in regard to race/ethnicity, class, age, and gender.

During the late teens, friendships are based on mutuality and intimacy, and opposite-sex friendships become more common. Same-sex friends have usually been the norm since preschool.

Finally, a new type of social relationship emerges in the romantic relationship as dating begins. Early in adolescence, these dates may consist of groups of boys and girls going to the mall on a "group date." Later, we begin to see one-on-one dating.

Influence on Behavior

Many studies have looked at specific instances of peer and friendship influence on behavior. I would like to share a few of these studies with you to give you a feel for the research in this area. We will look at the influence of peers on three behaviors: cigarette smoking, alcohol use, and marijuana use.

In a 2001 study by Cheryl Alexander and her colleagues at Johns Hopkins, adolescents completed questionnaires and were interviewed about the behaviors of their peers, friends, and themselves. Results found that those students who had best friends who smoked cigarettes were two times more likely to smoke than those without friends who smoked. In addition, it was discovered that teens were more likely to smoke when many in their school (peers) smoked.

Another troublesome behavior exhibited by teens is alcohol and marijuana use. A study by Rick Kosterman and his colleagues, at the University of Washington in 2000, examined the initiation of alcohol and marijuana use. Eight hundred and eight children, beginning at the age of ten, participated in this eight-year longitudinal study. They were interviewed every year between the ages of ten and sixteen and then again at age eighteen. The authors discovered that the risk of beginning alcohol or marijuana use rose at the age of thirteen, and teens were at greater risk of using these items if they were exposed to others who used them. Interestingly, the authors also found that parents could prevent or delay use by being proactive and setting clear family standards about drug use.

These two studies illustrate the influence of peers and friends on behaviors that may have long-term consequences on a teen's life.

Self-Esteem Theories

Self-esteem is what we think about ourselves, or our image of self. Two theorists that have addressed the development of esteem are William James (1842–1910) and Charles

Cooley (1864–1929). William James states that feelings of self are based on the discrepancy between the ideal and actual self, in other words, "Who I am" and "What I would like to be." The smaller the gap between these two selves, the better the person feels about self. Charles Cooley proposed the "Looking Glass Theory," which states that feelings of self are based on what others think of you. Your worth is reflected through the eyes of others.

In response to these theories, Susan Harter, a developmental psychologist at the University of Denver in 1987, created "The Harter Self Perception Profile for Children." This questionnaire combines concepts from both James's and Cooley's theories. Children are asked what others think of them (Looking Glass) as well as the differences between their actual performance and what they wish they could do (James's Theory). Harter assessed the following five areas of self-worth—or as she calls it, competence:

Scholastic Competence: how competent the child feels about schoolwork;
Athletic Competence: how competent the child feels about his athletic abilities;
Social Competence: how competent the child feels about his ability to be accepted by peers;
Behavioral Conduct: how competent the child feels about his ability to behave as he should; and
Physical Appearance: how attractive the child believes himself to be.

Answering questions on the Harter Profile is a two-step process: first the child would circle the statement that best describes his or her feelings. Next the child would indicate how it applies to self: true for me (1), somewhat true for me (2), neither true nor false for me (3), somewhat not true for me (4), or not true for me (5).

What follows is an example of a type of question on "The Harter Self Perception Profile" that taps into feelings about physical appearance:

Most kids are really good looking		But other kids are not attractive at all		
1	2	3	4	5

Through this questionnaire, Susan Harter discovered that both James and Cooley were right. The difference between real and actual self, and how others view self, influences feelings of self-esteem. She also found that of the five areas, physical appearance is the most important for positive feelings. In other words, children who find themselves physically attractive are more likely to like themselves. Behavioral conduct was the least important feature for positive feelings of self.

ADULT DEVELOPMENT

We will now progress to a discussion of development in adulthood. We will continue with the same format: physical, cognitive, and social development. You will notice that some sections will be noticeably shorter in the section on adult development. For although there are physical changes during adulthood, they are nowhere near as drastic as those in infancy. Again, you will see ages associated with each stage. According to Erikson's model, the three stages of adulthood are associated with early, middle, and late adulthood. Ages are included to provide a more concrete sense of the stage.

Early Adulthood (20 to 40 years)

The age categories in adulthood are based on the general literature, which divides adulthood into three phases, each phase spanning twenty years. However, there are big differences between a person at the beginning of a stage and a person at the end, between a twenty year old and a forty year old.

Most studies of development in adulthood have focused on cognitive and social changes, but obviously there are physical changes in adulthood as well. The promising news is that not all physical changes in adulthood are related to decline.

Physical Development

Unlike children, adults do have control over their physical development to a certain extent. During early adulthood, physical development is at a peak. Vision, hearing, and motor skills are at their best. Think about a career with physical demands such as a professional athlete. Unless you are a remarkable athlete along the lines of Willie Mays, Cal Ripken, George Foreman, or Willy Shoemaker, your career will peak and probably end during early adulthood.

Early adulthood is associated with childbearing in women and the beginning of physical changes that signify aging for both men and women. For many, one of these changes is weight gain. Reports by the American Obesity Association state that one-third of the adult American population is obese. Definitions of obesity are based on body mass index, which is calculated given one's height and weight. Obesity is the second leading cause of unnecessary deaths, and the causes of obesity are not clear-cut. It appears that obesity is caused by a combination of environmental factors (poor eating habits, inactivity) and biological factors (presence of obesity in family members).

From a psychological perspective, people who are obese are subject to discrimination that can have detrimental effects on self-esteem and self-image. The likelihood that a person will be obese increases during early adulthood and continues to increase until late adulthood.

Cognitive Development

One cognitive task that is a part of early adulthood is decision making, a concept first discussed in chapter 5. Many decisions are made during early adulthood, one of the first being occupational or career decision making. When and how do adults make this decision and how does it affect their lives? How did you decide on your career? Did you use one of the decision-making strategies from chapter 5? Most people select their career of choice as a function of exposure to the career through a family member, teacher, or friend.

A few studies have detected gender differences in occupational decision making. Studies by Carolyn Morgan and her colleagues at the University of Wisconsin and Pauline Lightbody and her colleagues at the University of Paisley (England) have found that women and men have different reasons for career decisions. Although both cite interest in the subject as a factor, women report interpersonal factors and the desire to have a fulfilling career. Men cite high pay and status as considerations for their decision making. How do we explain these differences? There is no definite answer about this phenomenon.

Social Development

Erikson's stage that corresponds to this period of development is called *intimacy versus isolation*. The challenge of this stage is to establish relationships that engender intimacy and love. Ideally, the social relationships that developed during adolescence make way for the more life-altering social relationships of early adulthood, the spousal relationship being one of the most important of these. According to William Doherty and Neil Jackson in their 1982 article "Marriage and the Family," research indicated that ninety percent of Americans will marry at some point in their lives. People today are marrying at later ages, but according to the 1998 U.S. Census data, the average age at first marriage for women is twenty-five, and for men, twenty-seven.

The ages of couples at the time of their first marriages are up compared to 1948, when the average age for a first marriage for a woman was twenty, and for a man, twenty-three. These delays in marriage may be attributed to a woman's decision to establish her professional identity before marriage. Expectations can also explain the delay. Women who once may have needed a husband for financial security now earn their own incomes, so they search for a man with qualities other than earning power, making the search less hurried. Similarly, men may also have different expectations. Men who once looked for women who would cook and clean for them now take care of their own household needs, so they search for women with qualities other than domestic skills. The changes in gender roles have influenced changes in mate selection and the timing of marriage.

It is also important to note that marriage is not the sole road to the intimacy that Erikson suggested we seek. Some couples, for various reasons, opt for long-term committed relationships. This type of arrangement is often seen in the elderly, where the financial penalties of marriage make cohabitation a more appealing option. This is also seen in homosexual couples, who provide another example of intimate, committed relationships outside of traditional marriage.

It is also during early adulthood that most people decide to start a family. Nancy Gibbs in a *Time* article "Babies vs. Careers," dated April 15, 2002, questioned which should come first for women who want both. This article was inspired by the book *Creating a Professional Life: Women and the Quest for Children* by economist Sylvia Ann Hewlett, Ph.D., of Harvard University. Hewlett's stance is that women who have to establish their careers and then wait until age thirty-five or older to have children are going to regret their decision because of the decrease in fertility. At the age of twenty, the risk of miscarriage is nine percent; it doubles by the age of thirty-five. At forty-two, ninety percent of a woman's eggs are abnormal, and twenty-seven is the age at which a woman's chances of becoming pregnant begin to decline.

So women are in a difficult position. Do I have children at a young age and possibly sacrifice my chance of having a career (it's harder to jump into the workforce when you are older), or should I establish my career and possibly sacrifice my chance of having a baby?

Despite this data, couples are starting families somewhat later than their parents did thirty years before. According to the Centers for Disease Control and Prevention in 2002, the average age of a mother upon the birth of her first child was twenty-five, compared to 1970, when it was twenty-one.

There is research on older and younger parents and their strengths and weaknesses. Older moms are more likely to have problems with fertility, as Hewlett discusses. They are also at increased risk of having a baby with disorders that include Down Syndrome, Fragile X, Klinefelter's Syndrome, and Trisomy 18. Fathers over age fifty-five are at increased risk of having a baby with Down Syndrome.

On the other hand, young mothers, especially mothers who are teenagers, are more likely to experience miscarriage, premature birth, and stillbirth. Given the limited earning potential of teen moms, young mothers are also more likely to live in poverty, which may affect their access to adequate food, shelter, clothing, and prenatal care.

The end of early adulthood leads to the portion of life referred to as middle age or middle adulthood.

Middle Adulthood (40 to 65 years)

For many, this period marks the beginning of the recognition that physical, cognitive, and social development are beginning to decline. Nevertheless, the lines between early, middle, and late adulthood are becoming blurred, as more and more middle age adults decline to conform to typical middle-age life. These days, middle adulthood is full of people having babies, starting new careers, returning to school, relocating, and remarrying or renewing their marriage vows. In the sections that follow, we will look at various developmental factors. Keep in mind, however, that there are many roads followed by adults in this life stage.

Physical Development

What physical attributes are associated with middle adulthood or middle age? Thinning hair, gray hair, thin skin, wrinkled skin, and weight gain? In some, these changes start to occur during early adulthood, but they become more noticeable during middle adulthood. There is great variability here, and with the development of cosmetics and advances in plastic surgery, it is easy to mask these changes. Susan Whitbourne, a developmental psychologist at the University of Massachusetts, Amherst, summarizes the changes in the appearance of the face and body.

Changes in Middle Adulthood

Changes in Skin

Wrinkling and sagging of the skin—due to loss of elasticity in the skin (skin stretches out but does not snap back, which results in sagging); thinning of fat and muscle under the skin; also, the sweat and oil glands in the skin become less active so lubrication of the skin diminishes.

Thinning of the skin—due to a loss of cells from the outermost layer of skin; this thinning results in less protection from heat and cold, and the skin is more likely to bruise.

Irregular pigmentation/age spots—changes in color of the skin, results in uneven skin coloring.

Changes in Face

Teeth—staining (from years of drinking coffee or tea or from smoking cigarettes); also gums recede.

Eyes—puffiness around the eyes as fluid and fat accumulate here; dark circles under the eyes which may make the eyes appear sunken.

Hair—graying, which may occur in some people in their thirties; thinning of hair in men and women, women may also develop facial hair (especially after fifty); older men may have more nostril and ear hair and longer eyebrow hair.

Changes in Body Build

Reduction in height—the vertebrae collapse during adulthood. With changes in nutrition and health, it is expected that fewer adults will experience this change.

Increase in body weight—around waist and hips.

One important physical change associated with women during this period in life is menopause, which marks the end of ovulation and menstruation for women.

The average age for menopause is fifty to fifty-five, although it may occur in women as young as forty. Menopause is most often associated with hot flashes, but other symptoms include irritability, fatigue, insomnia, and nervousness. This last cluster of symptoms may be a result of a decrease in estrogen, which can also lead to osteoporosis. Although estrogen deficiency is sometimes treated with estrogen replacement therapy, such treatment may place a woman at increased risk for other types of health problems, including cancer.

Psychological responses to menopause are mixed. For some women menopause represents a loss—a loss of womanhood, a loss of reproductive ability; for other women, it represents liberation—freedom from worry about contraception, the monthly discomfort associated with menstruation, and the use of feminine hygiene products.

Is there a male menopause? It appears not. We do know that men can father children until late in life, but research does indicate that the quantity and quality of sperm decrease with age.

Cognitive Development

Although research is mixed about cognitive changes during adulthood, it is certain that just as physical exercise is necessary to maintain physical health, cognitive exercise is important for cognitive health. The issue of whether or not cognitive abilities decline during middle adulthood is debatable. A 1990

study by K. Warner Schaie of Pennsylvania State University calculated the percentage of people who maintained stable performance on various abilities like inductive reasoning, spatial orientation, verbal meaning, number and word fluency; eighty percent showed no decline. Schaie believes that decline may not occur until the seventies. So, how do we explain all the observations/personal experiences that we have had with people at the end of middle adulthood or beginning of late adulthood that point to the contrary?

If you were to ask John Horn, a psychologist at the University of Southern California, whether or not cognitive abilities change with age, he would tell you that it varies. According to Horn, fluid intelligence (basic information-processing skills) may decline with age, while crystallized intelligence (application of knowledge accumulated through the years) appears to improve with age. Fluid intelligence is not altered by culture or environment; these abilities are measured through tests of attention span, general reasoning, and abstract abilities. Crystallized intelligence is influenced by culture and environment; these abilities are measured through tests of vocabulary, math skills, and general knowledge.

Social Development

According to Erikson's theory of psychosocial development, the stage associated with middle adulthood is called *generativity versus stagnation*. The focus here is to "pass it on," to become involved in activities that will result in improved conditions for future generations, and to help young people reach their potential. For some, this will occur through parenting, but it is important to note that this is not the only route to generativity. One can volunteer with youth groups or establish a relationship with a young relative. Those who do not master this stage will become stuck, or stagnate.

Another social experience during middle adulthood is a reflection and evaluation of one's current situation.

This is a time in life when adults begin to reflect on the decisions that they have made, and question whether or not they are pleased with their life choices. A midlife crisis, or some dramatic life change, may occur when the answer to that question is "no."

Although popular in mainstream culture, the *midlife crisis* is a point of controversy for psychologists. Daniel Levenson, who has studied lifespan development and published many articles in this area, believes that every person establishes "the dream," a fantasy of what one hopes to become. Most do not realize "the dream," and this is when the midlife crisis occurs. In 1978, Paul Costa and Robert McCrae developed a measure to assess midlife crisis in men. Men were asked to respond to statements like, "My life is boring; my job is meaningless." They found that many men do not go through a midlife crisis, and those who do, do so at a variety of ages.

A final common social experience during middle age is *empty nest syndrome*. It is during the end of middle adulthood that most parents send their children off to college, or find that their adult children have left home to establish their own lives. Like the bird who has pushed all her offspring out of the nest and is now left alone, the parents who are left behind will need to make adjustments to life without children in the home.

Although it is often assumed that both parents have a difficult time making this adjustment,

recent research shows that it is easier for women to adjust to an empty nest than men. Rebecca Clay, in a 2003 article for the *APA Monitor*, summarizes a recent study by Helen DeVries. In the DeVries' study, 147 mothers and 114 fathers with a child graduating from high school were interviewed. The mothers expressed great anticipation about their children's departure. Mothers talked about plans for their own development, such as returning to school and work. Fathers were more likely to talk about their regrets about time they had not spent with their children.

LATE ADULTHOOD (after 65 years)

The population of adults in this category is growing. As baby boomers reach late adulthood and people live longer than before, this developmental stage will become one of greater interest and study. To prove the existence of a growing elderly population, you only need to count the number of assisted living communities popping up all over the country or all the money spent by advertisers trying to woo this segment of the population.

Physical Development

The physical declines mentioned earlier continue, and some physical declines accelerate during late adulthood. Whitbourne and Weinstock have summarized some of these changes. Like the infant who displays great motor changes, the elderly also experience many physical changes that impact motor development. The overall results of these changes are decreased strength and bone fragility, placing them at great risk for injury from falls and slowed movement.

Although a loss in muscle mass begins during middle adulthood, this increases rapidly between the ages of sixty and seventy. This decrease in muscle mass results in a decrease in muscle strength. As muscle fibers degenerate, they are replaced with fat. Bone loss also begins in middle adulthood and increases more rapidly between the ages of sixty and seventy, with women experiencing more bone loss than men.

Osteoporosis is a condition associated with bone fragility, and although it may be seen in people of any age, it is more typically seen in elderly women. With age, joints become less flexible and they stiffen, making movement more difficult. There may also be inflammation of the tissue surrounding the joint, resulting in arthritis. Although arthritis is not limited to the elderly, it is often seen during late adulthood. In arthritis, movement may require more effort and may be painful. Although this sounds hopeless, it is important to note that there are individual differences in physical decline, as there are individual differences in all developmental processes.

Why does physical decline occur? Augustine DiGiovanna, in his 1994 book *Human Aging: Biological Perspectives*, suggests the possible existence of a "death gene" that tells cells to deteriorate and die. Nevertheless, as a result of improvements in health care, nutrition, and a host of other factors, life expectancies have increased and more and more adults are earning the title of centenarians. Yet there are still some groups who have shortened life expectancies. According to the Centers for Disease Control and Prevention, a white male born today has a life expectancy of seventy-five, while a black male born today will die about seven years earlier, at the age of sixty-eight. The same discrepancies hold true

for women. A white female born today has a life expectancy of seventy-nine, while her black counterpart will die about four years earlier, at the age of seventy-five.

An important component of development is adaptation to change, and this is especially evident during late adulthood. Changes in physical development can result in psychological problems as a once healthy, active, and independent person must rely on others to meet many needs. An inability to adapt to change may result in decreased self-esteem or even lead to feelings of depression.

Cognitive Development

The cognitive changes most often associated with this period are memory related. We will discuss two disorders that are associated with declines in memory: delirium and dementia, which is often associated with Alzheimer's disease. The symptoms of *delirium* are confusion, a sense of being disoriented over the course of several hours or several days. There may be impaired memory or speech. In the elderly, delirium may be a result of the improper use of medication. This can really pose a problem, since incorrectly taking medication can result in exacerbation of other health problems; it can also result in overdose.

Dementia is defined as a gradual deterioration of brain functioning that results in impaired judgment, memory, and other cognitive processes, such as language, problem solving, and decision making. When people talk of the disorder of dementia, they are often referring to Alzheimer's, which was discovered by Alois Alzheimer, a German psychiatrist, in 1906.

In Alzheimer's disease, the patient experiences gradual decline in cognitive abilities, most notably memory. Ultimately the Alzheimer patient loses memory of information, family, friends, and self, as well as how to perform typical tasks, for instance, how to bathe, dress, and walk. An official diagnosis of the disorder cannot be made until after death because diagnosis requires an autopsy to look for certain types of damage to the brain. Research into the prevention of Alzheimer's has focused on the use of ibuprofen to delay the onset of the disorder. There is currently neither a known cause nor a treatment for this devastating disease.

A final term that is often used to discuss the cognitive declines that are associated with old age is senility. *Senility*, in the technical sense, is neither delirium nor Alzheimer's. It is simply a decline in cognitive functioning as compared to previous functioning. Margaret Huyck and William Hoyer, authors of a book on adulthood, estimate that forty percent of the population over sixty-five has experienced such a decline.

Social Development

According to Erikson's theory of psychosocial development, the final psychosocial stage is called integrity versus despair. The goal of this stage is to realize and accept that one's life had meaning. If this is not realized, then one may despair that life was a waste, meaningless. This is a time for reflection and acceptance of not only the physical changes mentioned earlier, but also of one's social network changes. During late adulthood, a person may experience the loss of spouse and siblings, friends relocating, a reduced social network, and a sense of isolation.

For some elderly, the questions may not be "should I seek out social support," but "from whom do I seek social support?"

In addition, the elderly are facing their own mortality. Research suggests that ideas of death in the elderly differ quite significantly from those of the adolescent. In the elderly, death becomes accepted as a stage in the cycle of life. In dealing with their own impending death, people experience stages of dying. These stages were proposed by Elizabeth Kübler Ross, based on her work with terminally ill patients.

Stages of Dying

Denial—The person's reaction is one of disbelief, "this can't happen to me."

Anger—The reality of the situation sets in, and the person reacts with hostility to his given situation.

Bargaining—The person now seeks more time and may make "deals" with health care providers or God.

Depression—The person expresses great sadness and grief; this stage signifies that the final step is about to begin.

Acceptance—The person experiences a sense of peace and ties up "loose ends," unfinished business with family, friends, and work. The person is now ready to die.

The good news is that the overall quality of life for the elderly has improved. More and more elderly people spend their final years in relatively good health, traveling or pursuing other interests. Good medical care (plus a recognition of the special needs of the elderly) means that the quality of life in later years is not compromised as it once might have been.

DEVELOPMENT DURING ADULTHOOD: A SUMMARY		
	Early Adulthood	**Middle Adulthood**	**Late Adulthood**
Physical	At a peak, but increased risk of obesity begins	Changes in appearance of skin, face, and body build; women: menopause	Continuing physical changes; is there a death gene?
Cognitive	Occupational decision making	Crystallized intelligence is better than fluid intelligence	Memory-related disorders, such as delirium and dementia
Social	Committed relationships; *intimacy vs. isolation*	Mentoring youth; *generativity vs. stagnation;* adjustment to change; men: midlife crisis? Empty nest syndrome	Reflection on life; *integrity vs. despair*

CHAPTER SUMMARY

Our discussion of lifespan development in this chapter has focused on adolescence and adulthood. As with our discussion of infancy and childhood, we have organized each developmental period into three categories: physical, cognitive, and social changes.

Adolescence is marked by significant physical changes as girls and boys enter puberty, and physical appearance approaches that of an adult. Noteworthy events in the physical development of the adolescent are menarche and semenarche. Cognitive development involves formal operations, the final stage in Piaget's theory. Adolescents now have the ability to think hypothetically, and abstract concepts are understandable. Social development revolves around establishing a sense of self or identity. Key players in the identity development during adolescence are peers and friends.

Early adulthood is marked by peak physical functioning, although this also may become the period during which battles with weight emerge. An important cognitive task involves decisions about career, and social development focuses on developing intimate and loving relationships. Marriage and childrearing are common experiences during early adulthood.

Middle adulthood is the stage when physical declines become more evident. Changes in physical appearance can be seen in the skin, the face, and body build. Cognitive changes at this point are mixed. There may be declines in fluid intelligence (information processing abilities), but improvements in crystallized intelligence (application of accumulated knowledge). Social development focuses on being productive and mentoring members of the younger generation. In addition, other social experiences during middle age include the midlife crisis and empty nest syndrome.

Late adulthood is associated with further physical decline, which may result in psychological feelings of worthlessness or helplessness. Cognitive changes are most often associated with delirium and dementia, such as Alzheimer's. Social changes require reflection upon, and hopefully acceptance of, one's life. A decrease in one's social network may lead to feelings of isolation. The good news is that, overall, life expectancy has increased, and the quality of life has improved for the elderly as well. More attention is being paid to the needs and desires of the elderly, as evidenced by a surge in housing developments for those fifty-five and older, and products to improve comfort and lifestyle.

TEST YOUR RECALL AND RECOGNITION

True/False

1. The first menstrual period is called menarche.

2. Testosterone is responsible for the development of secondary sex characteristics.

3. Two examples of adolescent egocentrism are the imaginary audience and mental representation.

4. One important cognitive milestone reached during adolescence is the ability to think using hypothetical situations.

5. Seventy-five percent of Americans marry.

6. During early adulthood, physical development is at an optimal level.

7. Menopause occurs during early adulthood.

8. Kübler Ross' first stage of dying is anger.

9. Physical and cognitive exercise can impact the decline of health.

10. Life expectancy continues to increase in the United States.

Multiple Choice

1. By the age of eighteen most boys are
   a. taller than their same-aged female peers.
   b. shorter than their same-aged female peers.
   c. heavier than their same-aged female peers.
   d. both a and c.

2. Iris and her friends are going to the mall where they plan to meet a group of boys from their school. While at the mall, the boys and girls plan to attend a movie together. How would you describe this social interaction?
   a. a one-on-one date
   b. group date
   c. peer party
   d. none of the above

3. The personal fable in adolescence may explain
   a. why Justin, age sixteen, insists on driving without a seatbelt.
   b. why Veronica, age fifteen, has unprotected sex.
   c. why Shawn, age seventeen, drinks and drives.
   d. all of the above.

4. Kai, Allen, and Bernard spend most of their time together. They have other friends, but their parents describe it best when they say, "when you see one, you see the others." The term used to describe this small group of kids who enjoy each other's company is
   a. friends.   c. peers.
   b. acquaintances.   d. gang.

5. In 2000, the average age of a first-time mother was

a. twenty.
b. twenty-five.
c. thirty.
d. thirty-five.

6. _____ is to adolescence as _____ is to middle adulthood in women.

a. Growth spurt, menopause
b. Empty nest syndrome, imaginary audience
c. Menarche, menopause
d. Dating, cognitive decline

7. Empty nest syndrome refers to

a. the period when the home becomes empty of children.
b. the period when adults attempt to "find themselves."
c. symptoms of menopause.
d. exercises to halt cognitive decline.

8. Which of the following is an example of physical decline associated with late adulthood?

a. decrease in muscle strength
b. arthritis
c. changes in muscle mass
d. all of the above

9. About what age does a person enter late adulthood?

a. fifty
b. fifty-five
c. sixty
d. sixty-five

10. Even with the racial disparities in life expectancy, _____ outlive _____.

a. men, women
b. women, men
c. psychologists, nonpsychologists
d. none of the above

Fill in the Blanks

1. The growth of body hair during adolescence is an example of _____ sex characteristics.

2. The final stage in Piaget's theory of cognitive development is called _____.

3. Laura is one of twenty on the softball team. Although she likes all her teammates, she spends most of her time with Kim, who is also on the team. The teammates are Laura's _____, but Kim is her _____.

4. _____ sex friendships become more common during late adolescence.

5. Sexual identity development occurs during _____.

6. Adjustment to the empty nest appears to be more difficult for _____ than _____.

7. Decreases in estrogen after menopause may result in _____.

8. The _____ crisis is associated with middle adulthood.

9. Centenarians are people who are _____ or older.

10. Social support can impact _____ in the elderly.

ANSWERS TO QUESTIONS

True/False

1. true	6. true
2. true	7. false
3. false	8. true
4. true	9. true
5. false	10. true

Multiple Choice

1. d	6. c
2. b	7. a
3. d	8. d
4. a	9. d
5. b	10. b

Fill in the Blanks

1. secondary
2. formal operations
3. peers; friend (best friend)
4. Opposite
5. adolescence
6. men; women
7. osteoporosis
8. midlife
9. one hundred
10. overall health

ADDITIONAL RESOURCES

Books

Albom, M. 1997. *Tuesdays with Morrie.* New York: Doubleday.

Jones, R., ed. 1991. *Black psychology* (3rd ed.). Hampton, VA: Cobb and Henry Publishers.

Juska, J. 2003. *A round-heeled woman: My late-life adventures in sex and romance.* New York: Villard Books.

Katz, L. D., M. Rubin, and D. Suter. 1999. *Keep your brain alive: 83 neurobic exercises.* New York: Workman Publishing Company.

Video

Streetwise, directed by M. Bell. New York: Angelika Films. 1985.

Web site

AARP (American Association for Retired Persons) www.aarp.org

PERSONALITY

What exactly does a person mean when he says, "She's not attractive, but she has a great personality," or "He left the firm for his own reasons, but it was mostly because of personality differences with his supervisor?" How do you interpret a magazine cover that brandishes the intriguing headline "What is your personality type?"

Although we use the word "personality" all the time, it is a complex concept, and it lacks universal meaning. The fact is, we are all thinking of something different when we talk about personality.

There are many thoughts and theories of personality. In this chapter, we will cover some of the theories of personality, and in chapter 11, we will discuss the assessment of personality.

UNDERSTANDING PERSONALITY

Two terms that are important to understand in this chapter are personality and theory. *Personality* is defined as unique and enduring ways of thinking, feeling, and behaving. A *theory* explains a phenomenon, organizes facts, and makes predictions. Personality theories allow us to organize and understand thoughts, feelings, and behaviors of individuals.

The issue of personality can be used to revisit the person versus situation debate mentioned in the discussion on orientation/perspective in chapter 1. According to the above definition, personality is an enduring way of behaving that does not vary regardless of the situation. So for example, a shy, withdrawn person will avoid social interactions regardless of setting. Of course, we have all seen the usually shy and withdrawn person come out of her shell. That might be explained by the situation portion of the debate. According to that side of the debate, characteristics of a person vary depending on one's surroundings.

Remember, the psychological perspective is the lens that guides how phenomena are viewed or explained. So it should not surprise you that individual theories are guided by orientation. For example, Freud's theory of personality focuses on the unconscious and childhood experiences. Psychological orientation is used to give psychologists a framework, or guidelines, to help them understand a variety of psychological phenomena. In this chapter, we will explore how orientation is used to help us understand personality. Each of the varying theories clearly fits into a category of psychological orientation. In this chapter, we will focus on five personality theories: psychodynamic, humanistic/phenomenological, behavioral, trait, and social cognitive.

PERSONALITY THEORIES

Psychodynamic

The person most often associated with psychodynamic personality theories is Sigmund Freud. At the heart of Freudian theory is the *unconscious*. The unconscious is not an actual structure, but a construct. The unconscious contains thoughts and feelings of which we are not aware. Behavior is based on unconscious drives. Some of these drives are destructive, like greed and aggression, and others are necessary for survival, like hunger, self-preservation, and sexual instinct. Freud's references to sex are not just sex in the traditional sense (i.e., for procreation), but sex as synonymous with pleasure.

According to Freud, the personality consists of three parts: the id, ego, and superego. The *id* is present at birth. The id seeks immediate gratification and operates on what Freud refers to as the pleasure principle. "If it feels good, do it" is the motto of the id.

Neither the ego nor the superego is present at birth. Both develop during childhood. The *ego* is the center of reason and operates on what Freud refers to as the reality principle. "Let's consider the consequence" is the reasoning of the ego.

The *superego* is the conscience and is where morality is housed. "It might feel good, but it is bad for your health" is something that might be uttered by the superego.

These three structures are in constant conflict, and as you can guess, most of the conflict involves the id and the superego. The ego stands, figuratively, between the id and the superego. In an effort to cope with the anxiety produced by the conflict of the superego and the id, the ego uses defense mechanisms as a coping technique.

DEFENSE MECHANISMS

Denial—the refusal to acknowledge thoughts, feelings, or memories that present a threat

Example: An abused woman repeatedly brags to her friends about how much her partner loves her.

Displacement—applying negative feelings to a "safe" target rather than the source of the feelings

Example: After a day filled with criticism from his supervisor, a man goes home and yells at his dog.

Projections—placing your own thoughts, feelings, or behaviors onto someone else

Example: The brother of a successful businesswoman tells his parents that his sister is jealous of him.

Reaction Formation—espousing the opposite of an unacceptable feeling or thought

Example: The adolescent who says, "I don't like him; you know I think boys are gross," actually has a crush on the boy.

Regression—reverting to a behavior that is associated with an earlier period of development

Example: A healthy, seven year old starts wetting the bed.

Repression—pushing unacceptable thoughts deep into the unconscious where they are inaccessible

Example: Twenty years after receiving an honorable discharge from the military, a former prisoner of war is unable to recount any of his experiences that happened while in captivity.

Sublimation—a type of displacement; channeling unacceptable thoughts into an appropriate area, often associated with art

Example: Many artists will say that their art is the expression of their painful past experiences.

Psychosexual Development

Another psychodynamic theory in personality is Freud's theory of psychosexual development, one of the most well-known theories in the field of psychology. This theory is referred to as a *stage* theory because, like Piaget's theory of development, it progresses through sequential stages. Movement is forward only. Once you pass through a stage, you cannot go back. Please notice that the ages in Freud's stages are similar to those of Erikson. For each stage there is a target area of focus. Freud refers to this area as the erogenous zone, and it is the center of pleasure at this particular period.

Oral Stage: Birth to 18 months

The erogenous zone during the oral stage is the mouth. During the first eighteen months of life, the child's focus is on activities that involve the mouth, such as sucking, eating, and biting. If oral needs are not met, for example, if the child is weaned too soon, she will develop an oral fixation. This means that she did not accomplish the objective of the stage. A fixation at this stage could form the basis for a habit like nail-biting or even obsessive eating or smoking in the adult years.

Anal Stage: 18 months to 3 years

The erogenous zone during the anal stage is the anus. During this period, the child's focus is on activities that involve the anal region of the body, such as toileting. If the child's anal needs are not met through the parent's approach to toilet training—for example, excessive punishment when accidents occur—he will develop an anal fixation. A fixation at this stage could form the basis for behavior patterns in which the person holds on to things. This holding on may present as a person who is frugal or stingy. The opposite may be apparent as well, namely a person who lets go too easily, who may be too generous or a spendthrift.

Phallic Stage: 4 to 5 years

The erogenous zone during the phallic stage is the genital area. During this period, we see parallel challenges for boys and girls. Boys experience the *Oedipal Complex*. This is a reference to the play *Oedipus Rex* by Sophocles. During the Oedipal stage, a boy falls in love with his mother and wants her for himself, yet the father remains an obstacle. So, the child plans to eliminate his father. He then realizes that dad is bigger, stronger, and more powerful. Freud coined the term *castration anxiety* to explain this fear. Specifically, the child fears that the father will castrate him. This fear motivates the child not only to give up his pursuit of his mother, but also to identify with his father. Resolution of the phallic stage involves identification with the parent of the same sex.

In girls, there is the *Electra Complex*. Although quite similar to the Oedipal Complex (some refer to this stage as the Oedipal complex for girls), it contains some subtle differences. The girl begins to resent her mother and to love and envy her father. The reasons for the resentment toward her mother are because her mother made her a girl, which, according to the theory, is an inferior position. The envy of the father is because he possesses a penis, which is a symbol of power. This *penis envy* is the counterpart to the castration anxiety experienced by boys during this stage.

According to Freud, this dilemma can never be fully resolved, but the girl ultimately comes to identify with her mother. This particular portion of Freud's theory has received criticism from feminists and their supporters.

Latency Stage: 6 to 11 years
There is no erogenous zone associated with this stage because, according to Freud, sexual interest is dormant. One of the criticisms of Freud's theory of the latency stage is that it appears as if nothing happens to children during this period, when clearly there is a lot of change and development occurring.

Genital Stage: 11 to 12 years through adulthood
The erogenous zone for this stage is the genital area. This is the final stage in Freud's theory of psychosexual development and the period that is marked by sexual maturation. At this stage, sexual urges reappear. However, at this point, sexual interest is directed toward peers rather than toward oneself or caregivers.

When there is difficulty passing through the stages, problems may develop. As we learned, a person who did not work through the oral or anal stage may become orally or anally fixated and spend his adulthood trying to satisfy those unmet oral or anal needs.

Therefore, according to Freud, problems are caused by these conflicts with the unconscious. In order to treat these problems, you must tap into your unconscious. Freud's approach to treatment is referred to as psychoanalysis. We will cover this approach to treatment in chapter 13.

NeoFreudians

There are some offshoots of Freud's theories, and the creators of these modified theories are referred to as NeoFreudians. They include Carl Jung (1875–1961); Alfred Adler (1870–1937); Erik Erikson (1902–1994); Karen Horney (1885–1952); and Sigmund Freud's daughter, Anna Freud (1895–1982). Of special interest here are the theories of the first three psychologists, Jung, Adler, and Erikson.

The NeoFreudians whose ideas were most disturbing to Freud were those of Jung and Adler, both of whom worked alongside Freud. Although Jung and Freud were quite close at one time, Freud and Adler, although colleagues, were never congenial.

Carl Jung felt that Freud placed too much emphasis on sex and the past. According to Jung, there are two levels of personality: the conscious level and the unconscious level. Jung is most famous for his concept of the *collective unconscious*. This consists of a level of unconscious, which we inherited from our ancestors.

To clarify this concept, think about your physical being. You inherited your eyes from your father, your nose from your paternal great-grandmother, and your hair from your mother. Similarly, the collective unconscious is the product of generations and generations. Within this collective unconscious there are ancient and universal experiences that are referred to as *archetypes*. Jung spoke of archetypes as consisting of opposing forces that reside within each of us. We all have a masculine and feminine side, an introverted and extroverted side, and the goal is to integrate these opposing forces.

According to Alfred Adler, the goal is not to strive for gratification or pleasure, but to be the best we can be. Adler is credited with the development of the *superiority* and *inferiority complexes*. According to Adler, parents are influential in the development of a child's feelings of being superior or inferior. This theory has a social component that is not seen in Freud's original theory. We strive for superiority, which is the achievement of our ultimate goal in life. Of course, these goals vary from person to person.

Another interesting piece of Adler's theory of personality development focuses on the importance of *birth order*. Adler focused on the personalities of the oldest child, the middle child, the youngest child, and the only child. The oldest child begins as the prince or princess of the family. Upon the birth of the second child, that title is lost and the oldest child then makes efforts to regain that seat of privilege and power. The theory states that oldest children tend to be power seeking, conscientious, and organized.

The middle child, or second child, looks to the older child and, depending on the relationship, the older child may serve as a model for competition, threat, or companionship. In an attempt to keep in step with the older child, second-born children show more rapid development. Overall, these children are more competitive and hopeful about the future than their older siblings.

The youngest child, or the baby of the family, may take two routes. If pampered by older siblings, he may become dependent on others. If he doesn't receive attention from his siblings at first, the youngest child may work tirelessly to gain the attention of others.

Only children are in a unique position. Like the oldest child, they begin as the prince or princess of the family, but they never lose this title. These children struggle when they leave the cocoon of the home because they never learn to cooperate or share with other children. They may also demonstrate mature behaviors at an early age, because they initially spend most of their time with adults. There are many books on birth order, and many criticisms of this idea. Adler's contribution of this theory has elicited numerous debates among psychologists and the general public. He was deemed the first psychologist to bring psychology into the realm of the everyday person. He published psychology books and wrote self-help books as well.

Psychosocial Development

Finally, Erik Erikson's theory of psychosocial development evolved in response to Freud's theory of psychosexual development. Erikson believed that Freud's theory over-emphasized sex and that social components should be considered. In addition, Erikson's theory was one of the first to recognize life span development. This theory, as we learned in chapters 8 and 9, covers stages of development from birth through old age.

Erikson's stages of psychosocial development share similarities in age ranges with Freud's theory of psychosexual development. According to Erikson, difficulty in one stage may have implications for later development. During each stage, there is a psychological crisis that must be addressed. If the individual successfully addresses each crisis, he will acquire the first term or word used in the name of that stage, such as "trust" or "autonomy." If he does not address the crisis, he will experience the second term used in the title of the stage, which is "mistrust," or "shame and doubt." Ultimately, failure to resolve the crisis will have implications for later development.

Humanistic/Phenomenological

Carl Rogers developed a theory of psychotherapy, not personality, and one hallmark of Rogers' theory is its positive slant. Rogers emphasized that people are rational, and he stressed the importance of that which is at the conscious level. Rogers coined the term *unconditional positive regard* to suggest how people should be treated, and he stated that there are individual differences that must be accepted. The implications for this in a therapeutic context will be discussed in chapter 13. Unconditional positive regard consists of acceptance and warmth and leads to positive self-regard, in other words, feeling good about one's self.

Abraham Maslow is most often noted for his *hierarchy of needs* and the striving for *self-actualization*. In the hierarchy of needs, our most basic needs, such as food and water, are at the bottom. Next are safety needs, followed by belonging and love, then esteem, and finally self-actualization.

A person cannot even begin to consider a need if the needs below it on the hierarchy have not been met. So, for example, "I cannot begin to consider my need to belong or to be a part of something if I am not certain how I'm going to obtain a meal today."

Self-actualization is the highest of needs, and it is one that most people will never entirely meet. Being self-actualized means having the highest moral ideals. Duane Schultz and Sydney Ellen Schultz in *Theories of Personality* offer Mother Theresa, Martin Luther King, Jr., Ghandi, and Harriet Tubman as examples of people who would be considered to be self-actualized.

Behavioral

Behavioral theories of personality are actually antitheories in that behaviorists deny the existence of personality. Behaviorists would stand on the situation side of the person vs. situation debate. In chapter 7, we introduced behaviorists, including B. F. Skinner, John Watson, and Edward Thorndike, who were associated with operant conditioning, or instrumental conditioning. This type of conditioning involves the use of both positive and negative reinforcement to ensure that certain behaviors will happen in the future.

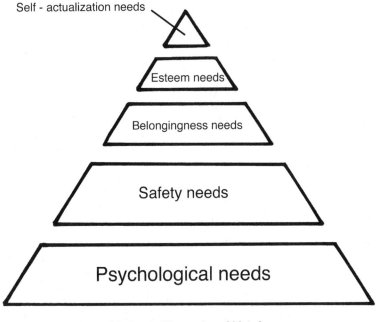

Self - actualization needs

Esteem needs

Belongingness needs

Safety needs

Psychological needs

Maslow's Hierarchy of Needs

According to Skinner, the emphasis of science should be on observable or overt behaviors. Skinner acknowledged the existence of the unseen or covert behaviors, but he felt that they were not useful in explaining behavior. Personality is an unseen concept and, therefore, not of interest to behaviorists. In addition, it is also important to remember that behaviorists feel that we are influenced by our environment, so the way we behave will change based on the feedback we receive from the environment. So, although a loud and rambunctious demeanor may be reinforced at the football game, it will not be reinforced in the library.

Trait

The trait theories view personality as consistent patterns in thought, feeling, and behavior that span time and situations. This consistency allows for predictions of how a person will behave in future situations. Three trait theorists—Gordon Allport (1897–1967), Raymond Cattell (1905–1998), and Hans Eysenck (1916–1997)—were responsible for developing these concepts.

Allport was a pioneer in personality research and presented the first lecture on personality in the United States. He proposed that any personality could be placed into one of three traits: cardinal traits, central traits, and secondary traits. A *cardinal trait* is one that is an all-consuming characteristic that guides behaviors, such as power. A *central trait* is one that influences behavior, but it doesn't have that all-consuming quality of the cardinal trait. Integrity is an example of a central trait. *Secondary traits* are what we would call attitudes or preferences.

Raymond Cattell was a student of Charles Spearman (1916–1997), who is famous for his theory of intelligence. Cattell's statistical training shines through in his theory. Cattell used *factor analysis*, which involves giving many measures (such as administering tests of personality to many people), then looked to see if certain characteristics clumped together. Cattell also proposed a theory of personality development that covers the entire lifespan, as does Erikson's theory.

Hans Eysenck developed three personality dimensions, and at least one of these will probably sound familiar. The three dimensions are extraversion-introversion, neuroticism-emotional stability, and psychoticism-impulse control. Each dimension can be placed on a continuum, and a person will be placed somewhere on that continuum.

THREE DIMENSIONS OF PERSONALITY

Extraversion
Focuses on people; the outside world; outgoing, social

Introversion
Focuses on self; inner thoughts and feelings; withdrawn, shy

Neuroticism
Difficulty controlling emotions; anxious, low self-esteem

Emotional stability
Demonstrates control of emotions; calm, composed

Psychoticism
Difficulty with impulse control; uncooperative, insensitive

Impulse control
Demonstrates control of impulses; warm, helpful

Big Five/Five Factor Model of Personality

Researchers Robert McCrae and Paul Costa believed that the theories of Cattell and

Eysenck were missing something, and this belief led to the development of the "Big Five" or the Five Factor Model of Personality. This model organized personality traits into five categories: extroversion, agreeableness, conscientiousness, emotional stability, and openness. The Big Five captures the most important dimensions of human personality, and it has been shown to apply cross culturally. So, you can interview people from a variety of Western and nonWestern cultures, and these five personality traits appear. This is exciting because such cross-cultural research findings support the idea that certain personality traits are universal.

THE FIVE FACTOR MODEL OF PERSONALITY

Extroversion—talkative, active, confident, gregarious, optimistic

Agreeableness—courteous, generous, accommodating, warm, considerate, sympathetic

Conscientiousness—competent, organized, responsible, ethical, consistent

Emotional Stability—unexcitable, calm, even-tempered, poised, unemotional

Openness—introspective, deep, sophisticated, creative, insightful

Social Cognitive

Social cognitive theories emphasize the role of the environment, social influence, and cognition on personality development. Three theorists associated with this approach to personality are Albert Bandura, Julian Rotter, and Walter Mischel.

Albert Bandura (1925–) is most often associated with his Bobo doll study, which illustrated the use of modeling. *Modeling* is synonymous with imitation, and it is easily seen in children who model others who are influential in the early years of their lives, usually their parents.

The now famous Bobo doll study was conducted in 1961 at a nursery school at Stanford University. Subjects were children between the ages of three and six. Seventy-two children participated in the study. Twenty-four, or one-third, of the children were assigned to the control group and did not witness the actions of the model. The remaining children were divided by gender and then either observed an aggressive model, or a nonaggressive model. The target of the aggression was a five-foot Bobo doll, which is a big balloon that rocks back and forth.

Those exposed to the aggressive model watched an adult hit the Bobo doll. Those exposed to the nonaggressive model did not see the adult model hit the doll. Actually, the model just ignored the doll.

Were there differences in how the children interacted with the doll based on the type of model with whom they had spent their time? Yes; those children exposed to the aggressive model were also more likely to hit the doll than were those exposed to the nonaggressive model. This study has farreaching implications for the origins of both positive and negative behavior.

Walter Mischel (1930–) developed the theory that behavior is based on situations, not traits. This contribution addresses the heart of the person-situation controversy introduced in chapter 1; his theory proposes that people make responses that they believe will lead to reinforcement in a situation. For instance, college students study hard to get high grades that they hope will lead to a good job or placement in a quality graduate program. If their studiousness results in a C as a final grade, they may become less industrious. In addition, Mischel's theory has resulted in much research to understand the stability of personality. His research concluded that people are less consistent in their behaviors than previously thought. For instance, people who are loyal in one situation may become "backstabbers" in another.

Julian Rotter (1916–) worked with Adler as an undergraduate student. Keep this in mind as you read ahead, and consider whether you think one of Rotter's most well-known theories conveys some of Adler's influence. One of Rotter's most famous ideas about personality addressed what he deemed locus of control. There are two types of locus of control: internal and external.

Internal Locus of Control

With internal locus of control, we believe that we receive reinforcement as a result of our own behavior. For example, the businesswoman who believes that she received a salary increase as a result of many hours of labor on a special project is relying on the internal locus of control.

External Locus of Control

We receive reinforcement as a result of something apart from ourselves, or outside our control. For example, the businesswoman who believes that she received a salary increase as a corporation-wide standard of living raise is operating under the external locus of control. As you might guess, people's locus of control can influence their behavior. People who believe that things just happen will be unlikely to make efforts to alter their

environment. Compare that position to someone who believes that she can influence or control her environment.

CHAPTER SUMMARY

The goal of a personality theory is to organize and explain thoughts, feelings, and behaviors. There are a variety of personality theories. These include, but are not limited to, psychodynamic, humanistic, behavioral, trait, and social-cognitive approaches.

The psychodynamic approaches are associated with Freud. The concept of the unconscious underlies all psychodynamic theories. Many psychologists have followed in the footsteps of Freud and created their own theories that present slight modifications on Freud's original theories. These psychologists include Jung, Adler, and Erikson.

The humanistic approach, associated with Rogers and Maslow, emphasizes individual differences and the importance of placing value on these differences. Behavioral approaches are associated with Skinner, and they emphasize observable events. The trait theorists such as Allport, Cattell, and Eysenck argue that personality is stable and predictable.

Researchers like Mischel have encouraged much healthy debate on the stability of personality and the person-situation debate. The social cognitive therapists, such as Bandura, Rotter, and Mischel, emphasize the importance of the environment, private events, and cognition in understanding and explaining behavior.

The theories that support the existence of personality are useful because they support the idea of personality as something that is stable and, therefore, predictable. Predictability is helpful because it allows us to determine when something is wrong. The parent brings his child to the pediatrician and says, "He has been very irritable lately; usually, he is a happy-go-lucky guy." The child's change in personality served as a red flag to let the father know that something is wrong.

The predictable nature of personality also provides us with a sense of stability and security. Have you ever tried to interact with someone who was "hot and cold" or totally unpredictable? This might be the boss who yells at you in the morning, warmly invites you to lunch in the afternoon, and then sneers at you as you leave in the evening? Such a person can be very difficult to work with.

In the next chapter, we talk about how we assess personality. Psychologists have a variety of techniques that they use to gain a sense of someone's personality. Some are as simple as the paper and pencil tests seen in magazines, and others involve intensive testing procedures and extensive interviews.

TEST YOUR RECALL AND RECOGNITION

True/False

1. Sigmund Freud's theories focus on conscious thought.

2. The id is present at birth.

3. The Oedipal and Electra complexes occur during the genital stage of development.

4. The concepts of an inferiority and superiority complex were developed by Adler.

5. Erik Erikson's theory is one of lifespan development.

6. At the top of the Maslow hierarchy of needs is the need for self-esteem.

7. Trait theories view personality as an inconsistent pattern of behavior.

8. Bandura's Bobo doll study illustrated the importance of introversion and extraversion.

9. Rotter is associated with the psycho-dynamic personality theories.

10. The Big Five refers to the five most important personality theories.

Multiple Choice

1. Which of the following concepts is *not* a part of personality, according to Freud?

   a. id   c. superego

   b. denial   d. ego

2. You walk past your favorite shoe store and notice a new pair of boots in the window. Although you barely have enough money to pay your current bills, you are tempted to purchase the boots. As you glance at the boots through the store window, something inside you says, "Do it; buy the boots. They will look fantastic with your new outfit." Which part of your personality is speaking?

   a. id   c. superego

   b. denial   d. ego

3. The source of pleasure, or erogenous zone, during the oral stage is the

   a. genitals.

   b. anus.

   c. mouth.

   d. none of the above.

4. What motivates resolution of the Oedipal Complex?

a. penis envy   c. displacement

b. castration anxiety d. repression

5. Greg is only four, but he seems very mature and wise. He is socially comfortable with adults, but finds it difficult to socialize with children his age. Greg is probably a(n) _____ child.

a. oldest   c. middle

b. youngest   d. only

6. Failure to meet the psychological crisis in Erikson's first stage of development could result in an

a. adolescent who follows the crowd because she does not have a strong sense of self.

b. elderly person who feels great regret about his choices in life.

c. adolescent who is mistrustful of those around her.

d. both a and b.

7. Which of the following would Maslow *not* consider to be an example of a self-actualized individual?

a. Mother Theresa

b. Martin Luther King, Jr.

c. Harriet Tubman

d. a newborn baby

8. Which of the following is *not* one of Eysenck's dimensions of personality?

a. internal-external

b. extraversion-introversion

c. neuroticism-emotional stability

d. psychoticism-impulse control

9. Lynne watches superheroes on television, and then she tries to imitate their super-human powers. As a result of this behavior, she has broken her arm, her father's lawn mower, and her brother's handlebars. Lynne's behavior is an example of

a. reaction formation.

b. introversion.

c. inferiority complex.

d. modeling.

10. The concept of locus of control is associated with

a. Freud.

b. Skinner.

c. Mischel.

d. Rotter.

Fill in the Blanks

1. William's parents were very strict about bottle-feeding and were determined that he be weaned from the bottle at the age of one. William now chain-smokes and overeats. William is fixated at the _____ stage of development.

2. Defense mechanisms are the _____ method of coping with the anxiety produced by the constant conflict between the _____ and _____.

3. The stages in Freud's theory of development are referred to as _____ stages.

4. Jung's two levels of personality are the _____ level and the _____ level.

5. The stages in Erikson's theory of development are referred to as _____ stages.

6. According to Rogers, people should be treated with _____ _____ _____.

7. Questions about the stability of personality were posed by _____.

8. Children in the Bobo study who observed the aggressive model were more likely to behave in a(n) _____ manner when presented with the Bobo doll.

9. "There is no such thing as luck. If you work hard, you will succeed." This comment is the voice of a person with a(n) _____ locus of control.

10. Trait theories of _____ emphasize the consistency of thoughts, feelings, and behaviors.

ANSWERS TO QUESTIONS
True/False

1. false
2. true
3. false
4. true
5. true
6. false
7. false
8. false
9. false
10. false

Multiple Choice

1. b
2. a
3. c
4. b
5. d
6. c
7. d
8. a
9. d
10. d

Fill in the Blanks

1. oral
2. ego's; id; superego
3. psychosexual
4. unconscious, conscious
5. psychosocial
6. unconditional positive regard
7. Mischel
8. aggressive
9. internal
10. personality

ADDITIONAL RESOURCES
Books

Allport, G. W. 1937. *Personality: A psychological interpretation.* New York: Holt.
Rogers, C. R. 1961. *On becoming a person.* Boston: Houghton Mifflin.

Web site

Society for Personality and Social Psychology, www.spsp.org

ASSESSMENT AND INDIVIDUAL DIFFERENCES

KEY TERMS

reliability, validity, Rorschach Inkblot Test, Thematic Apperception Test, A-B design, confounding variable, intelligence quotient, Gardner's Theory of Multiple Intelligences

Psychological assessments can be done in a variety of ways, depending on the situation that one is trying to understand. Assessments are basically the collection of information about a behavior/situation and are the first step in any approach to intervention. In psychology, examples of interventions include therapy or referral to someone else who can provide assistance, such as a physician for medication, a social worker for help with housing or job placement, or another specialist—for example, a speech therapist or physical therapist.

Assessment allows the psychologist to make decisions about which type of treatment will best solve the problem. The uses for assessment go beyond the field of psychology. Attorneys may use the results of a personality test to make a case for a client with an insanity plea. Parents may use the results from behavioral assessment to make decisions about the effectiveness of their approach to discipline. Educators may use the results from intelligence tests to make decisions about class placements, and physicians may use the results from biological tests to make decisions about medically based treatments.

In this chapter, we'll look at personality, behavioral, intelligence, and biological assessments, but it is important to first discuss

the issues of reliability and validity. Two of the tools that we use in making assessments are statistics and research methods, so some of the concepts introduced in chapter 2 will be applied here.

RELIABILITY AND VALIDITY

It is important that whatever type of assessment is used will provide consistent and stable findings. In other words, if you take an intelligence test today and then take the same test again three months later, assuming there have been no significant changes in your life, the second score should be relatively close to the first. The similar results indicate that there is good reliability in the test.

The second issue is one of validity. Does the test measure what it's supposed to measure? If you take a biological test, is it going to measure your math abilities, or is it going to measure what it is intended to measure—your biological functioning?

Any good assessment tool will possess both strong reliability and validity.

TOOLS FOR ASSESSMENT

Each type of assessment uses a different type of tool. For example, biological assessments use computerized axial tomography (CAT) and magnetic resonance imaging (MRI).

Personality assessments use tests like the Minnesota Multiphasic Personality Inventory (MMPI) and the Thematic Apperception Test (TAT). Intelligence assessments use tests like the Weschler Intelligence Scales for Children (WISC) and the well-known Stanford-Binet test. Behavioral assessments use procedures like direct observation. All these will be detailed in the pages that follow.

In this chapter, we will discuss four types of assessment: personality, intelligence, behavioral, and biological.

PERSONALITY ASSESSMENT

We learned in chapter 10 just how many different personality theories there are, so it will come as no surprise that there are just as many different ways to assess one's personality. We will focus on the interview, projective tests, and self-report/inventory tests.

Interview

The interview is typically the first step in the assessment process. It serves in the assessment of personality, and it is also one of the first steps in behavioral, intelligence, and biological assessments.

The interview is important for two reasons. One, it provides the clinician with an opportunity to establish a rapport, or a relationship, with the client. This rapport is important in order for the client to feel at ease with the clinician, and, consequently, be more forthcoming. Second, the interview provides an opportunity for the clinician to obtain information that may not be presented by any of the other tests that she plans to administer during assessment (such

as interaction style, social skills, and feelings about being in therapy).

There are two types of interviews: structured and unstructured. In a structured interview, the questions are listed before the interview begins. The Structured Clinical Interview for DSM-IV (SCID) is a commonly used structured interview. In an unstructured interview, the clinician uses cues from the client to determine what questions will be asked and which responses require probing to obtain more detail.

The interview process is not limited to the first meeting. The clinician may continue to interview the client throughout the assessment process.

Projective Tests

Projective tests are associated with the psychodynamic orientation. Since this orientation believes the unconscious to be key, these tests tap into the unconscious. The most famous of these tests are the Rorschach Inkblot Test and the TAT.

The Rorschach Inkblot Test was developed by Hermann Rorschach in 1942. The test consists of ten cards; each card contains a symmetrical and ambiguous blotch. The clinician presents the card to the client and the client describes what he sees. Interpretations of the responses on the Rorschach are then scored by the clinician. The ability to administer and score the Rorschach requires intensive study and training.

The TAT, which was developed by Henry Murray and Christina Morgan in 1943, uses ambiguous stimuli in the form of cards that contain pictures that present situations. The client is asked to create a story based on the picture. The cards are scored based on a scheme developed specifically for the TAT.

There is a children's version of the TAT called the Children's Apperception Test, or the CAT. In the CAT, the cards contain pictures of animals rather than people. There have also been recent attempts to make variations on the TAT that are culturally sensitive. All the people represented on the first TAT cards were white. These attempts have resulted in Tell-Me-A-Story (TEMAS) in which the subjects of the cards are Anglo-American, Latin American, African-American, and Asian-American. Guiseppe Constantino of Fordham University and Robert Malgady of New York University developed the TEMAS in 1983 in response to years of research that demonstrated that children of color were more responsive to culturally relevant projective tests. Unlike the TAT cards, which are strictly black and white, the TEMAS cards are colorful and portray children of color in different situations. They are more relevant to what children of color really experience.

In summary, the rationale behind projective tests is that the presentation of the ambiguous stimuli will elicit responses that reflect the true personality.

Self-Report/Inventory Tests

Unlike projective tests, self-report tests attempt to obtain information directly from the source. The projective tests employ an indirect method. Self-report/inventory tests are typically paper and pencil tests that require the respondent to answer questions about differing aspects of himself.

If you have ever taken a personality quiz in a magazine, then you have a rough sense of the self-report/inventory test.

The most commonly used self-report tests are the Minnesota Multiphasic Personality

Inventory (MMPI), and the California Psychological Inventory (CPI). The most recent version of the MMPI, the MMPI-2, has eliminated sexist language and updated the text. The test consists of 567 questions that require a true/false response. A version of the test, the MMPI-A, was developed for use with adolescents. The completed test may be scored by computer and then interpreted by a trained psychometrician.

A *psychometrician* is a person who has been trained to administer, score, and interpret objective psychological tests (like the MMPI and the WISC), but not the projective tests, which can take years of training to learn how to administer, score, and interpret. A psychometrician does not have to be a clinical psychologist or have a doctoral degree.

The CPI is a 462-item test that also uses a true/false format. This test may be used with adolescents and adults. Both the MMPI and CPI provide information about personality on different dimensions, such as depression, hysteria, paranoia (MMPI), and dominance, self-control, responsibility (CPI).

One problem with the self-report test is social desirability, or faking. People often want to portray themselves in a good light, so they may provide less honest responses. In addition, there is the issue of forgetting. Some questionnaires require that the respondent recall facts from his past. Inaccurate recall can impact the interpretation of the questionnaire.

BEHAVIORAL ASSESSMENT

Remember, behaviorists are concerned with observable behaviors. Assessments of behavior can also be used to draw conclusions about personality, so there is some crossover between this type of testing and personality testing.

In behavioral assessment, we look at four modes of behavior: overt behavior, cognitions, emotions, and physiological responding. Let us use fear of public speaking to illustrate. You have decided to get treatment for your fear of public speaking as you have a new job that requires you to travel the country and make public appearances where you will be asked to "say a few words." You go to see a psychologist for help with this problem. In an effort to understand how best to treat your problem, your therapist may ask, "What are you thinking when you have to speak in public (cognitions)?" "What sort of behaviors do you engage in? Do you bite your nails and wring your hands (overt behavior)?" "What are you feeling (emotions)?" Your therapist may hook you up to a machine that measures heart rate as part of a physiological assessment. In *multimodal assessment*, the psychologist simply asks about more than one mode of behavior.

The focus of behavioral assessment is the observation and recording of overt behaviors. Once collected, this information is used to make decisions about interventions. We will refer to this as the who, what, when, where, why, and how of behavioral assessment.

Who—Who will observe the behavior? If you plan to observe your own behavior, then you are *self-monitoring*. If you plan to have someone else observe the behavior, you are employing the services of an *outside monitor*. There are advantages and disadvantages to each approach. Self-monitoring is less expensive than an outside observer, and it's also less intrusive. However, an outside observer is more likely to be objective about the behavior than you are.

What—This is the behavior chosen to be studied. The important piece of "the what" is that the behavior receives a clear definition. One way to study behavior is to look at aspects of the behavior. Three often-studied aspects are *frequency, duration,* and *intensity*. How often does the behavior occur? How long does the behavior last? How much physical exertion is involved in the behavior?

When—Will the behavior be observed constantly? If so, *continuous recording* will be employed, which involves watching and recording the behavior every time it occurs. As you can guess, this may be difficult to do. If behavior occurs on a frequent basis, it may be difficult to keep track. On the other hand, if the behavior occurs on an infrequent basis, then the observer may find himself sitting around waiting to see something that will not happen for hours. *Interval recording* involves selecting a certain period to time, and only recording the occurrence of the behavior at that time. So, for example, I will record nail biting every day between the hours of 10:00 and 11:00 A.M. and again between the hours of 6:00 and 7:00 P.M.

Another method of recording is *product sample recording*, where a person collects the product of a behavior. For example, let us suppose a subject would like to decrease the number of cigarettes that he smokes each day. In an effort to collect data on this behavior, an observer could engage in continuous recording where each and every cigarette smoked during the course of the day is recorded. The observer could engage in interval recording and only record the number of cigarettes smoked between noon and four. Or the observer could engage in product sample recording and save the butts from each cigarette smoked. At the end of the day, the collected butts could be counted to discover how many cigarettes the subject smoked that day.

Where—What will the setting be for the behavioral observation? Will the subject be observed in a naturalistic setting? *Naturalistic settings* for children would include a school yard, classroom, or park. *Contrived settings*, like a clinic or laboratory, are arranged by someone else. There are advantages and disadvantages to each type of setting. Naturalistic settings tend to yield the true/honest form of the behavior, and lab settings may result in stifled behaviors. But in a lab setting, the researcher has much more control over when the behavior will occur.

Why—Behavioral assessment asks, "Is the behavior really a problem?" People are sometimes not the best judges of whether or not a behavior is a problem. A man may think that he drinks a lot of coffee, but the behavioral assessment will provide data to determine whether or not this is the case. Behavioral assessment is also important for evaluation purposes. Let's say a woman thinks that her intervention was successful, and she feels that she has cut down on the numbers of cigarettes smoked each day. But how can she be certain? Behavioral assessment will provide numbers that really track the trends in her cigarette smoking. Therefore, behavioral assessment may be used in the beginning of the process to determine if treatment is necessary, or it may be used at the end of the process to determine if treatment was effective.

How—What type of recording instrument will be used? The most basic instruments are pen or pencil and paper. Other instruments include tape and video recorders, pedometers, or golf-stroke counters. When considering how to record the data, an important consideration

is how easy or difficult it will be to use the instrument. It is important that the behavior is recorded when it occurs. So if the observer has to run home to enter the data into the computer after each instance of the behavior, then the recording instrument has not been properly selected.

Design of Behavioral Assessment

A-B design is the most basic research design. A stands for the *baseline*, which is the situation before intervention information is compiled. The collection of baseline data is required, for it serves as our point of comparison.

B stands for *treatment*, which is data collected during the treatment phase. An A-B design compares the baseline data to the treatment data for differences.

For example, you compare the number of cigarettes smoked before the use of the nicotine patch with the number smoked during use of the patch. Has the frequency of cigarette smoking decreased in the treatment phase as compared to the baseline phase? If so, then we can say the treatment had an effect.

In the A-B-A-B design, the A continues to stand for baseline and B for treatment. The sequence of this design is baseline-treatment-baseline-treatment. This design corrects for some of the problems of the A-B design, such as influence of confounding variables. A *confounding variable* makes it difficult for us to say that the intervention had an effect on the behavior.

Let us say, for example, that your baseline is the amount of cigarettes smoked each day for a week. You then begin to use the nicotine patch and record the number of cigarettes smoked, which is the treatment period.

You then stop wearing the patch and continue to record smoking frequency, which is the baseline again. You resume use of the patch and continue to record the frequency of smoking. But what if you discovered that during the first treatment phase, laws were enacted making smoking in restaurants illegal, and you tend to do most of your smoking in a restaurant that you frequent after work? Given this change, is the decrease in smoking frequency due to the intervention (nicotine patch), or is it due to the confounding variable (the change in the law)? In an A-B design, there is uncertainty, but in the A-B-A-B, there is more certainty.

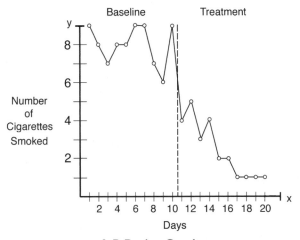

A-B Design Graph

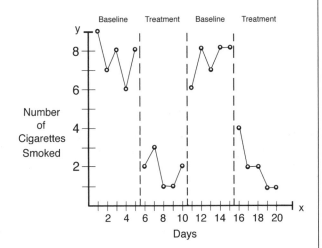

A-B-A-B Design Graph

INTELLIGENCE ASSESSMENT

First and foremost, we must agree on a definition of intelligence before we can measure it. But you will see that this is easier said than done.

I have a cousin who has very little formal education, yet he can disassemble, fix, and reassemble anything with a motor. I have years of formal education, but I find it challenging to change a tire. Who is more intelligent?

In our society, we tend to equate intelligence with years of school. If you ask the general public, most people respond that high academic performance is the measure of intelligence. But there are theorists who have developed definitions of intelligence that indicate that intelligence is so much more than book learning. We will start with a review of some of the theories of intelligence and then discuss how we assess intelligence.

Theories of Intelligence

One of the earliest theories of intelligence was developed by Charles Spearman at the beginning of the twentieth century. Called General Factor Theory of Intelligence, or "Spearman's g," it is an all-encompassing concept that states that you are either intelligent in all areas, or you are intelligent in no areas.

In 1983, Howard Gardner of Harvard University proposed that there are different types of intelligence, or *multiple intelligences*—intelligence is not an all or none concept. In other words, you can be intelligent in one way, and not so intelligent in another. To illustrate, let us return to the example of my cousin and me. He has the ability to take things apart, fix them, and put them back together. He does not use a manual or write anything down while he works. Thus, his ability to repair things requires that he hold in memory a visual representation of the object before dismantling it so that he can return the object to its predisassembled state.

According to Gardner, the ability to do this requires good spatial intelligence. Spatial intelligence is one of Gardner's types of intelligence.

More recent theories of intelligence include Sternberg's Triarchic Theory of Intelligence. Robert Sternberg is the 2003 President of the American Psychological Association and has

GARDNER'S THEORY OF MULTIPLE INTELLIGENCES

Type of Intelligence	Description	Example
Logical/Mathematical	Ability to understand numerical patterns, to think systematically	Physicist Stephen Hawking
Musical	Ability to appreciate and express components of music, such as pitch, rhythm, melody	Violinist Yo Yo Ma
Linguistic	Ability to manipulate the sounds and meanings of words; appreciation for the function of language	Poet Langston Hughes
Spatial	Ability to perceive visual-spatial patterns; to recreate those patterns	Sculptor Auguste Rodin
Bodily/Kinesthetic	Ability to use body to express self; can handle objects with ease	Dancer Mikhail Baryshnikov
Interpersonal	Ability to assess and appropriately respond to the needs, moods, feelings of others	Talk show host Oprah Winfrey
Intrapersonal	Ability to assess and appropriately respond to the needs, moods, feelings of self	A person who describes himself as being in tune with self
Naturalistic*	Ability to recognize and understand patterns in nature	Ocean explorer Jacques Costeau
Spiritual*	Ability to understand and express spiritual issues, such as issues about life, death, and the afterlife	Spiritual leader Mother Teresa
Existential*	Ability to understand and express issues related to the meaning of life	Philosopher Immanuel Kant

*The first seven intelligences were proposed in 1983; the final three, in 1998.

studied theories of intelligence for years. In a 2003 interview with Etienne Benson for the *APA Monitor on Psychology*, he recounted his own childhood experiences with tests. Many would probably be surprised to learn that Sternberg, a graduate of Yale and Stanford Universities, who has been so prolific as a researcher, did not perform well on IQ tests as a child. But a teacher who realized his potential provided Sternberg with encouragement that fueled his sense of academic competence.

The Triarchic Theory of Intelligence states that intelligence is made up of three components: analytical intelligence, creative intelligence, and practical intelligence. *Analytical intelligence* refers to the skills that most associate with intelligence, such as the ability to acquire new knowledge. *Creative intelligence* refers to a person's ability to respond to novel problems with innovative and creative solutions. *Practical intelligence* refers to the ability to adapt to situations; some would call this common sense. It requires the ability to adapt to situations and the understanding that what constitutes "smart" behavior depends on context.

For example, it may be smart for me to wear dark sunglasses while on the beach, but not while sitting on the witness stand in a courtroom. This theory is unique in that it acknowledges the importance of common sense, a type of intelligence that we all value and discuss but that is missing from the most widely accepted theories of intelligence.

So, how do we define intelligence? According to Sternberg and colleagues, it depends on whom you talk to. The general public and the academics have differing views. Members of the general public associate intelligence with good verbal skills (a person who is articulate), social gracefulness (sensitive to others, honest with self and others), and problem solving skills (logical and resourceful in their approach). You may be surprised to hear that the academics do agree with the general public on two characteristics—problem solving and verbal skills—but the third characteristic that academics associate with intelligence is practical intelligence. Interestingly, no one says anything about book knowledge.

In the next section, you will again be asked to consider definitions of intelligence as we look at how intelligence is measured through intelligence tests.

Intelligence Tests

The term associated with intelligence tests is Intelligence Quotient, or IQ. In this section, we will discuss IQ and how tests determine your IQ. Some of the most commonly administered tests are the Stanford-Binet, the Weschler Adult Intelligence Scale (WAIS), and the Weschler Intelligence Scale for Children (WISC).

The *Binet-Simon* test, one of the first, was developed by Alfred Binet and Theodore Simon in the early 1900s for French public school children. The objective was to predict academic abilities for the purpose of classroom placement. Many versions of this test have been developed since the original Binet-Simon. The current version is called the *Stanford-Binet Intelligence Scale* from Stanford University. The test measures four types of mental abilities that have been equated with intelligence: verbal reasoning, abstract/visual reasoning, quantitative reasoning, and short-term memory. Extensive training is required for administration, scoring, and interpretation of the tests. The final product of the Stanford-Binet is a score of mental age. Mental age is used to calculate a person's IQ. The following formula is used to generate an IQ score:

$$\text{IQ score} = \text{mental age} \div \text{chronological age} \times 100.$$

The Stanford-Binet has been researched and modified over the years based on testing individuals between the ages of two and twenty-four.

The *Weschler Adult Intelligence Scale* (WAIS), developed by David Weschler in 1939, yields the score most people associate with the term IQ. The current version of the WAIS is referred to as the WAIS-III. There are two sections to the WAIS: the verbal scale and the perform-ance scale. Items on the verbal scale include questions about general information (at what temperature does water boil?), vocabulary, and arithmetic; all tests on the verbal scale require a verbal response. Items on the performance scale include picture completion (subjects must identify what is missing in a picture), symbol search (subjects must find a match to a symbol), and picture arrangement (subjects must place pictures in sequence to tell a story). These tests result in three scores: a verbal scale score, a performance scale score, and a full-scale score. Knowing each of these scores is important in determining the person's strengths and weaknesses.

An examiner would consider both the com-bined score and the score on each of these scales. The full-scale IQ score provides the final result of the WAIS, the intelligence quotient, or the IQ. The average IQ score is 100 with a standard deviation of 15. Most IQ scores fall within two standard deviations of the mean. This means that most IQ scores range from 70 to 130. This test can be administered to anyone between the ages of sixteen and seventy-five.

Assessing Intelligence in Children

The technical name for the Weschler test for children is the *Weschler Intelligence Scales for Children* (WISC), and the most recent version of this test is the WISC-IV. This test also yields a full-scale IQ, and it is administered to chil-dren between the ages of six and sixteen. There is also the *Weschler Preschool and Primary Scale of Intelligence* (WPPSI), which is administered to children between the ages of four and six and a half. To assess intelligence in preverbal children, there are the Bayley Scales. The most recent version of the Bayley is the *Bayley II*. This test is administered to children between the ages of one month and three and a half years.

There are three scales: one scale assesses fine and gross motor skills; a second scale assesses perception, memory, and the start of verbal communication (remember the babbling and one-word sentences from chapter 8). A third scale assesses emotional, social, and personality development.

Issues of Cultural Fairness in Intelligence Testing

Historically, IQ tests have been standardized on predominately white, middle class, and male populations. Remember, one of the first tests, the original Simon-Binet, was normed on French children. This speaks to the issue of standardization in testing.

Tests are developed with the assistance of subjects who help researchers create questions. The subjects involved in test development need to represent the same groups of individu-als who will later take these tests. When this does not happen, (for example, when ques-tions about depression are developed based on feedback from men only, but the test is administered to both sexes), the sample is not necessarily representative of the population. The original Stanford-Binet, which was called the Binet-Simon, was tested on school children in Paris, so it would be inappropriate to use that same test to say something about the intellectual abilities of children from another culture (say, children from the U.S.). Lewis Terman of Stanford University recognized this and revised the test. Again, the smaller group (sample) that is used to develop the test must represent the larger group on which the test will be used (population). Otherwise, we would say there are problems with group norms. There has been much debate about whether or not intelligence tests are culturally biased. The facts: children of color, specifically black and Latino, tend to score lower on these standardized tests of intelligence. Why is there such emotion surrounding this issue? There are many reasons. First, as mentioned at the beginning of this chapter, the results from these tests are used to make decisions that are monumental. Will a child be placed in a special education class? Will a child be placed in an accelerated program? Will a teen get into the college of her choice, or get into college at all? Will an adult be admitted into a job-training program? Intelligence tests are used to make such decisions.

Second, this issue has many social implications. In the controversial book, *The Bell Curve*, authors Richard Hernstein and Charles Murray attribute differences in test scores to genetic differences (the nature versus nurture debate revisited). To label a group of people as genetically inferior is enough to raise great emotion.

Third, there are political implications. If a certain racial or ethnic group is considered intellectually inferior, then why put money into programs to help that group? Will this lead to a reduction in government-funded programs such as Head Start?

This debate stimulated a great deal of research in the 1970s and 1980s. Currently, researchers are rethinking how we define intelligence, which returns us to our quandary about the lack of a uniform definition of intelligence. Some researchers have suggested that we consider a broader definition of intelligence that includes skills like creativity, leadership, and responsibility. Others have suggested that we develop tests that are bias-free, tests like the Raven Progressive Matrices, where subjects are given a pattern with a missing piece and are asked to select the missing piece from a group of options.

Current research with these culture-free IQ tests still shows a difference in the scores of black and white children, which leads researchers to explore other reasons for the discrepancy, such as motivational factors. For example, some researchers, such as John Ogbu at the University of California at Berkley, have explored the lack of achievement among black children as being related to a fear of being seen by peers as "acting white." Clearly, the debate over discrepancies in test scores is a complicated and prickly issue, and the debate and research continues.

BIOLOGICAL ASSESSMENT

We have discussed in chapter 3 the work of psychologists who are interested in brain and behavior, but how do these professionals obtain information about the brain and the body? Their resources include tests such as Electroencephalography (EEG), Computerized Axial Tomography (CT or CAT scan), Positron Emission Tomography (PET scan), and Magnetic Resonance Imaging (MRI).

The EEG monitors and records electrical activity in the brain. Electrodes, or metal discs, are placed on the scalp. The electrodes pick up brain activity, which is interpreted as brain waves. These brain waves are recorded on paper.

The CT scan provides x rays of the brain, and these three-dimensional photographs can be taken from many different angles.

PET scans monitor activity in the brain. The PET scan results in colorful images of the brain. Different colors represent different levels of activity.

The MRI is similar to the CT scan, but radio and magnetic waves are used rather than x ray. The CT scan and MRI are static, but the PET and EEG are dynamic and show images of the functioning brain.

These physiological assessments may be used to make decisions about the diagnosis and treatment of problems such as the extent of brain damage as the result of injury, such as from a car accident. These tests may be used in conjunction with other tests. For example, behavioral assessments may be made to see if there is any noticeable change in behavior, in addition to the examination of the brain for structural changes.

CHAPTER SUMMARY

Assessment occurs at the beginning, middle, and end of any psychological intervention. There are different types of assessment. Assessment of personality may utilize an interview, projective tests (such as the Rorschach or TAT), and self-report/inventory tests (such as the MMPI or CPI). The who, what, when, where, why, and how of behavioral assessment addresses the many components of behavior and provides the psychologist with information that ultimately helps predict what leads to behaviors and the effects of the consequences that follow.

Intelligence tests tap into many aspects of intelligence, and they include the Stanford-Binet, WAIS III, WISC IV, and Bayley II. There are many theories of intelligence and much debate about the bias in intelligence testing.

Biological assessment involves the use of sophisticated medical equipment to help us see the brain and how it functions. EEG, CT scan, PET scan, and MRI are examples of biological assessment.

Assessment is the first step in any form of psychological treatment and is not limited to use by psychologists. Other professionals use assessments to make decisions about legal, educational, and medical matters. Assessments may be used in combination with each other. For example, in an effort to create a behavioral program for a child who engages in antisocial behavior, a psychologist may utilize an interview, a projective personality test, and some form of behavioral assessment. Assessment is one of the many important tools of the trade in psychology.

TEST YOUR RECALL AND RECOGNITION

True/False

1. The MMPI is used to assess intelligence in young children.

2. The goal of assessment with projective tests is to tap into conscious thought.

3. The CAT uses pictures of animals rather than human beings.

4. Structured interviews yield more valuable data than unstructured interviews.

5. The intelligence of a child cannot be assessed until she is six years of age.

6. The TEMAS and the Raven are examples of attempts to create culturally fair tests.

7. The goal of assessment with behavioral methods is to tap into unconscious thought.

8. As a result of social desirability, some subjects may fake their answers on measures of self-report.

9. Paper and pen are commonly used types of recording instruments.

10. The PET allows us to view the working brain.

Multiple Choice

1. Which of the following are necessary in any good assessment tool?

   a. reliability

   b. validity

   c. both a and b

   d. neither a nor b

2. Sherman has agreed to take a personality test. During the test, the examiner shows Sherman a card, and then asks him to tell her what he sees. Each time she shows him a new card, and asks for a response, Sherman thinks "What do I see? Not much, just some blotches, mostly black, but a few in colors." What type of test is Sherman probably taking?

   a. behavioral

   b. self-report

   c. projective

   d. inventory

3. The MMPI was recently revised. Why?

   a. to update the language

   b. to make it more eye-catching

   c. to remove sexist language

   d. both a and c

4. Both the MMPI-2 and the CPI

   a. require the subject to provide insightful responses.

   b. require the subject to respond "true" or "false."

   c. were developed by researchers in New Jersey.

   d. contain more than 600 items.

5. The SCID is a type of

   a. projective test.

   b. interview.

   c. biological test.

   d. questionnaire.

6. Of the four theories of intelligence listed below, which is most recent?

   a. general factor theory

   b. multiple intelligence theory

   c. Cattell's theory of crystallized and fluid intelligence

   d. triarchic theory of intelligence

7. Marnie takes the WAIS IV and obtains an IQ score of 100. Marnie's IQ score is

   a. above average.

   b. average.

   c. below average.

   d. undetermined.

8. The teacher of an elementary school would like to drink more water during her workday. Each time she consumes a bottle of water, she places it in the corner of her desk. At the end of the day, she counts the bottles to determine how much water she has consumed. She is conducting what type of observation?

   a. self-monitoring

   b. indirect

   c. secondhand

   d. paper and pencil

9. Which of the following is *not* a recording method used in behavioral assessment?

   a. golf stroke counter

   b. pedometer

   c. tape recorder

   d. all are recording methods

10. Which of the following is *not* a tool used for biological assessment?

    a. EEG

    b. FYI

    c. MRI

    d. PET

Fill in the Blanks

1. The interview is important for information gathering and rapport building. The two types of interviews are _____ and _____.

2. Although she has never taken a formal lesson, Riley's piano playing is phenomenal. Gardner would say that Riley has strong _____ intelligence.

3. IQ is short for _____.

4. The three scores that the WAIS yields are _____ score, _____ score, and _____ score.

5. Tests such as the Progressive Matrix are used to combat _____ unfairness in testing.

6. Every day between 1:00 and 4:00 P.M., Franklin records how often he cracks his knuckles. Franklin is engaging in _____ recording.

7. Rasheed wants to record his frequency of lip biting. Whenever he bites his lips, no matter what time of day, he must record the occurrence of the behavior in his notepad. Rasheed is using _____ recording.

8. Virginia decides to collect baseline data for her problem behavior and follow that with data collection during the intervention phase. Virginia is using a(n)_____ design.

9. Given her choice in research design, _____ _____ might prevent Virginia from accurately interpreting her data.

10. Cole went to the hospital where electrodes were connected to his head. The physician explained that the machine would help them record Cole's brain wave patterns. Cole is undergoing _____ assessment.

ANSWERS TO QUESTIONS

True/False

1. false	6. true
2. false	7. false
3. true	8. true
4. false	9. true
5. false	10. true

Multiple Choice

1. c	6. d
2. c	7. b
3. d	8. a
4. b	9. d
5. b	10. b

Fill in the Blanks

1. structured; unstructured
2. musical
3. intelligence quotient
4. verbal; performance; full
5. cultural
6. interval
7. continuous
8. A-B
9. confounding variables
10. biological

ADDITIONAL RESOURCES

Books

Guthrie, R. V. 1997. *Even the rat was white: A historical view of psychology.* Boston: Allyn and Bacon.

Spearman, C. 1927. *The abilities of man.* New York: Macmillan.

ABNORMAL BEHAVIORS

12

KEY TERMS

multiaxial system, anxiety, somatoform
disorders, factitious disorders, dissociative
disorders, phobia, body dysmorphic disorder

One of the greatest areas of public curiosity
in psychology includes abnormal behaviors,
also referred to as psychological disorders.
The multitude of news articles, books, and
movies that attempt to explain or are based
on these disorders evidence this concern.
However, there are numerous misconceptions
about what abnormal behavior is, and what
it is not.

This chapter is designed to clarify these
misperceptions, first by defining abnormal
behavior and then by providing descriptions
of the most common disorders. There are
many listings of abnormal behaviors in the
*Diagnostic and Statistical Manual of Mental
Disorders IV-TR (DSM)*, the classification
manual created by The American Psychiatric
Association that provides guidelines for diagnosis. This chapter doesn't attempt to cover
them all. For a full accounting, please refer to
the appendix in this book or the DSM-IV-TR
(which is the most recent version of the
DSM). However, here's one note of caution:
never engage in self-diagnosis or diagnosing
others. If, after reading these disorders, you
become concerned that you or someone you
know may suffer from one of them, take a
deep breath and re-think your concerns. If
your worries persist, please contact a mental
health professional.

CLASSIFYING DISORDERS

There are more than 300 disorders included
in the *DSM*, and we will briefly cover almost
fifty of the most commonly diagnosed disorders. But first, it's important to understand
that the diagnostic process is not just one
diagnosis. Judgments about individuals are
made on five separate dimensions that are
called *axes*. Each axis provides information
about a different aspect of the person and
his problem.

The multiaxial system provides the clinician
with a picture of the whole person. It allows
the clinician to consider social factors, medical
factors, the existence of other mental disorders, and overall level of functioning. Given
this system, two people could have the same
diagnosis, but look very different in terms of
their prognosis.

COMMON DISORDERS FROM THE DSM-IV-TR

We will cover the major diagnoses of the
DSM-IV-TR. For each disorder, you will find
a description of the symptoms associated
with the disorder. As indicated in the figure on
page 151, assessing the severity of a problem
or distinguishing symptoms of a disorder from
situational behavior is not always easy.

THE MULTIAXIAL SYSTEM AT WORK

Lisa and Michelle are both 16, both high school juniors, and both were recently diagnosed with Bulimia Nervosa, purging type. Although they have the same diagnosis, there are noticeable differences between the two. The multiaxial system provides us with information that goes beyond their Axis I diagnosis. In sum, Michelle has more problems to compound the bulimia. She also has a personality disorder (which is a challenge to treat), she has health problems, and she is probably under a great deal of stress as a result of academic problems. In addition, tests that score her overall level of functioning are low and suggest that she is having problems with daily life.

	Lisa	Michelle
Axis I-clinical disorders	Bulimia Nervosa, purging type	Bulimia nervosa, purging type
Axis II-personality disorder, mental retardation	None	Borderline personality disorder
Axis III-general medical condition	None	History of hospitalization for a heart condition
Axis IV-psychosocial and environmental problems	Parents recently divorced	Academic problems
Axis V-global assessment of functioning	85	50

The Axes of the DSM-IV-TR

Axis I—all mental disorders, except mental retardation and personality disorders

Axis II—mental retardation and personality disorders

Axis III—medical conditions

Axis IV—psychosocial and environmental problems (for example, work-related problems or family problems)

Axis V—general assessment of functioning; ranges from 0 to 100; the number 0 indicates that there is not enough information for assessment, 1 indicates serious danger to self and others, and 100 indicates optimal functioning.

Disorders Found in Infancy, Childhood, or Adolescence

This category includes disorders that occur before the age of eighteen and might include diagnoses of mental retardation, learning disorders, pervasive development disorder, attention deficit, and disruptive disorders.

Mental Retardation

Mental retardation is one of the two Axis II diagnoses and can be caused by a variety of factors. One of these, Fetal Alcohol Syndrome, was discussed in chapter 8. Other causes include anoxia (lack of oxygen during birth) and head injury or infection after birth.

In order to obtain a diagnosis of mental retardation, three criteria must be met. The patient must be diagnosed before the age of eighteen, have an Intelligence Quotient (IQ) of 70 or less, and experience difficulty completing everyday tasks of living. There are varying degrees of mental retardation, which are reflected in the level of functioning. Individuals with mild retardation may live independently with minimal supervision, and individuals with more severe retardation may require hospitalization throughout their lives.

Learning Disorders

Children with learning disorders are average or above average in intelligence, but they have problems with specific skills such as reading, math, or writing. *Dyslexia*, or *reading disorder*, involves the inability to decode words and comprehend text. Reading disorder is typically not diagnosed until after the first grade. According to the DSM, this disorder is more often seen in boys than girls; sixty to sixty-eight percent of those diagnosed with reading disorder are male.

Difficulties in math are known as *dyscalculia*, or *math disorder*. Children with this disorder have difficulty following the sequence of mathematical problems, recognizing numerical symbols, and naming math terms, just to name a few of the symptoms. It is estimated that one percent of the school population has math disorder.

Difficulty with writing, specifically composing written text, is known as *disorder of written expression*. This is associated with excessively poor handwriting in addition to poor paragraph structure and problems with punctuation. This disorder is often diagnosed in children who also have either reading disorder or math disorder.

Pervasive Developmental Disorder

Pervasive developmental disorder is often associated with autism, also known as *autistic disorder*. Children with autism are described as living in their own world. Symptoms of autism include impairment in social interactions communication, along with patterns of behavior such as rocking, hand flapping, and inflexible adherence to rituals and routines. In most cases, there is also a diagnosis of mental retardation.

Other pervasive disorders include *Asperger's disorder* and *Rett's disorder*. Some researchers refer to Asperger's as a mild form of autism instead of a distinct disorder. As with autism, Asperger's disorder causes severe social impairment. Children with this disorder also engage in patterns of behaviors and inflexible adherence to rituals and routine. Unlike autism, children with Asperger's show no cognitive impairment; these children typically have IQ scores that are in the average range.

Rett's disorder is referred to as a *progressive disorder* because at birth the child shows no impairment. Changes occur between the ages of five months and forty-eight months: head growth slows, and the child begins to experience declines in previously acquired motor skills. One motor activity characteristic of this disorder is a repeated hand-wringing motion. There is some preliminary evidence that suggests that a genetic mutation is the cause in some cases of Rett's. After the deterioration of motor skills, interest in social interactions also declines, but it may improve later in life. Children with this disorder are also diagnosed with very severe mental retardation. Interestingly, Rett's disorder has been diagnosed only in females, but autism and Asperger's are more common among males.

Attention-Deficit and Disruptive Behavior Disorders

Attention deficit hyperactivity disorder (ADHD) is one of the most common diagnoses in children. This disorder is characterized by impulsivity, distractibility, and difficulty with sustained attention. ADHD is more often diagnosed in boys than girls and has great implications for academic performance. Disruptive behaviors include *oppositional defiant disorder* and *conduct disorder*. As with ADHD, these disorders are diagnosed more often in boys than girls. In oppositional defiant disorder, the child demonstrates hostile behavior and is defiant or spiteful.

Problems of a more severe nature are seen in *conduct disorder*. The behaviors associated with this disorder are characterized by actions that violate societal norms, such as fighting, lying, and stealing.

Substance-Related Disorders

There is a diagnosis for just about every imaginable substance; the most common ones are alcohol, cocaine, and heroin. However, these are just the tip of the iceberg. The common substance-related disorders are

Alcohol-related disorders

Amphetamine-related disorders (uppers)

Cannabis-related disorders (marijuana)

Cocaine-related disorders (freebase, crack)

Hallucinogen-related disorders (LSD, Ecstasy)

Inhalant-related disorders (glue, paint thinners, gasoline)

Nicotine-related disorders (cigarettes, cigars, chewing tobacco, snuff)

Opioid-related disorders (morphine, heroin, codeine)

Phencyclidine-related disorders (PCP/Angel Dust)

Sedative, hypnotic, or anxiolytic-related disorders (sleeping pills and antianxiety medications)

Other substance-related disorders (poppers, steroids, laughing gas)

The important consideration for psychologists is the issue of *abuse* versus *dependence*. Abuse refers to a pattern of substance use that results in negative consequences. For instance, the abuse may interfere with social functioning and job performance. Dependence refers to the use of the substance that has gone beyond abuse.

Two symptoms often associated with dependence are *tolerance* and *withdrawal*. In tolerance, the user requires more and more of the substance to get the same effect. In withdrawal, when the user does not use the substance, he experiences painful physical symptoms that include stomach cramps and vomiting. People who drink alcohol may experience withdrawal symptoms as well; alcohol withdrawal may be associated with delirium or seizures.

Another problem, polysubstance-related disorder, is probably the most common type of substance-related disorder, as most substance users indulge in more than one substance. This might result in a diagnosis of dependence, but not abuse. A person who uses more than one substance may receive a dependence diagnosis for one, and an abuse diagnosis for the other.

Schizophrenia and Other Psychotic Disorders

Schizophrenic disorders are characterized by bizarre actions, irrational talk, and delusional thinking. It is typically first diagnosed in early adulthood, after which the person with schizophrenia may spend her life battling this illness. Symptoms of schizophrenia are divided into two categories: positive and negative symptoms. Positive symptoms are excesses in behavior or distortions of normal functioning; the two most common positive symptoms are hallucinations and delusions. A hallucinating person sees, hears, smells, tastes, and feels things even though the sensory receptors are not being stimulated. Auditory hallucinations are most common in schizophrenia.

Delusions are beliefs for which there is no support. Delusions of grandeur are frequent, such as "I am the king of Oklahoma," or persecutory delusions, "Someone is trying to steal my identity and take it to Pluto."

I met Angela while working as a therapist in New York City. Angela was a twenty-five-year-old, single, African-American female who was very cheerful and talkative. She was a college student and had no previous experience with therapy. Angela reported that she was excited about therapy and grateful for the opportunity to engage in some "self-reflection." She opened our second session by asking me if I had been following the impeachment proceedings (this was during the Clinton administration). When I replied, "No," she sighed and said, "Well, then you missed my letter." According to Angela, she had sent a letter to the president that was read during the hearings. Angela firmly believed that her letter would save the president from impeachment.

Other positive symptoms of schizophrenia include speech that is incoherent and disorganized behavior, such as unusual dress or disheveled appearance. The negative symptoms represent deficits or loss of normal functioning. These include lack of emotional expression (called inappropriate or flat affect), apathy or lack of energy, and speech that may contain many words, but in which the person is not really saying anything. What he says lacks a message or has poverty of content.

Paranoid, Disorganized, and Catatonic Schizophrenia

The DSM discusses several types of schizophrenia, including *paranoid*, *disorganized*, and *catatonic*. The paranoid schizophrenic has hallucinations and delusions that are persecutory or grand in nature. The disorganized schizophrenic exhibits frequently incoherent speech and behavior. Also, the person's facial expression does not match the emotions being expressed (flat or inappropriate affect). For instance, the person who discusses details of his mother's death while smiling would be described as demonstrating inappropriate affect.

In catatonic schizophrenia, the individual exhibits unusual motor activities. The patient may assume seemingly uncomfortable positions and remain in these positions for extended periods of time, or she may engage in excessive, unfocused motor activity. The book and film *Awakenings* chronicles Oliver Sacks's work with catatonic schizophrenics. Because of the use of antipsychotic medications, the symptoms (that is, motor disturbances) associated with catatonic schizophrenia are rarely seen today.

Much of the research in schizophrenia has focused on genetic factors, those that are inherited from our parents. Genetic studies in schizophrenia have often employed twins to understand the disorder. There are two types of twins: monozygotic, or identical twins, and dizygotic, or fraternal twins. Identical twins originated as one egg that divided into two embryos. They have the exact same genetic composition. Fraternal twins started as two eggs and are not more genetically similar than any other sibling pair.

Twin studies in schizophrenia, or in any area, are important for they allow us to tease apart the contributions of nature (genes) and nurture (environment). Because the genetic makeup of identical twins is the same, any differences that they exhibit can be attributed to the environment. If the chance of both identical twins having schizophrenia is high, then we can say that the disorder is greatly influenced by genetics. If, on the other hand, the chance of both members of an identical twin pair is not higher than the chance of both members of any sibling pair having schizophrenia, then we would say that the disorder is influenced by environment. In the case of schizophrenia, there is strong evidence of genetic influence, but there appear to be important environmental influences as well.

Other Psychotic Disorders

Psychotic, or psychosis, is another one of those terms that people use with great frequency, but what is meant by this term? In general, the term *psychotic behavior* is associated with the presence of hallucinations and delusions. In this section, we will discuss two psychotic disorders, shared psychotic disorder and brief psychotic disorder.

In shared psychotic disorder (Folie à Deux), a person shares a delusional belief with another. So if, for example, after several weeks of hearing about her daughter's power to save the president, Angela's mom came to believe that Angela did possess special powers, her mother would be diagnosed with shared psychotic disorder. One person may adopt the delusional belief of another, or several people may

adopt a belief, as in the case of children who adopt parent's delusional thinking.

In brief psychotic disorder, the person experiences at least one of the following symptoms: hallucinations, delusions, or disorganized speech or behavior. These symptoms last longer than one day, but no longer than one month.

Mood Disorders

Lots of people refer to having "the blues" or being "in a funk." Mood disorders are much more than this. A person with a mood disorder may be unable to function—getting out of bed in the morning may be impossible—and feelings of suicide may consume his thoughts. These disorders are more often seen in women than men, and they can strike all ages.

Major Depressive Disorder

Major depressive disorder is characterized by depressed mood, lack of interest in activities that were once seen as pleasurable, changes in eating and sleeping habits, fatigue, feelings of low self-worth, difficulty concentrating, and thoughts of suicide. These symptoms are different in children and the elderly. In children, there are also symptoms of irritability, social withdrawal, and physical complaints. In the elderly, there may be memory loss and disorientation. There is also a milder version of major depressive disorder, which is referred to as *dysthymic disorder*.

Bipolar Disorder

Bipolar disorder is often called manic depressive disorder, and it is characterized by cycling between the symptoms of major depressive disorder and the symptoms of a manic episode.

During a manic episode, a person may exhibit exaggerated feelings of self-worth, experience increased talkativeness with racing thoughts, have problems focusing, have a decreased need for sleep, overindulge in pleasurable activities that may have harmful consequences (for example, shopping sprees), and emphasize activities that have a goal, such as deciding to write a major novel. Unlike major depressive disorder, only one manic episode is necessary to elicit a diagnosis of bipolar disorder. There is also a less severe form of this disorder called *cyclothymic disorder*.

Seasonal Affective Disorder

Another mood disorder that has received a lot of coverage in recent years is *seasonal affective disorder* (SAD); the official DSM diagnosis for a person with SAD would be major depressive disorder with seasonal pattern. People with SAD tend to experience feelings of depression at specific times of the year, most often in the fall or winter, when the days shorten. These depressed feelings lift in the spring. It is believed that SAD might be caused by seasonal changes in the production of melatonin, a hormone that is suppressed by light and is produced at night. It is thought that the overproduction of melatonin during the winter months when there is less light might result in depression. Norman Rosenthal and fellow researchers documented light therapy for SAD, exposing the patients to bright, white light that slowed down melatonin production. This treatment is still a very new approach; many more experiments are needed for understanding the relationship between melatonin production and SAD.

Anxiety Disorders

Anxiety is an unpleasant emotional reaction whose most identifiable characteristic is fear. The common threat for the anxiety disorder is a stimulus, which is sometimes obvious and

tangible (like a snake), and sometimes unseen (like a thought). Anxiety disorders are more often seen in women than men, and such disorders can stifle one's way of life. We will cover each of the anxiety disorders: panic disorder, specific phobia, social phobia, obsessive compulsive disorder, posttraumatic stress disorder, acute stress disorder, and generalized anxiety disorder. Through the descriptions and examples of these disorders, you will gain an understanding of just how debilitating these conditions can be.

Panic Disorder

Panic disorder is characterized by recurring attacks of overpowering anxiety that can arise abruptly and without warning. The victims exhibit symptoms that include, but are not limited to, sweating, trembling, shaking, chest tightness, fear of dying, nausea, and fear of losing control. After a number of these types of experiences, sufferers may fear the possibility of having a panic attack in public. This may lead to a common complication known as agoraphobia, a fear of public places and open spaces, which may make the sufferer a prisoner in her own home. This disorder is seen most often in women.

Specific Phobia

Specific phobia is a fear of a particular object. This could be a type of animal, an object in the natural environment, or something like blood or needles. Fear of water (hydrophobia), enclosed spaces (claustrophobia), fire (pyrophobia), and being alone (monophobia) are just a few examples of specific phobias. For many people with specific phobia, the feared stimulus can easily be avoided. Climb the stairs rather than take elevators (the claustrophobic), or stay away from spiders (the arachnophobic). In some cases, however, the fear may interfere with daily functioning.

Social Phobia

The person with a social phobia has difficulty with social situations because of fears of being negatively evaluated. Although this includes the anxiety that can occur because of giving a public presentation, it is more pervasive than that. Any public act such as eating out, using a public restroom, or skating at an ice rink can give rise to fear.

Obsessive Compulsive Disorder

In obsessive compulsive disorder (OCD), there are two components: obsessions and compulsions. The obsessions consist of thoughts or images that are disturbing to the individual. In an effort to reduce the anxiety, the individual engages in some behavior; that behavior is the compulsion. The problem is that the compulsive behavior alleviates the anxiety, but only momentarily. So, the person repeats these behaviors over and over. Hand washing and endless re-checking of locks, faucets, and other things are common compulsive behaviors.

For instance, Kyle constantly worries about a home invasion. He is especially concerned about the locks on his front door. Therefore, whenever he is in his home, he spends most of his time checking the front door to make sure that it is locked. When he leaves the door, he questions whether or not it is securely locked, and then he returns to the door again to check the locks. Kyle's thoughts about home invasion constitute the obsessions; his behavior of constantly checking the locks on the front door constitute the compulsion.

Posttraumatic Stress Disorder

Some people refer to posttraumatic stress disorder (PTSD) as "shell shock," because the symptoms were first noticed in veterans of war. PTSD occurs as a result of any traumatic event: involvement in a war or act of terrorism, or being the victim of a violent crime or disaster. It may occur after being directly involved in one of these events, or even after just witnessing a traumatic event. The symptoms of PTSD are flashbacks of the event, avoidance of all things associated with the event, and emotional/behavioral problems, such as difficulty sleeping, exaggerated startle response, and irritability. In children, PTSD is also associated with behavioral problems. In order to obtain a diagnosis of PTSD, symptoms must have been in existence for more than one month. If symptoms last a month or less, the condition is known as acute stress disorder.

Generalized Anxiety Disorder

Generalized anxiety disorder (GAD) has no specific stimulus that serves as the feared object. In GAD, the individual experiences a pervasive, low-level anxiety. Some describe it as a constant feeling of impending doom. The individual has no control over this worry. Anxiety may be accompanied by irritability, restlessness, and fatigue. This constant anxiety interferes with the ability to work, go to school, and interact with others. This disorder is more often diagnosed in women than in men.

Somatoform Disorders

Somatoform disorders are related to a misperception of problems with the body in which, despite complaints of physical symptoms, a medical examination provides no information to support the patient's reported ailment.

Cognitive theorists believe that people with somatization disorder are oversensitive to physiological symptoms and then they incorrectly interpret them. Freud, from the psychoanalytic viewpoint, proposed that *conversion disorder*, one type of somatoform disorder, was due to an unresolved Electra complex.

Somatization Disorder

In this disorder, the person repeatedly complains of physical ailments, but they are not tied to any particular disease. When examined, no biological explanation is found for the physical complaints. The distinguishing feature is a diversity of complaints over many years that can range from pulmonary to gastrointestinal to neurological symptoms. These patients may describe their symptoms in exaggerated terms that lack true content. This disorder is chronic and rarely goes into total remission.

Conversion Disorder

In conversion disorder, the person loses the ability to move or feel sensations in a particular part of the body, often after a traumatic event. Again, a physical examination finds no physical evidence to support the complaints.

Pain Disorder

An individual complains of pain that impacts daily functioning—it keeps the individual home from work, school, or social events—but there is no biological support for the claims. Pain may be localized, or it may be all over. If the pain exists for less than six months, the diagnosis is pain disorder, acute. If longer than six months, the diagnosis is pain disorder, chronic.

One problem with diagnosing this disorder is due to the subjectivity of pain. What I find painful, you may not. Remember the Gate Control Theory to explain individual differences in pain? This theory suggested that pain sensations must pass through a "gate" in the spinal cord that can be closed, thus blocking

the pain. Although physicians may not always find
biological evidence of pain, that does not definitively determine that pain is not there.

Hypochondriasis

Unlike somatization disorder, a person with hypochondriasis (commonly called a hypochondriac) reports symptoms that he actually ties to a particular syndrome. In other words, this person does not say, "My leg hurts." He declares, "I have diabetes." Again, upon physical examination, the health care provider can find no biological evidence to support the reports. The hypochondriac constantly monitors his physical condition, and when he is assured he is well, he is typically so disbelieving that he continues to go from physician to physician looking for one who can confirm his physical diagnosis.

Body Dysmorphic Disorder

The person with body dysmorphic disorder reports distortion of the body. This person may look in the mirror and see his nose as extremely large, or his eyes as too close together. Although most complaints are related to the face and head, such as the presence of wrinkles and swelling, other parts of the body may also be targeted; for example, clients may report that one arm is longer or larger than the other. When others look at this person, they do not see these abnormalities. This disorder is not to be confused with anorexia where the distortion is restricted to weight concerns only.

Persons with this disorder may spend hours looking in the mirror examining their defect, or they may avoid mirrors altogether so they are not forced to look at the defect. This disorder is equally diagnosed in men and women. It is usually diagnosed during adolescence, which is not surprising, as this is the time when concerns with physical appearance take on greater importance.

Factitious Disorders

In contrast to those suffering with somatoform disorder, where clients report physical complaints that are not attributable to a true medical condition, those suffering with factitious disorder intentionally fake physical and/or psychological symptoms. Those with factitious disorder often have extensive medical knowledge, which helps them to assume the role of patient. This role may provide them with attention and release them from responsibilities.

Dissociative Disorders

Dissociative disorders are associated with a disruption in memory, identity, consciousness, or perception. We will discuss four dissociative disorders: dissociative amnesia, which is associated with a memory loss; dissociative fugue, which is associated with a disruption in both memory and identity; dissociative identity disorder, which is associated with the establishment of multiple identities; and depersonalization disorder, which is associated with a change in perception. The causes for these disorders are varied. Most researchers attribute this disorder to some form of severe trauma.

Dissociative Amnesia

The most common place to see dissociative amnesia is on soap operas where individuals forget their identity. This amnesia may be localized, where only a few hours of time are forgotten—maybe the first few hours after a traumatic event—or the amnesia may be generalized to the point that the person remembers nothing about himself or his life. Despite the frequent portrayal on TV, this type of amnesia is actually quite rare.

Dissociative Fugue

The symptoms associated with dissociative fugue include an inability to recall some or all of one's past, unexpected travel (or flight) from home, and confusion about one's identity. This is the plot of the movie comedy *Overboard*, starring Goldie Hawn and Kurt Russell. Hawn's character forgets her identity as the result of a boating accident. She is rescued by Russell's character and begins a new life as the wife of Russell and mother of his many, unruly children. Interestingly, people with dissociative fugue can recall information unrelated to their identity, such as how to cook or drive a car.

Dissociative Identity Disorder (DID)

This disorder was once referred to as multiple personality disorder (MPD), and it is often confused with schizophrenia. When people talk about split personalities, they are actually speaking of DID. In DID, the person experiences separate, distinct identities from the self. The original identity is referred to as the host, and the additional identities may differ from the host with regard to age, gender, and physical characteristics.

One of the most famous instances of DID involved a woman named Sybil Dorsett. (This is a pseudonym given to her by Flora Schreiber, the author of a popular book and film that chronicled this story.) Sybil demonstrated a total of sixteen identities (including Sybil, the host). These identities included Vanessa, a tall, attractive woman with great dramatic flair; Mike, a male carpenter with dark hair and brown eyes; Vicky, a confident and sophisticated blonde woman; and Marcia, an emotional female writer and painter. Each of these identities is separate and distinct.

Depersonalization Disorder

Depersonalization disorder is characterized by altered perceptions. People with this disorder have atypical sensory experiences. They may report feeling detached or removed from their bodies. They may describe being outside of their bodies and watching themselves from afar. Throughout these experiences, they remain aware of the fact that it is not reality, and, therefore, may worry about these experiences. This worry may lead to an impaired ability to function.

Sexual and Gender Identity Disorders

In this section, we will cover categories of disorders that make up the more general diagnosis of sexual and gender identity disorders. They are sexual dysfunctions, paraphilias, and gender identity disorder. Sexual dysfunctions can be described as disturbances in sexual desire or response. The paraphilias are characterized by a dependence on unconventional objects or illegal behaviors for sexual arousal. Gender identity disorder is simply described as a discrepancy between gender identity and biological sex.

Sexual Dysfunction

Anyone who has problems with sexual response or functioning may suffer from sexual dysfunction. These symptoms include erectile disorder and premature ejaculation in men, and female sexual arousal disorder and vaginismus in women. The causes of these problems may be psychological, for example, linked to long-standing feelings

about sex or relationship issues; or they may be related to medical conditions. For example, if a medical procedure has been performed, and as a result, the male is unable to maintain an erection; or, there may be both psychological and medical reasons.

Sexual Paraphilias

Sexual paraphilias are varied. The individual with a paraphilia derives sexual pleasure through unconventional, sometimes illegal means. In *exhibitionism*, sexual pleasure is obtained by exposing one's genitals to an unsuspecting person. In *fetishism*, sexual pleasure is derived through an inanimate object or a body part. Often-reported fetishes include shoes and feet.

In *frotteurism*, sexual pleasure is derived by rubbing against an unsuspecting person with one's genitals. In *pedophilia*, sexual pleasure is derived through sexual contact with children. With *sexual masochism*, sexual pleasure is derived through receiving pain. The complement to this is the sadist, who obtains pleasure from giving pain.

In *transvetic fetish*, sexual pleasure comes through wearing clothes, typically the underwear, of the opposite sex. It is important to note that this is not the same as gender identity disorder. Individuals with transvetic fetishism are comfortable being male or female, but they obtain pleasure through dressing like the opposite sex. In *voyeurism*, sexual pleasure is obtained through watching an unsuspecting person undress or have sex. What are the causes? There are strong behavioral explanations for these disorders. According to behaviorists, all behavior is learned. People with a paraphilia have been conditioned to associate an unusual object with sexual gratification.

Several years ago, there was a case in the news involving Marla Maples, who was then the wife of Donald Trump. Shoes belonging to Ms. Maples were missing. It was later discovered that these shoes had been stolen by one of Mr. Trump's male employees who was using them for sexual arousal and gratification. The behaviorist would hypothesize that at some time the person with a shoe fetish, for example, had a pleasant sexual experience while in the presence of a shoe.

Gender Identity Disorder

We are identified by our biological sex even before birth. As we grow, we develop a sense of self, or gender identity, as girl or boy. For most, biological sex is the same as gender identity. For people with gender identity disorder, biological sex doesn't have the same meaning. This is the person who will say, "I feel like a man trapped in a woman's body," or vice versa. One treatment for this disorder is sex reassignment surgery where the person undergoes an operation to make his biological sex the same as his gender identity.

Eating Disorders

Eating disorders are most commonly seen in young women and are often associated with certain careers, like dancing, modeling, and gymnastics; these careers place a premium on thinness. In our society, thin is considered attractive; it's desirable. There is definitely an environmental influence with this disorder.

According to the DSM, these disorders are more often seen in industrialized societies where thinness equals beauty. Anorexia nervosa and bulimia nervosa are most common in the United States, Canada, Europe, Australia, New Zealand, Japan, and South Africa. Individuals with this disorder are most likely to be white and female.

Anorexia Nervosa

Anorexia nervosa is characterized by excessive weight loss through dieting and excessive exercise. The person weighs less than eighty-five percent of the weight that would be considered normal for her given height, according to the American Psychiatric Association. The person with anorexia has a distorted body image wherein, although she is very thin, she believes herself to be overweight.

Severe and sudden weight loss may result in cessation of menstruation, cardiovascular problems, dental problems, and skin problems. If left untreated, it can result in death.

Bulimia Nervosa

Unlike the anorexic, the bulimic may be of normal weight. But like the anorexic, the bulimic believes herself to be overweight. However, the bulimic does not starve herself, but engages in binge eating. During binge eating, an individual will eat large amounts of food, like a gallon of ice cream or a five-pound box of chocolate. While she is bingeing, the bulimic describes a feeling of being out of control. After she binges, she purges. Purging involves the elimination of the food through vomiting, or the use of laxatives or diuretics. The bulimic forces her fingers down her throat to induce vomiting, causing scarring on the hands. This disorder may also result in dental problems and irregularities in the menstrual cycle.

Personality Disorders

Personality disorders are characterized by pervasive and inflexible ways of interacting with one's environment. These patterns are typically established during adolescence or early adulthood, and they impact every aspect of life, including social relationships and occupational/educational functioning. A brief description of each of the personality disorders follows.

Paranoid Personality Disorder

People with paranoid personality disorder are suspicious and mistrustful of others. This is not to be confused with paranoid schizophrenia. People with paranoid personality disorder do not experience the hallucinations or delusions associated with schizophrenia; they just believe everyone is out to get them.

Schizoid Personality Disorder

The person with schizoid personality disorder is not interested in social relationships with others, and as a result, spends much time alone. These individuals also exhibit very little expression of emotions (remember the term *flat affect* associated with schizophrenia?). This is not to be confused with the social isolation associated with autistic disorder. Individuals with schizoid personality disorder don't exhibit the repetitive patterns of behavior associated with autism.

Schizotypal Personality Disorder

This person may have unusual thought patterns and behaviors similar to the type seen in schizophrenia. Some would describe this person as eccentric. Although these people have unusual thought patterns and behaviors, they do not have the delusions or hallucinations associated with schizophrenia.

Antisocial Personality Disorder

This person exhibits a total disregard for the rights of others. This pattern of behavior begins in childhood or adolescence (conduct disorder) and continues into adulthood. Antisocial personality disorder is not a substance-related condition—these people are not violating societal norms because of the use of some substance. If it is determined that the antisocial behavior is associated with substance use, the diagnosis of antisocial personality disorder is not given.

Borderline Personality Disorder

One of the best illustrations of the symptoms of borderline personality disorder was Glenn Close's character in the film *Fatal Attraction*. People with borderline personality disorder are unpredictable; they run hot and cold, and they are impulsive in their actions. Their relationships with others are unstable, and their image of self constantly fluctuates. They ultimately fear the rejection and abandonment of others. In chapter 10, we discussed the enduring characteristics of personality. Very little about the person with borderline personality disorder can be described as enduring. These people engage in manipulative actions and/or self-injurious behavior (like cutting oneself).

Histrionic Personality Disorder

The person with this disorder tends to overexaggerate situations and emotions. The exaggeration is a way to gain attention. This disorder is often confused with other personality disorders, specifically borderline personality disorder, narcissistic personality disorder, and dependent personality disorder. Unlike borderline personality disorder, histrionic personality disorder is not associated with manipulative or self-destructive behaviors. Rather, the person with histrionic personality disorder is willing to be viewed in a less than positive light (for example, as needy) if this yields attention from others.

Narcissistic Personality Disorder

The person with narcissistic personality disorder is self-centered, has an inflated sense of self, and demonstrates inconsiderate behaviors. If you were to have a conversation with this person, it is highly unlikely that he would ask you anything about yourself.

This disorder is often mistaken for histrionic, antisocial, or borderline personality disorder. The element that distinguishes this disorder from the others is the grandiosity displayed by the person with the disorder, the stability of this self-image, and the lack of impulsivity.

Avoidant Personality Disorder

These people do not interact with others because they feel inadequate and are worried about negative evaluations. There is great overlap between avoidant personality disorder and social phobia. According to the DSM, this disorder may be a more severe form of social phobia.

Dependent Personality Disorder

This person is unable to make decisions on his own. He needs someone to take care of him. As a result he is clingy, submissive, and passive in his interactions with others. He worries about losing the support or approval of others.

Although people with borderline personality disorder have a fear of rejection, they respond to this fear by being manipulative and hostile. Those with dependent personality disorder, on the other hand, deal with this fear of rejection by becoming even more passive and agreeable.

Obsessive-Compulsive Personality Disorder

The person with obsessive-compulsive personality disorder is a perfectionist and has an inflexible way of living. These people value orderliness, efficiency, and control. The character of Felix Unger from the movie (and television series) *The Odd Couple* exemplifies one with obsessive-compulsive personality disorder. He also merits a diagnosis of hypochondriasis.

This is not to be confused with obsessive-compulsive disorder, or OCD. Although the names of the disorders are similar, the symptoms are quite different. OCD is characterized by obsessive thoughts, images, and ideas that are disturbing in nature. The anxiety caused by these obsessions is alleviated through the compulsions. This is very different from the inflexible patterns of behavior associated with obsessive-compulsive personality disorder.

CHAPTER SUMMARY

The Diagnostic and Statistical Manual of Mental Disorders (DSM) is the reference guide used by mental health care professionals to help with assessment, diagnosis, and treatment of abnormal behavior. Since defining the difference between normal and abnormal behavior is complex, psychologists follow standard criteria for diagnosis. People who suffer psychological disorders exhibit anxiety, fail to meet societal norms, may be dangerous to themselves, or have difficulty functioning.

Some of the numerous disorders detailed in the DSM and introduced here include disorders usually diagnosed in infancy, childhood, or adolescence; substance-related disorders; schizophrenic disorders; mood disorders; anxiety disorders; somatoform disorders; factitious disorders; dissociative disorders; sexual and gender identity disorders; eating disorders; and personality disorders.

Treatment approaches for many of these psychological disorders will be discussed in the next chapter.

TEST YOUR RECALL AND RECOGNITION

True/False

1. Mental retardation cannot be diagnosed after the age of eighteen.

2. Although adults and children may receive the same diagnosis, for example depression, the disorder will present differently depending on age.

3. In tolerance, the person uses the same amount of the drug and each time receives the same "high."

4. Cases of catatonic schizophrenia have decreased significantly because of the use of medication.

5. As a group, men are more likely to suffer from mood disorders than are women.

6. Seasonal affective disorder is a type of mood disorder.

7. DID was once referred to as MPD.

8. Gender identity disorder is a type of sexual paraphilia.

9. The bulimic who purges eats large amounts of food in a short period of time, and then eliminates it through the use of laxatives.

10. The personality disorders are placed on Axis III.

Multiple Choice

1. Which of the following diagnoses would be found on Axis II?
   a. Dissociative identity disorder
   b. Posttraumatic stress disorder
   c. Histrionic personality disorder
   d. Gender identity disorder

2. Gordon has an IQ of 130, but he has difficulty identifying letters and words. Based on this information, which diagnosis seems most appropriate for Gordon?
   a. mental retardation
   b. reading disorder
   c. math disorder
   d. pervasive developmental disorder

3. Wayne has used cocaine for the past year, but he now finds that he needs to take more and more of the drug to get the same "high." Wayne is starting to demonstrate
   a. withdrawal.
   b. abuse.
   c. tolerance.
   d. detox.

4. Patients in a hospital assume seemingly uncomfortable physical positions for extended periods of time. These patients have what type of schizophrenia?
   a. catatonic
   b. paranoid
   c. disorganized
   d. none of the above

5. The onset of schizophrenia is usually during
   a. adolescence.
   b. early adulthood.
   c. middle adulthood.
   d. late adulthood.

6. Rory has spent most of his life battling depression. About ten years ago, he experienced a brief manic episode. What diagnosis is most appropriate for Rory?
   a. major depressive disorder
   b. bioplar disorder
   c. seasonal affective disorder
   d. DID

7. Which of the following is *not* an anxiety disorder?
   a. specific phobia   c. GAD
   b. OCD   d. pain disorder

8. Since a boating accident during which she dropped her infant son into the icy waters of the Atlantic (his body was never recovered), Penelope has reported having no feeling in either hand. Penelope is suffering from
   a. somatization disorder.
   b. factitious disorder.
   c. conversion disorder.
   d. hypochondriasis.

9. The identities of a person with DID may vary
   a. with regard to gender.
   b. with regard to age.
   c. with regard to hair length.
   d. all of the above.

10. April loves to talk about April and only April. She never asks her coworkers about their thoughts or feelings and she brags that she is the most popular attorney in the firm. Which personality disorder would be most appropriate for April?
    a. narcissistic personality disorder
    b. dependent personality disorder
    c. schizoid personality disorder
    d. paranoid personality disorder

Fill in the Blanks

1. The manual used by mental health care professionals to help assess, diagnose, and treat mental disorders is referred to as the DSM. DSM stands for _____ _____ _____.

2. Autism is a type of _____ _____ _____.

3. Children with _____ _____ _____ may be described as defiant and disobedient, but they do not violate the rights of others.

4. The symptoms of schizophrenia are categorized as _____ and _____ symptoms.

5. A person with _____ _____ would find it difficult to make a speech at a party.

6. In gender identity disorder, _____ _____ does not match _____ _____.

7. Eating disorders are more often seen in individuals in certain professions, such as _____, _____, and _____.

8. Maria constantly worries that she will burn down her home; therefore, she constantly checks the stove to see if it is on. Maria's checking behavior is an example of a(n) _____.

9. People with _____
   _____ _____ are
   described as manipulative and
   unpredictable.
10. People with _____ _____
   _____ don't socialize because
   they just aren't interested in people.

ANSWERS TO QUESTIONS

True/False

1. true	6. true
2. true	7. true
3. false	8. false
4. true	9. true
5. false	10. false

Multiple Choice

1. c	6. b
2. b	7. d
3. c	8. c
4. a	9. d
5. b	10. a

Fill in the Blanks

1. *Diagnostic and Statistical Manual*
2. pervasive developmental disorder
3. oppositional defiant disorder
4. positive; negative
5. social phobia
6. biological sex; gender identity
7. dancing; modeling; gymnastics
8. compulsion
9. borderline personality disorder
10. schizoid personality disorder

ADDITIONAL RESOURCES

Book

American Psychiatric Association. 2000. *Diagnostic and statistical manual of mental disorders*, 4th edition-text revision. Washington, DC: APA.

Videos

Nasar, S. *A beautiful mind.* New York: Simon and Schuster, 1998.

Wedding, D. and M. A. Boyd. 1999. *Movies and mental illness: Using films to understand psychopathology.* Boston: McGraw Hill.

THERAPEUTIC APPROACHES TO TREATMENT

KEY TERMS

free association, dream analysis, systematic desensitization, flooding, aversive therapy, token economy system, hierarchy, time out, response cost, rational emotive behavior therapy

There are many diagnoses of psychological disorders and a number of differing perspectives or orientations held by psychologists. Every perspective leads to an individual approach in treatment or therapy. This leaves us with a vast array of treatments and approaches for a variety of disorders.

This chapter gives you an overview of treatments and therapies and how they are appropriate to different diagnoses. We will explore psychodynamic, humanistic, behavioral, and cognitive approaches to therapy, and we will place emphasis on some of the tools or techniques used by each orientation. In addition, we'll look at other types of therapies, such as group therapy or the issue of continuum of care.

By the end of this chapter, you may wonder, how does one ever choose a particular type of therapy, and how does one know which is best? Irvin Yalom, a pioneer in group therapy, summarizes the findings of years of research and makes it clear that more important than approach is the relationship between client and therapist. Carl Rogers, who was a pioneer in the humanistic orientation, contends that the most effective outcomes in therapy occur when the relationship is one in which there is trust, warmth, empathy, and acceptance.

Freud

PSYCHODYNAMIC APPROACH

Are you imagining Sigmund Freud with a client on the sofa? That's what most people think of when they hear about the psychodynamic approach to therapy. The therapy procedures we will discuss are known as psychoanalysis. The goal of analysis, as it is often called, is to tap into unconscious feelings that are causing problems, perhaps causing us to rely on defense mechanisms, and then to bring these problems into conscious awareness. Psychoanalysis in its purest sense is a time-consuming commitment. The client undergoing analysis sees her analyst about four times a week for anywhere from three to five years. Contemporary versions of the psychodynamic approach emphasize the importance of insight and conflicts within the unconscious, but therapy is brief—between six and twenty-five sessions. Greater emphasis is placed on alleviating the client's suffering, and the focus is on current situations. Brief therapy is often used to help clients who are suffering from posttraumatic stress disorder (PTSD). In such a case, the goal is to help the client interpret his current situation, deal with life stress, and tackle and lift the worst symptoms.

Some therapists with this orientation receive intense training that lasts for years and requires that they go into psychoanalysis themselves. These professionals then refer to themselves as analysts. In psychoanalysis, there are strategies to tap into the unconscious, which include free association and dream analysis.

Free Association

In free association, the client is asked to say whatever comes to mind, without censoring thoughts. The client will relax on the couch with the therapist sitting behind him. He will then begin to just "let it out" while the therapist listens and provides limited feedback.

The therapist does not distract the client, not even with his physical existence as he sits behind the client. The role of the therapist is to serve as a blank slate onto which the client can project his thoughts.

Dream Analysis

According to the psychodynamic orientation, the unconscious is released when we dream because the guard of ego is lowered during sleep. In dream analysis, clients are asked to talk about their dreams while the therapist interprets them. Any therapist with training

in psychodynamic approaches to therapy can use dream analysis techniques.

HUMANISTIC APPROACH

Unlike many of the other therapies, humanistic therapies emphasize those qualities of the therapist that are necessary for effective therapy. The therapist is to treat the client as a unique individual with strengths, and those strengths are emphasized during therapy. One type of humanistic therapy is the *client-centered approach*.

Carl Rogers, mentioned in chapter 10, was trained as a psychoanalyst but yearned to focus on the conscious, rather than the unconscious. This led him to develop a client-centered approach to therapy. This approach emerged from a humanistic perspective and emphasizes the characteristics of the therapist that are necessary for effective therapy. The therapist must exude warmth, concern for the client, and unconditional positive regard, which again is acceptance, no matter what the client's problem may be.

Some refer to this as a warm-and-fuzzy approach. The goal of Rogerian therapy is to help the client gain an understanding of self and function at an optimal level. The role of the therapist is not to cure the client, but to provide an environment where the client can cure himself. Rogers referred to this approach as nondirective therapy.

BEHAVIORAL APPROACH

Behavior therapy is based on the belief that behavior is learned. The techniques of behavior therapy utilize the principles of classical and operant conditioning. Techniques that use classical conditioning concepts include systematic desensitization, flooding, and aversion therapy. Techniques associated with operant conditioning include token economy systems, time out, and response cost.

Techniques That Utilize Classical Conditioning

Systematic desensitization is used to treat anxiety disorders, and it involves gradual exposure to the feared stimulus or event. The client and therapist work together to create a list that details situations related to the feared object and to organize this list from the least-feared situation to the most-feared situation. This list is called a *hierarchy*. The client then imagines each of these steps, one-by-one, until he can imagine the most feared situation without anxiety.

When anxiety is reported, the client uses relaxation exercises to induce a sense of calm. For the client who has difficulty imagining the anxiety-provoking situations in her hierarchy, the therapist may opt to use *in vivo desensitization*, where the client actually interacts with the feared stimulus or event.

A male client with a snake phobia could gradually work his way through the hierarchy as follows: he could imagine looking at the sketch of a snake in the dictionary. He could imagine seeing a snake in the grass of his backyard. He could imagine touching a snake. With *in vivo*, he would look at the sketch; look at a real, live snake in his backyard; then actually touch a snake.

In *flooding*, the client is exposed to the feared stimulus or event at full tilt, not gradually as with desensitization. Therefore, he would

begin with touching a snake. Flooding may be *in vivo* (real) or imagined.

Aversive therapies have been used to eliminate undesirable behaviors. As with all approaches to treatment that utilize classical conditioning, the goal is to form a negative association with a particular behavior. Aversion therapies have been used to treat disturbing sexual behavior, alcohol use, and cigarette use.

An example of an aversive therapy approach involves the use of a drug called antabuse, also known as disulfiram. A person who drinks alcohol after taking antabuse will become ill with nausea and vomiting. The idea is to create a negative association with alcohol use, so that ultimately, just thinking of alcohol would cause the person to become sick, and as result, he or she would abstain from drinking. Treatments with antabuse have not been as successful at treating alcohol dependence as was originally hoped. Researcher Richard Fuller found that when people really want to drink, they just don't take the antabuse.

Techniques That Utilize Operant Conditioning

Chances are you have been, or currently are involved in a *token economy system*. There are people who only use one airline. Why? Air miles. After they have accumulated a certain number of air miles, they can redeem them for a free flight, free upgrades, or other incentives.

Token economies provide reinforcement for a behavior in the form of a token. A token may take many forms, including a sticker, a poker chip, or points entered into a computer. At the end of some predesignated amount of time, tokens may be exchanged for a backup reinforcer. A backup reinforcer is a larger gift. If you have ever played an arcade game to receive tickets or tokens that you later exchange for one or several prizes, then you understand the concept of a backup reinforcer.

In a token economy, a token may be given in exchange for desirable behavior. For example, if I clean my room, I get to use the car; if I fly your airline, I get points; or if I read books, I get to go to a party. Tokens may also be removed as a result of an undesirable behavior. The removal of a reinforcer, as a result of an undesirable behavior, is called response cost. The classic example of response cost involves adults and a speeding ticket. If you exceed the speed limit and are pulled over by a police officer, a reinforcer will be removed; in this case your money. Or, if you were excessively speeding, the removed reinforcer could be your license. Response cost operates on the principles of negative punishment. As a result, the behavior will be less likely to occur in the future.

Token economies are often used in child behavior therapy. A child who has attention deficit hyperactivity disorder (ADHD) may be placed on a token economy system where he receives tokens for desirable behaviors: five tokens for putting away toys, ten tokens for completing homework. This system can be used at school as well: two tokens for waiting patiently in the cafeteria line, one token for raising his hand before speaking. At the end of a predetermined period of time, the child will have the option to cash in his tokens for a backup reinforcer: twenty tokens for thirty extra minutes of television, fifty tokens for a trip to the ice cream shop, one hundred tokens for a trip to an amusement park.

Another popular technique that uses negative punishment is *time out*. This approach is most commonly used with children. As a result of an undesirable behavior, a child is removed from her reinforcing environment. For example, she is sent out of the class, or she must sit on a chair in the corner of the room. As a result of this time out, the child should be less likely to engage in the undesirable behavior in the future. For children up to age five, the important rule for time out is that the length of the time out should equal the child's age times one minute. For example, a three-year-old child would receive a three-minute time out, a four-year-old a four-minute time out, and so on.

COGNITIVE APPROACH

The premise behind the cognitive therapies is that a change in thoughts or cognitions will result in a change in behavior. Two famous clinicians associated with the approach are Albert Ellis and Aaron Beck. There is also cognitive-behavior therapy that contains elements of both cognitive therapy and behavior therapy and emphasizes the importance of both in treatment.

Rational Emotive Behavior Therapy (REBT)

Albert Ellis's Rational Emotive Behavior Therapy (REBT), originally referred to as Rational Emotive Therapy (RET), involves challenging a client's irrational beliefs in an effort to get her to change these beliefs that are at the heart of her dysfunction. According to Ellis, people impose demands on themselves. This is referred to as "demandingness" and includes phrases like, "I must do this," or "I should do that." These unrealistic demands result in feelings of disappointment and inadequacy. Ellis's approach was published in the

Journal of Rational-Emotive and Cognitive Therapy in 1994. It encourages the client to discard these unrealistic demands on self and seek out new beliefs.

Beck's Cognitive Therapy

Aaron Beck's Cognitive Therapy is often used to treat depression. Through this approach, the therapist helps the client change his negative thinking patterns, which influence how he interacts with the world. Beck refers to *cognitive distortions*, which are things we tell ourselves to make our way through life. Examples include things like *all or nothing thinking*, such as "I must get all As or I am a failure." In 1980, psychologist David Burns suggested methods for making such assumptions. A person might say, "The New York City cab driver was rude during our trip; therefore, all people from New York City are rude." The cognitive-therapy approach to treatment involves working with the client to help him realize the ill-founded nature of such automatic thoughts.

One way therapists accomplish this change is by providing evidence to the contrary so clients see the flaws in their thinking. "So, the cab driver was rude. Did you meet anyone else on your trip? You talked to the hotel concierge; how was that? He was helpful and made your trip more enjoyable? Was he from New York? Yes?" In this scenario, therapist and client reach the conclusion together that not all people from New York City are rude.

In treating a client with major depressive disorder using Beck's approach, a therapist would work to help the client identify the thought processes that include automatic negative thinking and generate depression. Treatment involves correcting negative think-

ing and learning to generate more realistic evaluations of situations. The client takes a very active role in her treatment, and she will be asked to monitor and record her thoughts. The result of changing these thoughts will be changed feelings.

GROUP THERAPY

Our discussion of approaches to therapy, thus far, has focused on individual approaches, but therapy does not have to be a one-on-one experience. Group therapies are used to treat substance abuse disorders, anxiety disorders, and a variety of other abnormal behaviors. In group therapy, one or two therapists work with a number of individuals with shared problems. The advantages of group therapy include an opportunity for support and feedback from peers, and a feeling of not being the only one who struggles with a particular problem. There is no one perspective associated with group therapy.

In his classic book on group therapy, *The Theory and Practice of Group Psychotherapy*, Irvin Yalom divides the "therapeutic experience" into eleven factors. Some of these factors are unique to group therapy, and others apply to both group and individual therapy.

These factors include

- instillation of hope
- universality
- imparting information
- altruism
- corrective recapitulation of the primary family group
- development of socializing techniques
- imitative behavior

- interpersonal learning
- group cohesiveness
- catharsis
- existential factors

Group therapy instills hope in the members. A grieving family member may enter a bereavement group feeling as if the pain of mourning will never end. After entering the group, the person will meet others who are in various stages of grieving. This may provide the individual with a sense of what the future holds for him emotionally.

Individuals may find *universality* in group therapy. Knowing that you and your problems are not unique can provide a sense of relief. A young woman who was a recent victim of a sexual assault may experience feelings of isolation—of feeling like she is the only one to have had such an experience. Interacting with other survivors of sexual assault will allow her to see that she is not alone in her experience.

Groups may provide important information. I have run groups for women who are HIV positive, and an important part of the group involved providing information about the disease. This information may come from the therapist, or it may come from other group members. The participants can also give information in the form of advice. These women often served as great resources for each other about the side effects of different medications, strategies for disclosing HIV status, the physicians with the shortest office waits, and so on.

The fourth factor in group therapy is *altruism*. This term is often used in psychology to refer to actions that are purely selfless. Group therapy provides opportunities for participants to help others in a situation where the participants have no chance of personal gain for themselves. Offering words of comfort about a challenging crisis to a new group member is an example of altruistic behavior in group therapy.

The fifth element is the *corrective recapitulation of the primary family group*. In this case, the group resembles a family, with the therapist or therapists representing the parents. Group therapy may also provide an opportunity for members to re-enact crisis challenges from their families of origin. Therapists can observe these re-enactments and use them to gain insight into the clients.

Groups also begin to use *socializing techniques*, or social/observational learning as proposed by Albert Bandura in chapter 10. The dynamics of a group can be quite influential. For instance, some group members may provide each other with accurate feedback about specific behaviors. *Imitative behaviors* follow naturally from the social/observational learning. Group members will model behaviors of the therapist or other group members. In a group for people with children with behavior problems, one parent may admire another group member's optimistic approach to parenting and make efforts to adopt a similar outlook.

Yalom views the group as a social microcosm where there is much to be learned. In such *interpersonal learning*, members interact with each other, and the roles they assume in the group are reflective of their interactions and roles in society. The group member who always complains that no one takes him seriously may be the same person who brings a practical joke to the group each week and responds to every comment with a lighthearted remark. Within the safety of the group, he might begin to explore why he behaves this way. The group will begin to bond, and over time, there will be evidence of solidarity or *group cohesiveness*. This solidarity is important because it imparts a sense of acceptance, inclusiveness, and belongingness, which we learned in chapter 6 is an important motivator.

The next element, *catharsis*, is typically associated with psychoanalytic approaches, but it can refer to the fact that the group allows for open expression of feelings, both negative and positive. Groups can become very emotional, and members may make themselves vulnerable by doing and saying things in an effort to get problems off their chests. Group therapy encourages this outpouring of feelings.

Finally, in a group, there needs to be an acknowledgment of the larger issues in life, the *existential factors*. Group members must take responsibility for their actions and the consequences of their behavior. They must come to realize that life may be unfair or unjust and that they must accept their own mortality. Irvin Yalom emphasizes that these guidelines are related to each other and that not all of these elements are necessary for an effective group experience.

An alternative type of group experience is the self-help group. In these groups there is no mental health professional. Instead, group members take responsibility for the effectiveness of their own group. Examples of these include Alcoholics Anonymous, Narcotics Anonymous, and Gamblers Anonymous. Essentially, these groups consist of a number of people who share the same problem, and who gather to help each other.

OTHER APPROACHES

There are other therapies that are worth mentioning. Some are categorized by the people involved, rather than by approach. Just as a therapist may work with one person or a group of people, a therapist may also work with two people, a couple, or a family.

Couples Therapy

Couples therapy was once referred to as marital therapy. The name changed because today committed partners aren't always married to each other. The goal of the couples therapist is to help the couple with problems in their relationship; help may take a variety of approaches, based on orientation. In behavioral couples therapy, couples may use some of the strategies used in individual therapy. One of these approaches is *contracting*. Couples, along with their therapist, will sit down and develop a contract that speaks to some behavior change they would like to achieve. Both members of the couple and the therapist will sign the contact to symbolize their commitment to the plan.

For example, Darlene and Thomas create a contract stipulating that Darlene is to clean the bathroom once a week, take out the trash twice a week, and wash the dishes daily. Thomas's tasks are to make the beds daily, cook dinner daily, and shop for groceries once a week. At the end of the week, each member would receive reinforcement if they've honored their end of the contract. As you can see, this approach is based on the basic principles of behaviorism from chapter 7.

Another approach to couples therapy is *cognitive couples therapy*. In any relationship, there are misinterpretations, and this is certainly the case in intimate relationships. A husband says,

"Is that a new pair of shoes?" The wife interprets this as "you are wasting money." While on a road trip a partner says, "How fast are you driving?" The other person interprets the question as "you are a crummy driver." As with individual cognitive therapy the goal of couples therapy is to change the irrational, unproductive thinking that sabotages the relationship.

Family Therapy

As the name implies, family therapy involves all the members of the family. Family may be defined as the immediate family, those in one household, or the extended family, including people who do not live together yet are connected and identified as a unit. One theory often associated with family therapy is the *family systems approach*. According to the systems approach, a person does not live or develop in a vacuum. In order to understand a person's problems, the therapist must also understand the dynamics of his or her family. This is because the family is a unit. A good analogy for the family is that of a machine with interlocking parts. If one part is removed or changed, the change will impact the workings of the entire machine. The same holds true with the family. If the brother stops using drugs, the change impacts not only the brother, but also every member in that family system. Therefore, family therapy with a systems approach will take the concept of the family as an intertwined unit into consideration by involving every member and anticipating the consequences of change on the system.

Continuum of Care

Fifty minutes once a week is hardly sufficient for some people in individual, couples, or group therapy; more intensive approaches to therapy may be required. Today, the options for therapy for this segment of the population

are quite varied. Gone are the days when the only option was long-term hospitalization in a psychiatric hospital.

Today's options include home-based treatment services, where a mental health professional comes to the home of the client to provide services; partial and full-day treatment programs, where patients attend a facility during weekdays and go home on nights and weekends; and therapeutic group homes, where ten or fewer residents live in a community setting. These patients may leave home to attend a day treatment program, or treatment may be provided in the home. Hospital treatment is also available, where patients receive treatment in a psychiatric hospital (which may be located on the psychiatric floor of a general hospital or may be a hospital devoted solely to the treatment of mental disorders). The length of stay varies depending on variables that include the severity of illness and the type of treatment.

CONTINUUM OF CARE OPTIONS

- Home-based services
- Partial and day treatment
- Therapeutic group homes
- Hospital treatment

Electroconvulsive Treatment

Electroconvulsive therapy (ECT) is not what it used to be. If you've seen the films *One Flew Over the Cuckoo's Nest* or *A Beautiful Mind*, the phrase ECT probably conjures disturbing images of a patient strapped to an operating table having violent convulsions. Although ECT is still used as a last resort—for cases of prolonged depression that have not responded to therapy or antidepressants, such as Prozac, Elavil, or Nardil—today, doctors use lower electric currents and unilateral ECT, where current is passed only through one side of the brain. This eliminates some of the confusion and memory impairment that was once associated with ECT.

Multimodal Approaches

Many treatment approaches to mental disorders are *multimodal*. That is, different strategies may be used to treat one problem. Severe depression, or an episode of depression in a person with bipolar disorder, may be treated with antidepressants and therapy. The same holds true for many other disorders that may not respond to therapy alone.

CHAPTER SUMMARY

A variety of approaches to therapy exist in the field of psychology. One of the more familiar is psychoanalysis, often associated with Sigmund Freud. The goal of psychoanalysis is to provide the client with a better understanding of self. This goal is also the focus of client-centered therapy, or Rogerian therapy, associated with Carl Rogers. The behavioral approaches are based on the belief that behavior is learned. Behavioral approaches to therapy utilize concepts from classical and operant conditioning. There are a variety of techniques associated with a behavioral approach.

The cognitive therapies are based on the belief that a change in cognition will result in a change in behavior. Albert Ellis and Aaron Beck are most often associated with these approaches. There is also a combination of cognitive and behavioral approaches, referred to as cognitive-behavioral therapy (CBT).

Therapies may also vary in composition and involve individuals, groups, couples, or families.

The continuum of care refers to the wide array of mental health services available outside the traditional office visits. These include home-based services, partial and day treatment programs, therapeutic group homes, and hospital treatment. Multimodal approaches involve treating psychological disorders with more than one approach, such as a combination of therapy and psychotropic medication.

TEST YOUR RECALL AND RECOGNITION

True/False

1. Free association and dream analysis are techniques used in psychoanalysis.

2. During free association, the client is asked to say the first thing that comes to mind.

3. Both systematic and *in vivo* desensitization use a gradual approach to treatment.

4. Specific phobias are commonly treated with behavioral therapies.

5. Behavior therapy focuses on introspection from the client.

6. Beck's approach to treatment is commonly used to treat depression.

7. Group therapists can use any orientation.

8. The goal of cognitive couples therapy is to have each partner gain insight into the childhood experiences of the other.

9. In unilateral ECT, current is passed through both sides of the brain.

10. The continuum of care refers to the variety of mental health services available today.

Multiple Choice

1. Which of the following techniques is *not* used in psychoanalysis?

    a. dream analysis

    b. free association

    c. flooding

    d. none of the above

2. Rogerian approaches to therapy are unique in that there is an emphasis on the

    a. characteristics of the therapist.

    b. genetic makeup of the client.

    c. both a and b.

    d. neither a nor b.

3. June's fear of heights must be addressed, since her new job is on the thirty-seventh floor of a high-rise building. June agrees to go to the building with her therapist and take the elevator to the observation deck on the seventieth floor. Which therapeutic approach are June and her therapist using?

    a. systematic desensitization

    b. flooding (*in vivo*)

    c. flooding (imagined)

    d. *in vivo* desensitization

4. Michelle was caught cheating on a math exam. In response to this behavior, her parents have removed her telephone from her room. Which behavioral strategy are her parents using?

    a. positive punishment

    b. time out

    c. positive reinforcement

    d. response cost

5. Ellis's approach to therapy is abbreviated

    a. RAT.   c. DID.

    b. REBT.   d. PTSD.

6. Individuals with which of the following disorders would probably *not* respond well to group therapy?

    a. alcohol abuse

    b. schizoid personality disorder

    c. phobias

    d. heroin dependence

7. Beth and her husband, Fred, have decided to see a therapist along with their children, Elizabeth and Frederick. Sometimes, the therapist asks to see the parents without the children. Other times, the therapist will see the children without the parents. Sometimes, the therapist will see each member separately, and other times the therapist will see the entire group. What type of therapy is this?

    a. family therapy

    b. group therapy

    c. psychoanalysis

    d. undetermined

8. Oscar attends a partial-day program. Which of the following statements is *not* true regarding Oscar's treatment experience?

    a. Oscar returns home each afternoon.

    b. Oscar participates in group therapy.

    c. Oscar socializes with friends.

    d. Oscar has the option to live in the facility.

9. ECT may be used to treat which of the following?

   a. OCD

   b. major depressive disorder

   c. heroin dependence

   d. DID

10. Which of the following is an option in the continuum of care?

   a. home-based services

   b. hospitalization

   c. therapeutic group home

   d. all of the above

Fill in the Blanks

1. _____ _____ is responsible for the development of client-centered therapy.

2. In systematic and *in vivo* desensitization, the client creates a listing of the least-feared and most-feared stimuli. This list is called the client's _____.

3. Response cost utilizes the principles of _____ conditioning.

4. Kay is three years old; her time out should last _____ minutes.

5. Aversion therapy utilizes the principles of _____ conditioning.

6. Antabuse has been used to treat _____ abuse and dependence.

7. A change in thought will result in a change in behavior; this is the premise behind _____ approaches to therapy.

8. The example of cognitive distortions, offered in the section on Aaron Beck, is _____.

9. During group, Steve begins to sob uncontrollably about his inability to secure unemployment. He then begins to scream at the top of his lungs that he feels inadequate and helpless. The group allows him to vent, and then provides emotional support. This scenario illustrates _____ at work in group therapy.

10. Ever since she started attending the group, Emma has found that she uses many positive self-statements that she often hears other group members use. Emma is _____ the behavior of the others in the group.

ANSWERS TO QUESTIONS
True/False

1. true	6. true
2. true	7. true
3. true	8. false
4. true	9. false
5. false	10. true

Multiple Choice

1. c	6. b
2. a	7. a
3. b	8. d
4. d	9. b
5. b	10. d

Fill in the Blanks

1. Carl Rogers

2. hierarchy

3. operant

4. three

5. classical

6. alcohol

7. cognitive

8. all or nothing thinking

9. catharsis

10. modeling

ADDITIONAL RESOURCES

Books

Beck, A. T. 1976. *Cognitive therapy and the emotional disorders*. New York: International Universities Press.

Yalom, I. D. 1995. *Theory and practice of group psychotherapy*, (4th ed.). New York: Basic Books.

Videos

Analyze this, directed by H. Ramis. Motion picture, United States: Warner Studios, 1998.

One flew over the cuckoo's nest, directed by M. Forman. Motion picture, United States: Warner Studios, 1975.

SOCIAL PSYCHOLOGY

> attitudes, cognitive dissonance, influence,
> attribution, attraction, helping behavior,
> deindividuation, groupthink, mob behavior

Have you ever behaved in a certain way just because everyone else did? Perhaps you stood up at an assembly because the rest of the crowd did, or followed a line that went nowhere because there were fifty people in front of you. The scope of social psychology is quite broad, but the emphasis is on understanding how our behavior is influenced by people around us, and how we influence them.

This is one of the areas in psychology that is rich with classic studies, and it is one of the areas that people generally find very intriguing. In this chapter, we'll cover concepts in social psychology such as attitudes, influence, attribution, attraction, helping behavior, and deindividuation.

RESEARCH METHODS IN SOCIAL PSYCHOLOGY

Before we discuss social psychology, let us talk briefly about research methods in social psychology. We've talked about the tools, or research methods, used by psychologists to learn more about human behavior. These include experiments where researchers learn about behavior by asking subjects to complete questionnaires or submit to interviews. These are examples of self-report strategies. We have also discussed the disadvantages of self-report, one of these being inaccurate data that yields invalid results. This is an especially important issue in social psychology, where people are asked to talk about behaviors for which there are societal expectations. If I asked you if you were going to help a person in trouble, wouldn't you say "yes"? If I asked you if you were going to conform to the group, wouldn't you say, "no"? These responses illustrate a concept in psychology known as *social desirability*. This means that we try to present ourselves in a positive light. In this case, we do it so that the experimenter will view us favorably.

To obtain data that truly reflects the real behavior of people, social psychologists use additional tools in their research. We will discuss two of these tools: confederates and debriefing. Most simply put, *confederates* are fake subjects. They look and behave as if they are just subjects in the study like everyone else. In reality, they are acting. This allows the researcher to gain a true understanding of how the presence of others influences behavior.

The deception involved in the use of confederates allows the researcher to create real-life situations and observe the subject's behavior, which may differ from behavior in a naturalistic setting. The subject's responses to the confederates are more likely to be honest than are responses given to an experimenter. Later in this chapter, you'll learn how the Milgram and Darley and Lantané studies illustrate the utility of confederates. As we describe these studies, you will see that some of these studies involve deception: subjects believe that they are among other subjects, but they are really with confederates; subjects think there is some real crisis when it's actually a staged event.

At the end of these studies, subjects may feel stressed or anxious. In an effort to bring the subject back to a pre-experiment state of mind, researchers use a technique called *debriefing*. After the experiment is over, the experimenter takes the subjects aside and debriefs them— in other words, explains the true nature of the study. (For example, "This person was a part of the study; you did not cause anyone harm.") Providing such information is required by the ethical guidelines of the American Psychological Association and were created to protect the subjects' well being.

Studies in social psychology include some of the most famous and memorable in all of psychology. Stanley Milgram's study on obedience and Leon Festinger's study on cognitive dissonance are two examples. Because these areas touch upon issues that we all deal with in our everyday lives, they are some of the most fascinating in psychology.

ATTITUDES

An attitude is a feeling, position, or stance about an idea or object. We all have many attitudes about a variety of different subjects. The first step in understanding our attitudes is to look at attitude formation and attitude change.

Attitude Formation

How do attitudes develop? Why do you adhere to a particular political viewpoint?

Why do you dislike a particular group of people? Attitudes may form through learning, either via direct experience or observational learning, or through modeling.

For example, attitude formation is of interest to researchers studying racism. For instance, how do children learn to have opinions about another group of people based on skin color? We know that children pick up subtle clues from their parents. The parents may feel a particular way about a certain group of people, and the children assimilate those beliefs and opinions. They may develop an attitude about a racial group even when there hasn't been any outward behavior or discussion to prompt those beliefs.

The same thing can happen with attitudes about socioeconomic class, age groups, religious sects, or political groups. The influence of our parents, teachers, peers, and the media may have more of an impact than we previously believed.

Attitude Change

Attitudes, our opinions or beliefs, can be changed even when we are not aware that it is happening. One of the classic studies in attitude change is Leon Festinger's study of cognitive dissonance from 1959. In this study, students were given an excruciatingly boring task to complete. Upon completion of the task, some subjects were given $1, then they were asked to tell the others that the task was enjoyable. Others were given $20, and they were also asked to tell people that the task was enjoyable. In addition, there was a control group: involvement of these subjects was minimal. They completed the task, and then responded to interview questions only.

Later, when asked to rate the task, those who were given $1 were more likely to rate the task as enjoyable, informative, and important, and to say that they would do a similar activity in the future than those people who received $20. The students who received $1 were experiencing *cognitive dissonance*. This means that there was a state of unease caused by the discrepancy between the request to tell others the task was enjoyable and the fact that they thought it was boring. To alleviate this discomfort, or aversive state, they needed to change one of the thoughts, so they changed their attitudes about the task. Those who received the $20 did not experience the discrepancy because the payment of $20 justified the lie.

Based on this theory, Festinger developed a *theory of cognitive dissonance*, which states that if a person is asked to do or say something that is in conflict with her opinion, she will change her opinion to match what she says or does. A person is more likely to make these changes in opinion when there is insufficient justification for the discrepancy between opinion and behavior. ("I only received $1 for that boring task, so I did not do it for the money, I did it because it was enjoyable.") A person is less likely to make these changes in opinion when there is sufficient justification for the discrepancy between opinion and behavior. ("I received $20 for that boring task; I only did it for the money because it was really boring.")

A real-life example of attitude change might involve the motorist who looks at his speedometer and sees that he is traveling eighty-five miles per hour. Knowing that speeding is dangerous, he can make one of two adjustments: he can say, "I'm a very good and safe driver," or he can reduce his speed.

INFLUENCE

Even though most people like to think of themselves as independent and free-thinking, our behaviors are greatly influenced by the viewpoints and actions of the people around us, whether or not we know them well. The section that follows looks at two types of influence: conformity and obedience.

Conformity

Think of an individual in the midst of a group. Conformity occurs when the individual gives into the wants of the group, although the inclinations of the individual are to do otherwise. Of course, our inclination to comply with the group is important when we really want to belong to the group. But research has shown that even when it's not so important to belong, people tend to want to conform.

In a study done by Solomon Asch in 1956, subjects were given two cards. The procedure for the study was as follows: subjects were informed that they were participating in a study about visual perception. When they arrived for the study, they were ushered into a room where chairs were arranged in a row. The subject was always the last to arrive and was forced to sit in the last chair in the row. Unbeknownst to the subjects, the other seats were occupied by confederates. The experimenter then showed the two cards. One card had three parallel lines of increasing length, and each line was numbered. The second card contained just one line, which was obviously the same length as one of the three lines. Subjects were asked to select which one of the three lines matched the lone line. The true subject was the last to respond.

During the first trial, the confederates all responded with the same, correct answer. During the second trial, the confederates all responded with the same, correct answer. On the third trial, however, confederates selected the wrong line. Asch discovered that when the confederates unanimously answered incorrectly, the subject was more likely to answer incorrectly as well.

But, when even *one* confederate answered correctly, the chances of the subject answering correctly increased. In other words, having just one individual who holds your view can make a difference in whether or not conformity occurs.

This study has been backed up by other research, and we can all probably recall a time when we conformed to the majority's false opinion. How many times have you agreed that you liked some fashion item that you truly found hideous? How many times have you laughed at a joke that you found offensive? How many times have you spent more than you could afford to keep up with the neighbors? We all conform, but why? We do so because being the one person who doesn't conform is not always a comfortable position.

Obedience

There are times when obedience is important, and times when it can be detrimental. We are comforted by the thought that a young child will take his mother's hand and wait with her before crossing the street. At the same time, when a commanding officer in the military gives an order to attack, and the soldiers bomb a village full of women and children, we question the soldiers' reasoning.

Both scenarios illustrate the concept of obedience. There are times when obedience is desirable, as in the case of the child-parent

relationship. There are times when obedience may lead to horrible consequences, as in the case of the soldiers who were simply following orders.

What is it that makes people obedient? Researcher Stanley Milgram's curiosity about obedience was spurred by the horrific events of the Holocaust and by a general interest in why people would do the wrong thing just because they were given instructions. In the famous Milgram study conducted in 1963 and published in 1974, men between the ages of twenty and fifty responded to an advertisement seeking participants for a study on memory. When they arrived, they were placed in front of a panel with a row of switches. These subjects were asked to be a teacher, to read a list of words to a learner in an adjacent room, and then ask for a response. Unbeknown to the participants, the learner was a confederate.

When the learner provided an incorrect response, the subjects were instructed to press a lever on the panel and deliver a shock. With each error, the experimenter told the subjects to intensify the level of shock administered. Subjects continued to obey the experimenter even when the shock reached a dangerous level for the learner. Two-thirds of the subjects obeyed the directions of the experimenter and delivered the highest level of shock possible.

Milgram followed this study with others that examined factors that make obedience more or less likely. Results of these later studies, published in 1974, found that the more physical and/or emotional distance between the victim and the subject, the more likely there would be obedience to demands. In addition, the more distance between the authority figure and the subject, the less obedience.

ATTRIBUTION

Why do we do the things we do? What made little Joey kick the dog? Why did your mother say that to her sister? Why did you run over the garbage can? Attribution theory is how we explain the causes of individual and social behavior. This might refer to a person's personality. Joey is prone to temper tantrums. It could be a temporary internal state, such as stress. Mother's words were sarcastic and rude because she has always been a little jealous of her sister, and in a moment of stress those feelings burst out. You told your neighbor, Mr. Jones, that if he left his trash can in your driveway one more time, you were going to flatten it; and so, at the end of the day, you did. Attribution theory also takes into account the immediate situation in which a particular behavior might occur.

In 1958, Fritz Heider proposed that we explain behaviors as being a function of either an internal or external factor. In 1967, Harold Kelley took Heider's proposition to another level and examined the factors that make us suspect an attribution is due to an internal or external factor. He identified the factors as distinctiveness, consistency, and consensus.

Distinctiveness is the variability of response to the behavior. Michael asks his younger brother, Norman "Why did you break the vase?" Norman responds, "The devil made me do it." Before we react, we have to consider how Norman usually responds when he does something wrong. Is his answer generally so glib? If this is unusual for him, then we might attribute the behavior to external factors. Perhaps he was very angry with Michael at the moment. If this is his usual response, then we might attribute the behavior to internal factors. Norman has a pattern of such behaviors and responses.

Consistency examines whether the behavior is an ordinary or out-of-the-ordinary occurrence. How often does Norman break things? If he has never broken anything before, then we would say that some external factor was responsible, such as the vase was slippery or the table was unstable. If, on the other hand, Norman broke a flowerpot on the porch yesterday, then we might attribute the broken vase to some internal factors.

Consensus allows us to consider if Norman is the only person to break something on this table. If several people have walked by the table only to have its contents fall off and break, then we could attribute Norman's experience to external factors. If, however, other family members walk by the table all the time and break nothing, then we would attribute that to some internal factors.

One problem in making these decisions about attribution is called the *fundamental attribution error*, which was proposed in research by Lee Ross in 1977. We tend to over-attribute the behaviors of others to internal factors and over-attribute our own behaviors to external factors. For instance, Michael is quick to tell his father that Norman broke the vase because he was running by the table. But when Michael breaks something on the same table weeks later, he is just as quick to tell his father that the table's leg is unstable.

ATTRACTION

This section will not focus on intimacy, love, or commitment—in spite of the title. Rather, it will explore what factors determine whether or not two people will like each other. There are innumerable sayings to explain attraction: birds of a feather flock together, absence makes the heart grow fonder, like attracts like, opposites attract. Is there any merit to these sayings? We will discuss four factors that help us understand attraction: similarity, proximity, physical attractiveness, and complementary attributes.

Similarity

A number of research studies suggest that we are attracted to people with whom we share similar attitudes. We tend to be attracted to these people because their agreement validates our viewpoint. A study by Theodore Newcomb in 1961 tracked the perceived attraction of a group of students who lived together. Although similarity in values did not initially predict attraction, it did by the end of the semester. Those whose views were similar were also those who were most likely to report being attracted to each other.

Proximity

Proximity, called the *exposure effect* by Robert Zajonc in 1968, demonstrates that the more we are exposed to a stimulus, the more we will like it. This holds true for attraction. We are more likely to be attracted to people who live near us and to those whom we see on a frequent basis. This is quite logical because people who live near us are also probably similar in many ways; perhaps they share our economic standing or our preferences for a particular urban or rural environment.

Physical Attractiveness

People are attracted to people whom they find physically attractive, and there has been a lot of research on the effects of physical attractiveness on the development of the person. Research done by Ellen Berscheid in 1985 shows that attractive people receive preferential treatment and are perceived by others as having desirable characteristics. This certainly comes as no surprise, but why do we like these people more? One explanation is that being seen with an attractive person may be a reinforcer, because it reflects positively on the less attractive person. For instance, "I'm a great person because I have a gorgeous date."

It seems fitting that people are attracted to others who possess some characteristic that they feel they lack. A socially awkward person finds a social butterfly very attractive; an impulsive person appreciates a person who acts only after weighing all the options. Although this may sound logical, research by Amnon Till and Eric Freedman in 1978 finds data to the contrary. In Till and Freedman's cross-cultural study, college students from the United States, Australia, and New Zealand were asked to describe their preferences for dating and marriage partners. They were also asked to describe self-perceptions. The results showed that subjects were in search of a partner with similar (psychological and physical) characteristics rather than a complementary partner. A review of the literature done by K. Daniel O'Leary and David Smith in 1991 concurs with the results of the Till and Freedman study; it doesn't support the line of reasoning that says "opposites attract."

HELPING BEHAVIOR

Every day we are faced with decisions about how and when to help other people. Perhaps a lost child cries for his mother in the supermarket. You may see a couple engage in a public disagreement, which escalates with the woman punching the man; or a young man on the street approaches you and asks for money for a meal. Who do you help?

We are faced with these dilemmas all the time; sometimes we help; other times we do not. One of the deciding factors that influence our decisions to help is usually how many other people are around to join us in helping.

In 1964, a young woman named Kitty Genovese was returning home from work. She was only a few feet away from her door when she was brutally attacked and repeatedly stabbed. Kitty Genovese yelled for help. Thirty-eight witnesses saw what was going on, but only one person called the police. By the time they arrived, Kitty Genovese was dead.

This incident inspired John Darley and Bibb Lantané in 1968 to create a study that helps us understand helping behavior. These researchers recruited college students for the study and set up the following scenario. Subjects were asked to talk to other students (who, unbeknown to the subject, were confederates) through an intercom about their adjustment to college. Subjects were led to believe that they were talking to one, two, or five other people. As the discussion proceeded, the subject heard through the intercom that one of the other students was having a seizure. Did the subject help? The subject was more likely to help when he thought that there was only one person on the intercom. The subject was less likely to help when he thought that there were five people on the intercom. This finding, called the *bystander effect*, states that the reason people are less likely to help when others are around is diffusion of responsibility. In other words, "I thought someone else would do it."

DEINDIVIDUATION

When caught in the throes of some group behavior, people may lose their individual identities and behave in ways that are uncharacteristic of their typical selves. This may be exciting and fun, as in the case of the lacrosse team members who rush the field in victory and carry their coach around the stadium on their shoulders. It may also be disturbing and undesirable in the case of mob behavior and groupthink.

Mob Behavior

Just the term *mob behavior* conjures up images of an unruly, angry group of people engaging in horrible behavior. Consider the lynch mobs that terrorized African Americans during the twentieth century, the clusters of men who sexually assaulted women during a parade in New York City, and the response of groups after the Rodney King verdict. In this last case, the Los Angeles police officers were found not guilty of assaulting Rodney King, an African-American motorist, who was pulled over by the police. This verdict was surprising because the assault was captured on videotape. The response in Los Angeles was horrific: people started fires, assaulted innocent bystanders, and looted local establishments.

Much of the reason for this destruction is because people feel anonymous in groups and, therefore, less responsible for their actions. In addition, there is the presence of peer pressure at work. One researcher, Ed Diener, studied mob behavior in 1980, and he found that people seek out deindividuation experiences when they feel badly about their own identities.

Groupthink

Studies by Irving Janis (1918–1990), a social psychologist at Yale University, suggest that group members may make decisions— sometimes bad ones—in an effort to maintain the harmony of the group, rather than considering what is best. Janis coined this psychological phenomenon, which is called groupthink. Much of the research on groupthink has focused on decisions that are made in the political arena or in corporate America.

Consider this example: you are vice president of a corporation. You and your colleagues discover that your company has chosen to work with another corporation, which is known for its repeated violations of child labor laws. Do you decide to cease work with this corporation, knowing that such a decision might upset the other members in your company, or do you ignore the issue? The decisions that are made as a result of groupthink may have important consequences. At first glimpse, this may seem benign compared to the outcome of mob behavior. However, sometimes important decisions are made that cause a loss of sense of self and that allow one to behave in ways that are atypical of one's usual behavior. People tend to seek out such group experiences when they feel bad about their own identities.

CHAPTER SUMMARY

The focus of social psychology is to gain an understanding of human behavior and understand how others impact our behaviors.

The areas of social psychology include, but are by no means limited to, attitudes, influence, attributions, attraction, helping behavior, and deindividuation.

The focus of attitude research is twofold and deals with both attitude formation and attitude change.

Influence covers human behaviors such as obedience and conformity. There are times when obedience and conformity can be helpful, such as when the child crosses the street with his mother, and when they can be disruptive, such as when people follow rules without considering the implications.

Attributions (theories that explain the causes of our behavior) may be internal or external and are subject to misinterpretation.

Attraction, the idea of people liking each other, is another subject of study in social psychology. People are attracted to others who possess a host of characteristics, such as similarity, proximity, and physical attractiveness.

Research in helping behaviors has explored under what conditions helping behavior is likely to occur. For example, people are more likely to respond to a person in distress if there is no one else available to help.

Deindividuation is the losing of one's identity while in a group. Such loss may occur with mob behavior or with groupthink.

TEST YOUR RECALL AND RECOGNITION

True/False

1. The process of debriefing occurs only at the beginning of the experiment.

2. The Milgram study illustrates the concept of conformity.

3. Attitudes are formed through interactions with parents, other relatives, teachers, and peers.

4. Festinger is associated with the term *cognitive dissonance.*

5. Physically attractive people reap few benefits from their good looks.

6. The research supports the saying "opposites attract."

7. "I did not help the lost child because there was a security guard in the store, and helping is her job." This statement illustrates diffusion of responsibility.

8. In Darley and Latané's study on helping behavior, a confederate pretended to have a heart attack.

9. In groupthink, the group makes decisions in an effort to maintain group harmony.

10. People may seek out deindividuation experiences when they are feeling good about their own identity and want to share those good feelings with the crowd.

Multiple Choice

1. Which of the following researchers did *not* create one of the classic studies in social psychology?

   a. Watson   c. Milgram
   b. Festinger   d. Darley and Lantané

2. Which of the following statements illustrates cognitive dissonance?

   a. Attractive people are thin, and I am thin.
   b. Ice cream is bad for my digestive system, and I love to eat ice cream.
   c. Television is bad, and I don't own a television.
   d. Exercise improves my health, and I exercise three times a week.

3. In the Milgram study, subjects thought they were going to participate in a study about

   a. exercise.
   b. adjustments to school.
   c. memory.
   d. alcohol use.

4. The Milgram study contributed a better understanding of which concept?

   a. attraction   c. helping behavior
   b. attitudes   d. obedience

5. "Why did he do that?" This question would be answered by which concept?

   a. attribution   c. attitudes
   b. attraction   d. helping behavior

6. Olivia is very attracted to Steve. She loves his dimples and his perfect smile. They live across the hall from each other, so she sees him often. Whenever she spends time with him, they talk for hours about their favorite sitcoms from the 1960s. Why is Olivia attracted to Steve?

   a. proximity
   b. similarity
   c. physical attraction
   d. all of the above

7. Identify the independent variable (*hint*: see chapter 2) in the original Darley and Latané study.

   a. the emergency
   b. the number of people on the other end of the intercom
   c. the response time
   d. the gender of the subject

8. Phil has always loved football, so he was thrilled when he received tickets to the Super Bowl. When his team lost, his seatmates began yelling obscenities at the winning team. They then leapt out of their seats and ran toward the field; before Phil knew what was happening, he was punching and being punched by stadium police. Phil's experience illustrates

   a. groupthink.

   b. mob behavior.

   c. bystander effect.

   d. cognitive dissonance.

9. One reason people engage in undesirable group behavior is that, while in the group, they feel

   a. attractive.

   b. confident.

   c. anonymous.

   d. none of the above.

10. What is one of the goals of debriefing?

   a. To ensure lawsuits.

   b. To return the subject to a pre-experiment state of being.

   c. To tell the subject about the results of the study.

   d. To obtain contact information from the subject.

Fill in the Blanks

1. The _____ in a study pretends to be a subject, but in actuality is a member of the research team.

2. _____ _____ is described as a discrepancy between opinion and behavior and creates a state of unease.

3. Although he knows that it is unsafe to drink and drive, Mitch, who has had several drinks, collapses under the pressures of his buddies and agrees to drive his friends to the twenty-four-hour diner. Mitch's behavior is an example of _____.

4. The Jonestown tragedy, where people followed the orders of their leader, Jim Jones, and committed suicide, provides an example of _____.

5. The three parts of Kelley's theory are _____, _____ and _____.

6. According to the _____ _____ _____, we are more likely to attribute the success of others to external factors.

7. Three factors that influence attraction are _____, _____, and _____.

8. I failed the exam because it was too long. This is an example of a(n) _____ attribution.

9. The _____ people present during an emergency, the less likely it is that someone will help.

10. _____ is a result of efforts to maintain harmony.

ANSWERS TO QUESTIONS

True/False

1. false	6. false
2. false	7. true
3. true	8. false
4. true	9. true
5. false	10. false

Multiple Choice

1. a	6. d
2. b	7. b
3. c	8. b
4. d	9. c
5. a	10. b

Fill in the Blanks

1. confederate
2. Cognitive dissonance
3. conformity
4. obedience
5. distinctiveness; consistency; consensus
6. fundamental attribution error
7. proximity; attractiveness; similarity
8. external
9. more
10. Groupthink

ADDITIONAL RESOURCES

Book

Aronsen, E., ed. 1984. *Readings about the social animal*, 4th ed. New York: W. H. Freeman and Company.

Video

History's mysteries: Silent witnesses—The Kitty Genovese murder. Television Broadcast. New York: A & E Television, 1999.

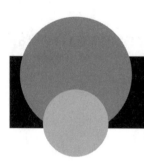

GLOSSARY

A-B design
A research design for behavioral assessment and intervention that allows for before and after comparison. A stands for baseline, which is the situation before intervention; B stands for treatment.

A-B-A-B design
A research design for behavioral assessment and intervention similar to the A-B design. In this design, the A stands for baseline and B for treatment. The sequence of this design is baseline-treatment-baseline-treatment.

abscissa
The x-axis or horizontal line on the graph.

absolute threshold
The point at which fifty percent of people would detect sensory information.

abstract
A component of a research article that provides a summary of the article.

acute stress disorder
A less severe form of posttraumatic stress disorder (PTSD) where symptoms last for less than one month.

adjustment disorders
A group of disorders that do not warrant a diagnosis in any of the other mental disorder categories and can include marital problems, social difficulty, bereavement, and academic problems.

adolescence
The period between twelve and eighteen years of life.

adolescent egocentrism
A stage of adolescence when teens view themselves as different from others. Two examples of this thinking include imaginary audiences and personal fables.

adolescent moratorium
Erikson's period of transition between childhood and adulthood; he describes this period as a break during which teens are free to ponder who they are and who they will become.

adulthood
The period after eighteen years; it can be divided into early adulthood, middle adulthood, and late adulthood.

afterimage
A visual image that continues after a stimulus is taken away.

Alcoholics Anonymous (AA)
A twelve-step program for those who abuse alcohol. Through group meetings, A.A. endorses a life of abstinence from alcohol use.

all or nothing thinking
An example of a cognitive distortion, such as "I must get all As or I am a failure."

alternative hypothesis
A prediction made by the experimenter that states the manipulation of the independent variable has an effect on the dependent variable.

altruism
A term used in psychology to describe actions that are purely selfless.

Alzheimer's disease
A type of dementia in which the patient loses memory of information, family, friends, self.

anal stage (18 months–3 years)
A component of Freud's theory of psychosexual development; during this period, the child's focus is on activities that involve the anal region of the body such as toileting.

analytical intelligence
In the Triarchic Theory of Intelligence, this refers to the skills most associated with intelligence, such as the ability to acquire new knowledge.

anorexia nervosa
Eating disorder characterized by excessive weight loss through dieting and/or excessive exercise; people with anorexia have a distorted body image in that although very thin, they believe themselves to be overweight.

anxiety
Unpleasant emotional reaction whose most identifiable characteristic is fear.

Apgar test
Test administered to newborns at one minute after birth, five minutes after birth, and sometimes ten minutes after birth. This test, based on a range of 0 to 10, rates the infant's appearance, pulse, grimace, activity, and respiration. A score of 4 or lower is cause for concern; scores between 7 and 10 indicate that the baby is healthy.

apparent motion
Perceptual illusion wherein a stationary object appears to move but doesn't actually move.

appendix
The part of a research article that includes supplemental information.

aqueous humor
Portion of the eye; the aqueous humor is filled with fluid and provides nutrients to the cornea and lens.

archetypes
Ancient and universal experiences within the collective unconscious.

Asperger's disorder
Mild form of autism that causes severe social impairment. Unlike autism, though, children with Asperger's show no cognitive impairment.

assimilation
One of four paths adopted by teens during their search for ethnic identity, this occurs when the teen rejects the norms of the minority group in favor of those of the majority group.

attachment
Close emotional relationship between child and caregiver.

attention-deficit disorder (ADD)
Disorder usually first diagnosed during childhood. Characterized by impulsivity, distractibility, and difficulty with sustained attention; may also include hyperactivity (attention deficit hyperactivity disorder, ADHD).

attitude
Feeling, position, or stance about an idea or object.

attraction
Degree of like or dislike for another person.

attribution
Assigning of blame for a behavior to internal or external factors.

attribution theories
Conclusions people draw for the causes of behavior.

auditory canal
Outer part of the ear through which sounds travel on the way to the eardrum.

auditory nerve
Group of axons that carry information from the ears to the brain.

autistic disorder or autism
Often associated with pervasive developmental disorder, symptoms of this disorder include impairment in social interactions and communication, as well as patterns of behavior such as rocking, hand flapping, and inflexible adherence to routines and rituals.

autonomic nervous system
Carries information to the internal organs of the body, such as the heart and lungs. Within the autonomic system are both the parasympathetic nervous system and the sympathetic nervous system.

autonomy versus shame and doubt (18 months–3 years)
Component of Erikson's theory of psychosocial development in which the child must learn to develop a sense of control and independence.

aversive therapies
Techniques used to eliminate undesirable behaviors by forming a negative association with those behaviors.

axes
Dimension used in judging individuals with psychological disorders.

axon
Long, tail-like portion of the neuron that carries information away from the cell body and toward other neurons.

baseline
In A-B design of behavioral assessment, the A stands for baseline, which is the situation before intervention information is compiled.

behavior therapy
Form of therapy that uses the principles of learning to change certain responses or activities.

behavioral neuroscience
Broader animal research term than physiological psychology that encompasses examination of the biological basis of behavior.

behavioral perspective
Psychological orientation that focuses on behaviors that can be seen. Some behavioral psychologists refer to these behaviors as public events, and they are the opposite of the private events that occur in the unconscious. Behaviorism asserts that behaviors are influenced by the environment.

biculturalism
One of four paths adopted by teens during their search for ethnic identity, this occurs when the teen opts for an identity that reflects both the majority culture and the minority culture of which he is a part.

Big Five/the five factor model of personality
Theory of personality that organizes personality traits into five categories: neuroticism, extroversion, openness, agreeableness, and conscientiousness.

bimodal
In statistics, a measure of central tendency where there are two numbers that appear most often in a distribution.

binocular cues
Visual cues that require the use of both eyes.

biological motivator
Instinctive actions necessary for survival.

biopsychology
Field of study that examines the effects of biology on behavior.

bipolar cells
Specialized cells in the visual system that consist of one axon and one dendrite. They connect rods and cones to ganglion cells.

bipolar disorder
Disorder characterized by the cycling between symptoms of depression and mania.

birth order
Adler's theory of personality development that focuses on the importance of birth order. It states that there are differences in character and behavior based on the order that children are born within families.

blind studies
Part of experimental research used to decrease subject or experimenter bias. Subjects and/or the experimenter are unaware of assignment to treatment conditions. There are two types of blind procedures: single-blind and double-blind.

body dysmorphic disorder
Disorder characterized by the patient seeing gross distortion of the body when there are no actual physical abnormalities.

bonding
Process through which a close relationship is formed between child and caregiver.

brain
Key component of the central nervous system.

breakdown
Process by which the neurotransmitter is broken down by enzymes and then removed from the synapse, so the synapse may receive new messages.

bulimia nervosa
Eating disorder characterized by distorted body image, binge eating, and purging of food.

bystander effect
Social phenomenon in which people are less likely to help others when others are present rather than when they are alone.

California Psychological Inventory (CPI)
Self-report personality test; the test consists of 462 questions that require a true/false response.

Cannon-Bard theory
Early theory of emotion that maintains that emotions and physiological changes occur simultaneously, not one after another.

cardinal trait
In the study of personality, a trait that is an all-consuming characteristic that guides behaviors.

case study
Comprehensive investigation of one particular subject.

castration anxiety
Part of Freud's Oedipal Complex where the son realizes that the father is bigger, stronger, and more powerful than he; this motivates the son to give up pursuit of his mother and relate to his father.

catatonic schizophrenia
Type of schizophrenic disorder characterized by unusual motor activities. For example, the patient may assume seemingly uncomfortable seating postures and remain in these positions for extended periods of time.

catharsis
Refers to the fact that the group therapy environment allows for open expression of feelings, both negative and positive.

cell body, or soma
Portion of the neuron from which the axons and dendrites extend; houses the cell nucleus.

central nervous system
Portion of the nervous system that consists of the brain and spinal cord.

central tendency
Statistical measurement that allows for a description of a group of scores; the three measures of central tendency are mean, median, and mode.

central trait
In the study of personality, a trait that influences behavior, but doesn't have the all-consuming quality of the cardinal trait.

cephalocaudal development
Motor development that occurs from the head downward.

cerebellum
Portion of the hindbrain that coordinates the body's movement, receiving information from the cerebrum and directing the position of the arms and legs as well as the degree of muscle tone. It allows the body to move slowly and smoothly.

cerebrum
Outer part of the brain that is wrinkled in appearance, also known as the cerebral cortex.

childhood
Period between two and twelve years of age.

chunking
Strategy used to expand the capacity of short-term memory; common stimuli are grouped together as a single unit of information.

ciliary muscles
Eye muscles on each side of the lens that assist with focusing.

classical (or Pavlovian) conditioning
Type of learning in which a neutral stimulus gains the capability to induce a response that was initially induced by another stimulus.

client-centered (or person-centered) approach
Therapeutic approach that emphasizes specific characteristics of the therapist that are necessary for effective therapy. The therapist must exude warmth, concern for the client, and unconditional positive regard.

clinical psychologists
Psychologists who specialize in the diagnosis and treatment of people with psychological disorders.

cochlea
Snail-shaped structure of the inner ear that is filled with fluid and houses the Organ of Corti.

cognitive couples therapy
Strategy in couples therapy that strives to change the irrational, unproductive thinking that sabotages the relationship.

cognitive dissonance
Discrepancy between thoughts/actions that causes a feeling of discomfort.

cognitive distortions
Things we tell ourselves to make our way through life. Cognitive therapy would help the client to realize the ill-founded nature of these automatic thoughts.

cognitive perspective
Psychological perspective purporting that our behaviors are influenced by our thoughts.

cognitive psychology
Field of study that investigates mental processes such as language, problem solving, and decision-making.

cognitive therapy
Therapy that involves changing faulty thoughts. Approaches include Ellis' Rational Emotive Behavior Therapy (REBT), formerly known as Rational Emotive Therapy (RET) and Beck's Cognitive Therapy.

cohort effects
Major disadvantage of cross-sectional studies that involves differences among the groups being studied that are not related to the study (e.g., age, familiarity with material, etc.).

collective unconscious
Concept associated with Carl Jung; a level of unconscious and latent memories inherited from people's ancestors and shared by all.

community psychologists
Psychologists who focus on changing the behavior of groups, rather than individuals, and the prevention of problem behaviors.

compensatory model
Logical approach to decision making that allows appealing options to compensate for unappealing options.

computerized axial tomography (CT or CAT scan)
Three-dimensional x-ray photographs of the brain taken at many different angles.

concrete operations
Third stage in Piaget's theory of cognitive development; children are no longer dependent on perceptions for decision making and now engage in activities that demonstrate this progression.

conditioned response (CR)
Learned reaction that is elicited by the conditioned stimulus (CS).

conditioned stimulus (CS)
Originally a neutral stimulus that has, after conditioning, the ability to induce a conditioned response (CR).

conduct disorder
Condition characterized by actions that violate societal norms, such as lying, fighting, and stealing.

cones
Receptor cells that are responsible for color vision.

confederates
Fake or staged subjects who help the researcher to fool the actual subjects in an experiment.

conformity
Behavior that occurs when an individual yields to social pressure.

confounding variables
When variables are connected in a manner that proves difficult for researchers to sort out their individual effects.

consensus
In attribution theory, the agreement of factors to support a suspicion about attribution.

consistency
In attribution theory, the examination of whether the behavior is an ordinary or out-of-the-ordinary occurence.

constancy
Concept associated with perception; allows for stability in our perception of the world.

continuous recording
Assessment method that involves watching and recording a particular behavior everytime it occurs.

continuous schedules of reinforcement
Reinforcer is delivered after every instance of the behavior.

continuum of care
Varied collection of mental health services including home-based treatment, partial-day and full-day treatment, therapeutic group home, and hospital treatment.

contracting
Strategy used in couples therapy where the couple sits down with the therapist and develops a contract that addresses some behavior change they would like to realize.

contrived setting
Laboratory or clinic settings, where researchers have more control over when the observable behavior will occur.

control group
Group that does not receive treatment in an experimental study.

conversion disorder
Inability to move or feel sensations in a particular part of the body, often after a traumatic event, with no physical evidence to support complaints.

Cooley's looking glass self
Theory of self-image in which we see ourselves as others see us.

cornea
Portion of the eye; the bulge in the sclera.

corpus callosum
Structure that connects the left brain and the right brain.

corrective recapitulation of the primary family group
Element of group therapy where the group resembles a family, with the therapist representing the parent.

correlational research
Research method that examines relationships between variables.

counseling psychologists
Psychologists who concentrate on the treatment of less severe problems such as adjustment problems.

couples therapy
Treatment of couples with relationship problems.

creative intelligence
In the Triarchic Theory of Intelligence, this refers to a person's ability to respond to novel problems with innovative and creative solutions.

cross-sectional studies
Provides information about developmental changes by interviewing several groups of differing ages at one point in time.

crystallized intelligence
Type of intelligence that is a result of experience.

cyclothymic disorder
Less severe form of bipolar disorder.

death gene
Name given to a gene that supposedly tells cells to deteriorate and die.

debriefing
After an experiment, the researcher takes the subject aside and explains the true nature of the study.

decision making
Procedure of calculating options and choosing from among them.

deductive reasoning
Problem-solving method that begins with the whole scenario and then allows you to break things down to see if your idea applies to the present situation.

defense mechanism
Techniques used by the ego in an effort to cope with the anxiety produced by the conflict of the superego and the id.

deindividuation
Phenomenon that when in a group, people may lose their individual identities and behave in ways that are uncharacteristic of their usual behavior.

delirium
State of temporary mental confusion.

dementia
Gradual deterioration of brain functioning that results in impaired judgment, memory, and other cognitive processes.

dendrite
Finger-like structure of the neuron. Receives information from other neurons.

denial
Type of defense mechanism; the refusal to acknowledge thoughts, feelings, or memory that present a threat.

dependent variable
In an experiment, the variable that is thought to be changed by the action of the independent variable.

depersonalization disorder
Feeling of detachment or removal from the body.

descriptive statistics
Branch of statistics that allows us to organize and describe data.

desensitization
Technique used in classical conditioning to mitigate a patient's reactions to feared stimuli.

detoxification (detox)
Treatment approach in which a person is placed in a setting where he or she is refused access to alcohol and/or drugs.

developmental psychologists
Psychologists who study the growth and development of infants, children, adolescents, and/or adults.

difficult child
One of the three distinct temperaments found in babies; the child described as difficult is said to have difficulty accepting change, demonstrates a generally negative mood, and has irregular sleeping and eating habits.

discussion
Part of a research article where the researcher shares the findings of the study.

disorder of written expression
Learning disorder characterized by difficulty with composing written text, poor handwriting, poor paragraph structure, and problems with punctuation.

disorganized attachment
Term that describes those children who, upon entering a new environment, exhibit less clear, disoriented behavior in response to the mother's departure and return.

disorganized schizophrenia
Type of schizophrenic disorder characterized by frequently incoherent speech and behavior. Also, the person's facial expression often does not match the emotions being expressed.

displacement (defense mechanism)
Type of defense mechanism that diverts negative feelings to a "safe" target.

displacement (in language)
Element of language that allows people to talk about something that is not physically present such as the past, future, and other abstract concepts.

dissociative amnesia
Sudden loss of memory that may be localized (where only a few hours of time are forgotten) or generalized (where persons remember nothing about themselves or their lives).

dissociative disorders
Group of disorders associated with a disruption in memory, identity, consciousness, or perception.

dissociative fugue
Disorder in which people lose memory of self, flee from home, and establish a new identity.

dissociative identity disorder (DID)
Formerly known as multiple personality disorder, a condition characterized by experiences of separate, distinct identities from self. The original identity is referred to as the host, and the additional identities may differ from the host with regard to age, gender, and physical characteristics.

distinctiveness
In attribution theory, this is the variability of responses to behaviors.

dizygotic or fraternal twins
Babies who started as two eggs and are no more genetically similar than any sibling pair.

double-blind study
Experimental method whereby neither the experimenter nor the subject is aware of assignment to treatment conditions.

dream analysis
Tool used in psychoanalysis wherein clients are asked to talk about their dreams while the therapist interprets them.

duration
In behavior assessment, it is how long a behavior lasts.

dyscalculia
Learning disorder associated with difficulties in math. Children with this disorder have difficulty following the sequence of mathematical problems, recognizing numerical symbols, or naming math terms, among other symptoms (sometimes called math disorder).

dyslexia
Learning disorder that involves the inability to decode words and comprehend text (sometimes called reading disorder).

dysthymic disorder
Milder version of major depressive disorder.

eardrum
Portion of the outer ear that vibrates in response to sound waves.

easy child
One of the three distinct temperaments found in babies, the child described as easy is said to adjust to changes in environment without difficulty, demonstrates a generally positive mood, and has regular sleeping and eating habits.

educational psychologists
Psychologists who specialize in how we teach and how we learn.

ego
One of the three parts of personality, according to Sigmund Freud. The ego is the center of reason, and it operates on what Freud refers to as the reality principle.

egocentrism
Restricted capacity to share another person's point of view.

Electra Complex
According to Freud, a stage in development in which the father becomes the target of a daughter's romantic interest; similar to the Oedipal Complex in boys.

electroconvulsive therapy (ECT)
Shock therapy where a current is passed through one side of the brain to produce a cortical seizure and convulsions. It is used as a treatment for mood disorders that have not responded to other approaches.

electroencephalography (EEG)
Instrument that monitors and records electrical activity in the brain. Electrodes, or metal discs, are placed on the scalp. The electrodes pick up activity in the brain, which is interpreted as brain waves that are recorded.

embryo
Term used to describe the organism during the embryonic period.

embryonic period
Second stage of prenatal development that encompasses weeks two through eight after fertilization.

emotion
Feelings such as joy and sadness that are aroused by external or internal stimuli.

empathy
Ability to understand the feelings, moods, emotions of others.

empty nest syndrome
Occurrence in middle adulthood when children reach their own adulthood and leave home; some parents go through a period of adjustment in which they must get used to life without children in the house.

endocrine system
Group of organs that release hormones directly into the bloodstream. They are the hypothalamus, pituitary, thyroid, parathyroid, adrenal, pineal, gonads and pancreas.

enzyme-linked immunosorbent assay test
Test that can detect even low levels of human chorionic gonadotropin, a sure sign of pregnancy, in the urine. Also referrred to as ELISA.

existential factors
Element of group therapy that states members must take responsibility for both their actions and the consequences of their behaviors.

experimental group
Also referred to as the treatment group in an experimental design, this group receives the intervention or treatment.

experimental psychologists
Psychologists who use scientific procedures to gain a better understanding of a process, such as memory and motivation.

experimental research
Research method in which the experimenter manipulates circumstances and then measures the effects of those manipulations on behavior.

external locus of control
Tendency to attribute reinforcement as a result of something apart from ourselves, outside our control.

external validity
Extent to which the findings of a study may be generalized to the population that the study is designed to represent.

factitious disorder
Disorders associated with faking an illness to assume the role of a sick person.

factor analysis
In the study of personality, a theory that involves giving many measures (such as administering tests of personality to many people) and then making note of certain characteristics that could be clumped together.

family systems approach
Theory often associated with family therapy based on the idea that a person does not live or develop in a vacuum. In order to understand a person's situation, the therapist must also understand the dynamics of the person's family.

family therapy
Therapeutic sessions that focus on all members of the family.

fetal period
Third stage of prenatal development that lasts from eight to thirty-eight weeks following fertilization.

fetus
Term used to describe the organism during the fetal period.

fixed interval schedule (FI)
Type of reinforcement schedule whereby the reinforcer is delivered after a set amount of time has passed.

fixed ratio schedule (FR)
Type of reinforcement schedule whereby the reinforcer is delivered after a set number of responses.

flooding
Classical conditioning technique used in treating anxiety disorders wherein the client is exposed to the feared stimulus or event at full tilt.

fluid intelligence
Type of intelligence that is not a result of experience, such as reasoning ability, memory for numbers, and attention span.

forebrain
Largest portion of the brain, it contains the corpus callosum, limbic system, hypothalamus, thalamus, and cerebral cortex.

forensic psychology
Field of psychology that combines psychology and law to gain an understanding of human behavior.

formal operations
Fourth and final stage of Piaget's theory of cognitive development; children have the ability to think hypothetically and systematically.

free association
Method of therapy used in psychoanalysis wherein the client is asked to say whatever comes to mind, without censoring his/her thoughts.

frequency
In behavior assessment, it is how often a behavior occurs.

friends
People who have the same likes and dislikes, engage in shared activities, demonstrate reciprocity and trust.

frontal lobe
One of the four lobes of the cerebral cortex, it controls body movement and concentration, and it coordinates information from other lobes.

functional fixedness (set)
Ability to perceive an object only in terms of its most common use.

functionalism
Approach to psychology that focuses on the what and why of the working of the mind.

fundamental attribution error
In attribution theory, the idea that we tend to overattribute the behaviors of others to internal factors and overattribute our own behaviors to external factors.

ganglion cells
Specialized cells in the visual system that link together to form the optic nerve and then send information to the brain.

Gardner's theory of multiple intelligences
Theory proposed by Howard Gardner that suggests there are different types of intelligence or multiple intelligences. They are logical, mathematical, musical, linguistic, spatial, bodily-kinesthetic, interpersonal, intrapersonal, naturalistic, spiritual, and existential.

gate control theory
Theory that explains individual differences in pain tolerance. The theory posits that there is a "gate" in the spinal cord that controls messages that go to the brain. When the gate is open, more pain is experienced than when the gate is closed.

gender identity disorder
Disorder that causes people to strongly identify as being, or wanting to be, of the opposite sex.

general factor theory of intelligence (also known as Spearman's g)
Early theory of intelligence that states intelligence is all-encompassing; there is one general type of intelligence.

generalized anxiety disorder (GAD)
Disorder with no specific stimulus that serves as the feared object. The individual experiences a chronic level of anxiety that may be described as a constant feeling of impending doom.

generativity versus stagnation (middle adulthood)
Component of Erikson's theory of psycho-social development; the adult in this stage attempts to be a productive member of society.

genital stage (12–adulthood)
Component of Freud's theory of psychosexual development. The erogenous zone during this stage is the genital area and the stage is marked by mature sexuality.

germinal period
First phase of prenatal development; the period from fertilization to two weeks.

gestalt perspective
Orientation in modern psychology that focuses on the individual's perceptions of the world.

gestational period
Span of pregnancy, which in humans is forty weeks from the date of the last period, or thirty-eight weeks from conception.

glands of internal secretion
Another name for the endocrine system, a group of organs that broadcasts hormonal messages to all cells.

goodness of fit
Reference that describes when the temperament of child and caregiver are in sync.

grasping reflex
Unlearned reaction to stimuli where a baby attempts to grasp an object when pressure is applied to his palms.

group cohesiveness
Solidarity that is formed when members of a group begin to bond during the course of their therapy.

group therapy
Therapist works with a number of individuals with shared problems or concerns simultaneously.

groupthink
Group members make decisions in an effort to maintain the harmony of the group, rather than considering which decision is the best.

gustatory
System of taste; closely linked to the olfactory system.

health psychology
Field of study that focuses on how psycho-social factors relate to health and the treatment of illness.

helping behavior
In the study of influences on behavior, it is believed that one of the deciding factors in our decisions to help others is usually based on how many other people are around to join us in helping.

heuristics
Techniques that provide guidelines or "rules of thumb" for problem solving.

hierarchy
In systematic desensitization, a list that details situations related to the feared object or event that is organized from the least-feared situation to the most-feared situation..

hierarchy of needs
Maslow's arrangement of needs according to priority, which states that basic needs such as food and water must be met before less basic needs, such as belongingness and love.

hill climbing
Approach to problem solving where movement is forward and does not digress from the goal. This allows for an evaluation of distance from the starting point and distance from the goal.

hindbrain
Portion of the brain that contains the medulla, the pons, and the cerebellum.

homeostasis
Body's physiological need to return to a previous balance.

human chorionic gonadotropin
Chemical found in the urine of pregnant women.

humanistic perspective
Psychological perspective that views the individual as one with potential who is constantly striving to meet that potential. The emphasis is on an individual's free will and uniqueness.

hypochondriasis
Disorder characterized by disproportionate anxiety concerning health problems and an abnormal worry about developing a serious disease.

hypothesis
Prediction made by the experimenter. There are two types of hypotheses: null and alternative.

id
One of three parts of the personality, according to Sigmund Freud; the id is present at birth, seeks immediate gratification, and operates on what Freud refers to as the pleasure principle.

identity versus identity diffusion (12 to 18 years)
Component of Erikson's theory of psychosocial development; adolescent attempts to find an identity. Parents and especially peers are instrumental in this phase. This stage gave rise to the popular term "identity crisis."

imaginary audience
Type of adolescent thinking; believes that others are watching at all times.

imitative behaviors
Part of the group therapy process where group members model behaviors of the therapist and other group members.

in vivo desensitization
Technique used in classical conditioning to treat anxiety disorders, where the client actually interacts with the feared stimulus or event.

incus
One of the three bones of the middle ear, also referred to as the anvil.

independent variable
Variable that is manipulated by the researcher in a scientific study.

inductive reasoning
Beginning with very specific ideas or hints, a hypothesis is drawn based on those observations, which leads to a conclusion that can be tested.

industrial/organizational psychology
Focuses on the work environment and what can be done to increase employee satisfaction, which then impacts employee productivity and staff turnover.

industry versus inferiority (6–12 years)
Component of Erikson's theory of psychosocial development; the child is now firmly rooted in an educational plan. The acquisition of knowledge is the key component in this stage. Not only parents, but also teachers and others in the child's community are influential during this stage.

infancy
Period between birth and two years.

inferential statistics
Branch of statistics that allows us to draw conclusions about a research study.

inferiority complex
Severely negative opinion of oneself, believed to be the result of parental influence on the child's feelings of self-worth.

influence
Power or capacity of causing an effect in indirect or intangible ways; things that determine how we will behave in certain situations.

information-processing model
This model compares the workings of the human brain to the complexity of a computer.

initiative versus guilt (3–7 years)
Component of Erikson's theory of psychosocial development; at this time, the child begins to take the lead in behaviors, and this stage of exploration and creativity must be supported. Parents are instrumental in determining whether or not the child's initiative-taking is supported.

insecure-avoidant attachment
Term that describes those children who, upon entering a new environment, rarely cry when the mother leaves but then express anger toward her when she returns.

insecure-resistant attachment
Term that describes those children who, upon entering a new environment, are extremely upset when the mother leaves and then express anger toward her when she returns.

integrity versus despair (late adulthood)
Component of Erikson's theory of psychosocial development; a sense of acceptance of one's choices in life are key during this stage. Otherwise the person will end life with a sense of regret, a sense of despair.

intelligence quotient (IQ)
Intellectual functioning as measured by tests such as the Weschler Adult Intelligence Scale (WAIS) and Stanford-Binet.

intensity
In behavior assessment, it is how much physical exertion is involved in the behavior.

intermittent schedule of reinforcement
Reinforcer is not delivered after each and every instance of the behavior.

internal locus of control
Tendency to attribute the receipt of reinforcement to our own behavior.

interpersonal learning
In group therapy, this is where members of the group interact with each other, and the roles they assume in the group are reflective of their interactions and roles in society.

interval recording
Involves selecting a certain period to time and only recording the occurrence of the behavior at that instance.

intimacy versus isolation (early adulthood)
Component of Erikson's theory of psychosocial development; social relationships that are established during adulthood, such as with spouses or children, are a part of this stage. A pattern of intimacy must be established. Instrumental in this pursuit are family and friends.

introduction
Part of research article that contains a literature review. This covers other research articles on the topic, a rationale, and the hypothesis for the current study.

iris
Colored portion of the eye.

James theory of self-esteem
Also referred to as the discrepancy theory. Self-image is based on the difference between the actual self and the ideal self.

James-Lange theory
Early theory of emotion that maintains that physiological change precedes emotion. According to the theory, some stimulus in the environment results in a physiological change, which is then interpreted as an emotion.

language acquisition device
Concept developed by Noam Chomsky that states children are born with an internal device that allows them to understand and produce language.

latency stage (6–11 years)
Component of Freud's theory of psychosexual development in which there is no erogenous zone at this stage and sexual interest is dormant.

learning
Permanent change in behavior or knowledge that results from experience.

learning disorders
Group of disorders characterized by an uncommon difficulty with specific skills such as reading, math, and language.

lens
Portion of the eye that changes shape to help place objects into focus.

lifespan theory
Theory that explore development from birth through old age.

limbic system
Part of the brain that is responsible for emotions and that motivates such behaviors as aggression, hunger, and thirst.

longitudinal approach
Research method in which one group of subjects is studied over an extended period of time.

long-term memory
According to the Information Processing Model, a type of memory that has an unlimited capacity to hold information for a lengthy period of time.

magnetic resonance imaging (MRI)
Biological assessment method psychologists use to obtain information about the brain and behavior. MRIs are similar to the Computerized Axial Tomography (CT or CAT scan), but radio and magnetic waves are used rather than x rays.

major depressive disorder
Characterized by depressed mood, lack of interest in activities that were once seen as pleasurable, changes in eating and sleeping habits, fatigue, feelings of low self-worth, difficulty concentrating, and thoughts of suicide.

malleus
One of the three bones of the middle ear, also referred to as the hammer.

manipulation
Also referred to as the independent variable. The

variable that is controlled or manipulated by the experimenter.

marginalization
One of four paths adopted by teens during their search for ethnic identity, this occurs when the teen lives with the majority culture but exists on the edge of society; this teen is viewed as an outcast and is rejected by both the majority culture and his culture of origin.

mean
Measure of central tendency; the mean equals the sum of the scores divided by the total number of scores.

meaningfulness
Important characteristic of language; allows for shared understanding of communication.

means-end analysis
Approach to problem solving that combines hill climbing and subgoals.

measures of variability
Category of descriptive statistics that provides information about the spread of scores in a distribution. There are three measures of variability: range, interquartile range, and standard deviation.

mechanoreceptors
One of the three types of skin receptors; these receptors are sensitive to pressure.

median
Measure of central tendency; it is the middle number in an array of numbers.

medulla
Portion of the hindbrain that regulates breathing, heart rate, and blood pressure.

menarche
Associated with adolescence; a girl's first menstrual period.

menopause
End of menstrual periods in females, usually occurring sometime between forty-five and fifty years of age.

mental representation
Milestone in Piaget's sensorimotor period when babies are capable of creating mental images.

mental retardation
Disorder usually first diagnosed during child-

hood; characteristics are an IQ of seventy or less and problems completing everyday tasks of living.

metacognition
Ability to think about thinking.

metamemory
Ability to think about memory.

methadone
Drug that prevents heroin users from experiencing withdrawal symptoms.

method
Part of a research article that explains what exactly the researcher did and includes a section on subjects or participants (what gender, how old, how many), and a section on equipment (EEG, MRI) or materials, such as a particular questionnaire or test that was used.

midbrain
Located between the forebrain and hindbrain, it controls sensory processes such as vision and movement.

midlife crisis
Problematic and chaotic period of doubts and review of one's life.

Minnesota Multiphasic Personality Inventory (MMPI)
Self-report personality test; the test consists of 567 questions that require a true/false response.

mixers
One of five categories of social status used to describe a child's social standing, children in this group are those who interact with everyone and are liked by some but not by others.

mob behavior
Condition wherein people feel anonymous in groups, and therefore less responsible for their actions.

mode
Measure of central tendency, it is the number that appears most often in an array of numbers.

modeling
Tendency to replicate the behaviors of those people most influential in one's life.

monocular cues
Visual cues that require the use of only one

eye and are sufficient for most judgments of distance and depth.

monozygotic or identical twins
Originated as one egg that divided into two parts. These twins have the same genetic composition.

moro reflex
Reflex where a baby extends his arms and legs in response to a loud sound.

motivation
Urge or need that directs our behavior.

multiaxial system
Judgements about individuals are made on five different dimensions or axes. This system provides the clinician with a picture of the whole person.

multimodal
In statistics, an array of numbers with more than two modes.

myelin
White, fatty substance that covers the axon. Protects the axons and speeds the transmission of information.

naturalistic observation
Subject's natural habitat. Observations in these settings are said to yield the true/honest form of the behavior being observed.

nature versus nurture
Enduring psychological issue that questions whether people are products of their genetic makeup or their environment.

negative correlation
Type of correlation wherein as one variable increases, the other decreases.

negative punishment
Means of weakening behavior through the removal of a reinforcer.

negative reinforcement
Means of strengthening behavior through the removal of an aversive stimulus or something else the subject finds unpleasant.

nerves or tracts
Bundles of axons.

neurons
Cells in the nervous system that receive and transmit information.

neuropsychology
Field of psychology that focuses on the connection between brain and behavior and the effects of damage to the brain on behavior as a result of brain injury.

neurotransmitter
Substance that carries the information that is transmitted by neurons. Acetylcholine, dopamine, serotonin, and norepinephrine are types of neurotransmitters.

neutral stimulus
Type of stimulus that elicits no response.

no correlation
Type of correlation wherein there is no direct relationship between the two variables.

nocioceptors
One of the three types of skin receptors; these receptors are sensitive to pain.

noncompensatory model
Decision-making model that does not allow some options to compensate for others.

nonverbal expression
Emotions that are conveyed without the use of words.

null hypothesis
Prediction made by the experimenter that states that there is no treatment effect; there is no difference between groups.

obedience
Engaging in a behavior as a result of a command from an authority figure.

object permanence
Toward the end of the sensorimotor period, this is when babies develop the ability to hold mental images.

obsessive compulsive disorder (OCD)
Anxiety disorder characterized by uncontrollable and continual thoughts (obsessions) and urges to carry out irrational rituals (compulsions).

occipital lobe
One of the four lobes of the cerebral cortex, it controls vision.

Oedipal Complex
Component of Freud's theory of psychosexual development in which the mother becomes the target of her son's romantic interest, but

the child fears the wrath of father (castration anxiety).

olfactory
System of smell; closely linked to the gustatory system.

olfactory bulb
Axons from the receptor cells for smell are sent to the olfactory bulb and then travel to other parts of the brain.

olfactory epithelium
Receptor cells for smell; located in the nasal cavity.

operant (or instrumental) conditioning
Behavior is controlled by consequences that will be either reinforcing or punishing.

opponent-process theory
Theory of color vision proposed by Ewald Hering that states there are three sets of cones that determine what color is visualized. Some cones detect yellow-blue, others red-green, and others black-white.

oppositional defiant disorder
Condition characterized by hostile behavior, where the child is defiant or spiteful.

optic chiasm
Point where some fibers from the optic nerve of each eye cross over to the other side of the brain.

optic nerve
Ganglion cells (group of axons) link together to form the optic nerve, which carries information from the eyes to the brain.

oral stage (birth–18 months)
Component of Freud's theory of psychosexual development; the erogenous zone during the oral stage is the mouth. During the first eighteen months of life, the child's focus is on activities that involve the mouth, such as sucking, eating, and biting.

ordinate
Y axis, or the vertical line on a graph.

Organ of Corti
Structure of the inner ear that contains receptor cells.

orientation
Perspective or school of psychology that influences how the psychologist views the phenomenon or situation.

outside monitor
In behavioral assessment, an outside party employed to observe the behaviors to be assessed.

oval window
Connects the middle ear to the inner ear.

pain disorder
Disorder where the patient complains of pain, but there is no biological support for those claims.

panic disorder
Anxiety disorder characterized by panic attacks that occur suddenly and without warning.

papillae
Taste buds located in the bumps on your tongue, which are constantly being replaced.

parameters
Used to describe data from a population.

paranoid schizophrenia
Type of schizophrenic disorder characterized by hallucinations and delusions that are persecutory or grand in nature.

parasympathetic nervous system
Portion of the autonomic nervous system that prepares the body for relaxation.

parietal lobe
One of the four lobes of the cerebral cortex, it controls both the sensory area and visual/spatial abilities.

peer group
Considered equals in the community, may consist of classmates, teammates, or neighbors.

penis envy
Part of the Electra Complex, this is when the daughter resents her mother for making her a girl and envies the father for having a penis, which she sees as a symbol of power.

perception
Interpretation of sensory information.

peripheral nervous system
Includes the somatic nervous system and the autonomic nervous system.

person versus situation
Enduring psychological issue that questions whether personality remains the same or changes depending on the circumstance.

personal fable
Type of adolescent thinking in which the adolescent believes that he/she is different from everyone else.

personality
Unique and enduring ways of thinking, feeling, and behaving.

personality disorders
Characterized by a pervasive and maladaptive way of interacting with one's environment.

pervasive developmental disorder
Disorders in this group are usually diagnosed during childhood; the disorder most often associated with this category is autism. Other pervasive disorders include Asperger's disorder and Rett's disorder.

phallic stage (4–5 years)
Component of Freud's theory of psychosexual development; the erogenous zone during this stage is the genital area.

pheromones
Chemical secretions that signal specific messages to other animals.

phi phenomenon
Illusion of movement created by presenting visual stimuli in a quick progression.

phobia
Intense fear of an object or situation that can be debilitating.

physiological perspective
Perspective in modern psychology that examines the connection between the body and mental health.

pinna
Outer part of the ear consisting of cartilage and covered by skin.

placebo
Commonly referred to as a "sugar pill," this is a drug with no active ingredients. It is often used in experimental research to ensure that subjects remain "blind" to their assigned condition.

pons
Portion of the hindbrain that connects the cerebrum to the cerebellum.

population
Large compilation of animals or people from which a sample is taken.

positive correlation
Type of correlation where an increase in one variable is accompanied by an increase in the other variable, or a decrease in one variable is accompanied by a decrease in the other variable.

positive punishment
Means of weakening behavior through the application of an aversive stimulus or event.

positive reinforcement
Means of strengthening behavior through the application of a reinforcer.

positron emission tomography, (PET scan)
Monitors activity by taking colorful images of the brain. Different colors represent different levels of brain activity.

postpartum depression
Disorder that can occur after giving birth that is characterized by depression and thoughts of harming self or the baby.

posttraumatic stress disorder (PTSD)
Disturbed behavior attributed to a major stressful event that surfaces after the event is over.

practical intelligence
In the Triarchic Theory of Intelligence, this refers to a person's ability to adapt to situations (some call this common sense).

prematurity stereotyping
Tendency to hold different expectations for premature infants, labeling them as weaker, less social, smaller, less cognitively competent, and less behaviorally appealing than full-term babies.

preoperational stage
Second stage in Piaget's theory of cognitive development; children make decisions about their world based on their perceptions.

proactive interference
Old information blocks the retrieval of new information.

problem solving
Cognitive process; approaches include algorithms, heuristics, and trial and error.

product sample recording
Involves collecting the product of a behavior.

productiveness
Element of language that pertains to our ability to use words in an endless number of combinations to create an untold number of expressions.

progressive disorder
Disorder wherein the child shows no impairment at birth, but changes occur later on and get worse.

projection
Type of defense mechanism in which thoughts, feelings, and behaviors are placed onto someone else.

proximodistal development
Motor development that occurs from the center outward.

psychoanalysis
Type of insight therapy associated with the psychodynamic perspective. Approaches include dream analysis and free association.

psychodynamic perspective
Emphasizes the importance of early childhood experiences on adjustment in adulthood. This viewpoint also explores the role of the unconscious in our everyday lives.

psychological motivator
Actions that bring about a sense of well being.

psychology
Scientific study of behavior and mental processes; the study of the mind and its activities.

psychometrician
Person who has been trained to administer, score, and interpret objective psychological tests.

puberty
Stage of development associated with adolescence, changes in physical development, and the onset of sexual maturity.

punishment
Positive or negative event that follows a response and that will weaken behavior.

pupil
Opening in the middle of the iris that opens or closes in response to changes in light.

qualitative
Data that is not countable, such as phrases and comments from interviews.

quantitative
Data that is countable, such as numbers.

random sampling
Every member of the population has an equal chance of being selected for the sample.

range
Measure of variability; calculated by subtracting the smallest number from the largest number in an array of numbers.

rational emotive behavior therapy
Technique that involves challenging a client's irrational beliefs in an effort to change the beliefs that are at the heart of the dysfunction.

reaction formation
Behaving in a way that is completely opposite of one's true feelings.

real movement
As compared to apparent motion, this is when an object actually moves.

recall
Technique used to assess learning that involves retrieving information from long-term memory when the information is not in front of you.

receptor cell
Specialized portion of the body sensitive to particular kinds of stimuli. This cell transmits information to the brain, which interprets it and takes the necessary action.

recognition
Technique used to assess learning that involves retrieving information from long-term memory when the information is in front of you but is hidden among other information.

reference
Section of a research article where the work of others is acknowledged.

reflex
Unlearned, automatic response to stimuli.

regression
Type of defense mechanism in which one reverts to a behavior that is associated with an earlier period in development.

rehabilitation psychology
Focuses on helping people with disabilities adjust to the social, physical, and emotional demands of daily living.

rehearsal
Strategy to facilitate the transfer of information from short-term to long-term memory; involves repeating or practicing the information.

reinforcement
Positive or negative event that follows a response that will strengthen behavior.

reliability
Degree to which the results of a test are consistent and stable.

repression
Type of defense mechanism in which distressing thoughts and feelings are pushed deep into the unconscious, where they are inaccessible.

response cost
Removal of a reinforcer as a result of undesirable behavior.

results
Part of the research article where statistical analyses are presented, including tests conducted and the findings.

retina
Contains the receptor cells for the eye.

retroactive interference
New information blocks the retrieval of old information.

Rett's disorder
Progressive disorder wherein the child shows no impairment at birth, but changes occur between the ages of five and forty-eight months: head growth slows, and the child begins to experience declines in previously acquired motor skills.

reuptake
Process by which the neurotransmitter leaves the synapse and returns to the terminal button where it had been stored, so the synapse may receive new messages.

rods
Receptor cells that detect light and dark and assist with night vision.

rooting reflex
Unlearned reaction to stimuli where a newborn turns his head toward the source of food when his cheek is stroked.

Rorschach Inkblot Test
Type of projective test that consists of ten cards; each card depicts a symmetrical and ambiguous blotch. The clinician presents each card to the client, and the client describes what she sees.

sample
Subset of the population.

schemas
Things that we expect to happen, given a certain situation, a type of person, or some experience.

schizophrenia
Disorder characterized by disturbances in thought that affect perceptual, social, and emotional processes.

sclera
White of the eye.

seasonal affective disorder (SAD)
Disorder referred to as mood disorder with seasonal pattern; associated with feelings of depression at specific times of the year, most often the fall or the winter (when the days shorten).

secondary trait
In the study of personality, a trait that is sometimes considered an attitude or preference.

secure attachment
Term that describes those children who, upon entering a new environment, cling to their mothers but gradually move away from them to explore.

self-actualization
Highest level in Maslow's hierarchy of needs; the development of one's potential to the highest extent.

self-esteem
What we think of ourselves, or our image of self.

self-monitoring
In behavior assessment, when a subject plans to observe and record his/her own behavior.

semenarche
Associated with adolescence; the first ejaculation.

senility
Decline of cognitive functioning usually associated with late adulthood.

sensation
Experienced when the senses are stimulated.

sensorimotor period
First stage in Piaget's theory of cognitive development; children in this stage learn from their senses and interactions with the world around them.

sensory adaptation
Measured weakening in sensitivity due to prolonged stimulation.

sensory memory
Component of the information processing model of memory that is very brief in duration.

sensory threshold
Determines when receptor cells will detect information.

separation
One of four paths adopted by teens during their search for ethnic identity, this occurs when the teen rejects the mainstream culture and adopts the values of the minority culture.

set
When one solves problems based on previous experiences with problem solving, while demonstrating an inability to look beyond routine solutions.

sexual dysfunction
Problem with sexual response or functioning. These include erectile disorder and premature ejaculation in men and female sexual arousal disorder and vaginismus in women.

sexual paraphilias
Group of sexual disorders where the individual derives sexual pleasure through unconventional behaviors, sometimes through illegal means.

shaping
Reinforcement of closer and closer approximations of a desired response.

short-term memory
Limited capacity for information stored for a brief period of time.

signal detection theory
Theory that states that sensory thresholds may differ depending upon the presence of background stimuli and the nature of the signal.

single-blind study
Psychological study where either the experimenter or the subject is unaware of assignment to treatment conditions.

slow to warm child
One of the three distinct temperaments found in babies, the child described as slow to warm is said to adapt to change, but he does so slowly; and he demonstrates a relatively negative mood.

social cognitive theory
Personality theory that emphasizes the role of the environment, social influence, and cognition on personality development.

social desirability
Idea that we try to present ourselves to others in a positive light.

social motivator
Actions that are learned and are pursued to help a person achieve success.

social phobia
Abnormal fear of social situations.

social psychologists
Psychologists who specialize in how individuals are impacted by their social interactions with others (other individuals or other groups).

socializing techniques
Social/observational learning, as proposed by Albert Bandura in chapter 10.

sociocultural perspective
Emphasizes the role of society and culture on behavior.

sociometric rejectees
One of five categories of social status used to describe a child's social standing, children in this group are actively disliked by their peers.

sociometric stars
One of five categories of social status used to describe a child's social standing, children in this group are considered popular and liked by most.

soma
Part of a neuron also known as a cell body.

somatic nervous system
Carries information to the central nervous

system (brain and spinal cord) and to the senses (sight, smell, taste, hearing, touch).

somatization disorder
Associated with complaints of physical ailments, but these complaints are not tied to any particular disease. When examined, no biological explanation is found for the physical complaints.

somatoform disorders
Related to a misperception of problems with the body in which, despite complaints of physical symptoms, a medical examination provides no information to support the patient's reported ailment.

specific phobia
Fear of a particular object or situation; fear of water (hydrophobia), enclosed spaces (claustrophobia), fire (pyrophobia), and of being alone (monophobia) are examples of specific phobias.

spinal cord
Bundle of axons that connect the brain to the rest of the body. These fragile cables are housed inside a string of bones that is called the spine. The spinal cord is responsible for carrying messages to and from the brain; the spinal cord is also involved in reflex actions.

sports psychologists
Psychologists who specialize in working with athletes to help them improve their athletic performance, as well as to help them maintain a healthy mental state.

stability versus change debate
Enduring psychological issue that asks whether people change or remain the same. Often used by developmental psychologists to address the physical, cognitive, and social changes associated with aging.

stage theories
Theories characterized by progressive stages in development that must be passed through to get to the next in a forward movement. Subjects can be stalled at various stages, but typically cannot revert to one already passed through.

stages of dying
Proposed by Elizabeth Kübler Ross, the five stages that characterize the feelings of the terminally ill. The five stages are denial, anger, bargaining, depression, and acceptance.

standard deviation
Measure of variability; provides information about the distance between a score (or scores) and the mean.

Stanford-Binet test
Measures four types of mental abilities that have been equated with intelligence: verbal reasoning, abstract/visual reasoning, quantitative reasoning, and short-term memory.

stapes
One of the three bones of the middle ear, also referred to as the stirrup.

startle reflex
Responding to a sudden or loud noise by jumping, or in infants by crying.

stepping reflex
Unlearned reaction to stimuli where a baby responds with a stepping motion when pressure is applied to his feet.

stereoscopic vision
The ability to use both eyes; stereoscopic vision contributes to the ability to see the world as three-dimensional.

stimulus
Feature of the environment that brings about a response.

stroboscopic movement
Illusion of movement that is apparent when someone stands under a strobe light.

structuralism
Approach to psychology based on the idea that the mind can be separated and studied as distinct components.

sublimation
Type of defense mechanism similar to displacement. In sublimation, unacceptable thoughts are channeled into an appropriate area, often associated with art.

substance abuse
Refers to a pattern of substance use that results in bad consequences; the abuse may interfere with social functioning and job performance.

substance dependence
Refers to use of a drug that has gone beyond abuse. Two features associated with dependence are tolerance and withdrawal.

superego
One of the three parts of personality, according

to Sigmund Freud; the superego is the moral component of personality.

superiority complex
Exaggerated opinion of oneself, believed to be the result of parental influence on the child's feelings of self-worth.

survey
Research method where interviews and questionnaires are used to collect information.

sympathetic nervous system
Portion of the autonomic nervous system that prepares the body for action.

synapse
Space between neurons; also referred to as the synaptic space or the synaptic cleft.

systematic desensitization
Technique used to treat anxiety disorders that involves gradual exposure to the feared stimulus or event.

tastants
Chemicals that interact with taste receptors.

taste buds
Located in the papillae on the tongue, they are constantly being replaced. New taste buds develop every one or two weeks. In addition, the number of taste buds changes as we grow older, which impacts sensitivity to taste.

teacher negatives
One of five categories of social status used to describe a child's social standing; children in this group are liked by some but not by others, and they are often liked by teachers.

temperament
Characteristic mood, activity level, and emotional reactions of an individual.

temporal lobe
One of the four lobes of the cerebral cortex, it controls hearing, smell, balance, and some vision.

teratogens
Agents that can cause abnormal growth or development in a developing fetus.

Thematic Apperception Test (TAT)
Type of projective test that uses ambiguous stimuli in the form of cards that contain pictures that present situations.

theory
Explains a phenomenon, organizes facts, and makes predictions.

thermoreceptors
One of the three types of skin receptors; these receptors are sensitive to temperature.

time out
Popular technique of operant conditioning that uses negative punishment, where a child is removed from her reinforcing environment as a result of an undesirable behavior.

token economy system
Technique used in operant conditioning that provides reinforcement for a behavior in the form of a token that can then be exchanged for a backup reinforcer.

tolerance
Symptom often associated with drug dependence, whereby the user requires more and more of the drug to get the same effect.

tracts
Bundles of axons, also called nerves.

trait theory
Theory that views personality as consistent patterns in thought, feeling, and behavior that span time and situations. This consistency allows for predictions of how a person will behave in future situations.

treatment
In A-B design of behavioral assessment, the B stands for treatment, which is the data collected during the treatment phase.

treatment group
Also referred to as the experimental group or the group that receives the independent variable.

trial and error
Approach to problem solving where attempts at a solution are made until the goal is reached.

trichromatic theory
Theory of color vision proposed by Thomas Young and revised by Hermann van Helmholtz. All color is the result of mixing the three primary colors; red, yellow, and blue. There are

three types of cones and each cone responds to one of these three primary colors.

trust versus mistrust (0–18 months)
Component of Erikson's theory of psychosocial development; child must learn to trust the environment.

tuned out
One of five categories of social status used to describe a child's social standing; children in this group don't interact much, and they are not disliked but rather are ignored by peers.

Type I error
Incorrect decision by the experimenter that the treatment has an effect, when in actuality it does not.

Type II error
Incorrect decision by the experimenter that the treatment has no effect, when in actuality it does.

umami
Some researchers believe this to be the fifth taste, after sweet, sour, bitter, and salty.

unconditional positive regard
Therapeutic technique that consists of complete acceptance and warmth for the client by the therapist; leads to positive self-worth in the client.

unconditioned response (UR)
Reaction that is automatically produced when an unconditioned stimulus is presented.

unconditioned stimulus (US)
Event that produces a response without any conditioning.

universality
Primary benefit to group therapy, individuals find relief in knowing that they are not alone in their experience.

validity
Ability of a test to measure correctly what it was designed to measure.

variable
Characteristic or event that can be altered in an experiment.

variable-interval schedule (VI)
Type of reinforcement schedule whereby the reinforcer is delivered after a certain amount of time has elapsed, on the average.

variable-ratio schedule (VR)
Type of reinforcement schedule whereby the reinforcer is delivered after a certain number of responses, on the average.

verbal expression
Emotions that are conveyed through the use of words.

vomeronasal organ
Site for receptor cells to pheromones.

Weschler Adult Intelligence Scale (WAIS)
Type of IQ test first developed by David Weschler in 1939 and modified over the years. Versions of the Weschler also exist for child and preschool populations.

withdrawal
Symptoms obtained by stopping the use of an addictive drug. The user experiences painful physical symptoms that can include stomach cramps and vomiting.

working backward
Approach to problem solving where the starting point is the goal and then movement occurs back from the goal.

zygote
One-celled organism formed by the unification of a sperm and an egg.

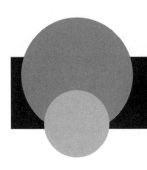

REFERENCES

Albers, S. M. 1998. The effect of gender-typed clothing on children's social judgments. *Child Study Journal*. 28: 1137–59.

Alexander, C. M. and others. 2001. Peers, schools, and adolescent cigarette smoking. *Journal of Adolescent Health*. 29 (1): 22–30.

Allee, J. G. ed. 1997. *Webster's Dictionary*. Ownings Mills, MD: Ottenheimer Publishers.

American Academy of Pediatrics. 1991. *Caring for your baby and young child*. New York: Bantam.

American Psychiatric Association. 2000. *Diagnostic and Statistical Manual of Mental Disorders*, 4th ed. text revision. Washington, DC: American Psychiatric Association.

American Psychological Association. 2002. A renaissance for humanistic psychology: The field explores new niches while building on its past. (Electronic version). *Monitor on Psychology*. 33 (Sept.): 42–45. Retrieved 5 April 2003, from http://www.apa.org.

——. 2002. *Ethical principles of psychologists and code of conduct 2002*. Retrieved April 16, 2003, from http://www.apa.org/ethics.code 2002.html.

——. 2001. *Publication manual of the American Psychological Association*. 5th ed. Washington, D.C.: American Psychological Association.

——. 2000. *Diagnostic and statistical manual of mental disorders*. 4th edition, text revision. Washington, DC: American Psychological Association.

Angie, N. "Does testosterone equal aggression? Maybe not." *New York Times*, June 20, 1995. A1.

Asch, S. E. 1956. Studies of independence and conformity: A minority of one against unanimous majority. *Psychological Monographs*, 70: (9) whole no. 416.

Atkinson, R. C. and R. M. Shifrin. 1968. Human memory: A proposed system and its control processes. In *The psychology of learning and motivation: Advances in research and theory*. Edited by K. Spence and J. Spence. Vol. 2, pp. 89–195. New York: Academic Press.

Bandura, A., D. Ross, and S. A. Ross. 1961. The transmission of aggression through imitations of aggressive models. *Journal of Abnormal and Social Psychology*. 63: 575–82.

Baron, J. 1988. *Thinking and deciding*. Cambridge: Cambridge University Press.

Beausang, C. C. and A. G. Razor. 2000. Young women's experiences of menarche and menstruation. *Health Care for Women International*. 21 (6): 517–28.

Benson, E. 2003. In search of a more perfect union: APA's 2003 president brings his formidable energy and a lifetime of experience to bear on the task of unifying psychology. *APA Monitor on Psychology*, 34 (4) (January). Retrieved from http://www.apa.org/monitor/jan03/union.htm.

Berndt, T. J. 1982. The features and effects of friendship in early adolescence. *Child Development*. 53 (6): 1447–60.

——. 1990. Distinctive features and effects of early adolescent friendships. In *From childhood to adolescence: A transitional period? Advances in adolescent development: An annual book series.* Edited by R. Montemayor and G. R. Adams (Vol. 2, pp. 269–87).

Berscheid, E. 1985. Interpersonal attraction. In *The handbook of social psychology.* Edited by G. Lindzey and E. Aronson (Vol. 2, pp. 413–84).

Bock, K. and S. M. Garnsey. 1998. Language processing. In *A companion to cognitive science (Blackwell companions to philosophy).* Edited by W. Bechtel and G. Graham. Malder, MA: Blackwell Publishers.

Brehm, S. S. and S. M. Kassin. 1993. *Social psychology,* 2nd ed. Boston: Houghton Mifflin Company.

Broadbent, D. 1958. *Perception and communication.* Oxford: Pergamon.

Brown, R. 1973. *A first language: The early stages.* Cambridge, MA: Harvard University Press.

Burns, D. D. 1980. *Feeling good: The new mood therapy.* New York: Morris. Centers for Disease Control and Prevention. 2002. *Fast stats.* Retrieved 6 May 2003, from http://www.cdc.gov/nchs.fastats.

Cherry, C. J. and J. Bowles. 1960. Contribution to the study of the cocktail party phenomenon. *Journal of the Acoustical Society of America.* 32: 884.

Clay, R. 2003. An empty nest can promote freedom, improved relationships (Electronic version). *APA Monitor.* 34 (4): 40–44.

Constantino, G. and R. G. Malgady. 2000. Multicultural and cross-cultural validity of the TEMAS (Tell-Me-A-Story) Test. In *Handbook of cross-cultural and multicultural personality assessment. Personality and psychology series.* Edited by R. H. Dana. (pp. 481–513).

Costa, P. T. and R. R. McCrae. 1978. Objective personality assessment. In *The clinical psychology of aging.* Edited by M. Storandt, I. C. Siegler, and M. F. Elias. New York: Plenum Press.

Costos, D., R. Ackerman, and L. Paradis. 2002. Recollections of menarche: Communication between mothers and daughters regarding menstruation. *Sex Roles.* 46 (1–2): 49–59.

Darley, J. M. and B. Lantané. 1968. Bystander intervention in emergencies: Diffusion of responsibility. *Journal of Personality and Social Psychology.* 8: 377–83.

Davis, G. A. 1973. *Psychology of problem solving: Theory and practice.* New York: Basic Books.

Diener, E. 1980. Deindividuation: The absence of self-awareness, and self-regulation in group members. In *Psychology of group influence.* Edited by P. B. Paulus. Hillside, NJ: Erlbaum and Associates.

DiGiovanna, A. G. 1994. *Human aging: Biological perspectives.* New York: McGraw-Hill.

Doherty, W. J. and N. S. Jackson. 1982. Marriage and the family. In *Handbook of developmental psychology.* Edited by B. B. Wolman. (pp. 667–80). Englewood Cliffs, NJ: Prentice Hall.

Dybing, E. and Sanner, T. 1999. Passive smoking, sudden infant death syndrome (SIDS), and childhood infections. *Human and Experimental Toxicology.* 18: 202–5.

Ekman, P. and others. 1987. Universals and cultural differences in the judgments of facial expressions and emotion. *Journal of Personality and Social Psychology.* 53: 712–17.

Elek, S. M., D. B. Hudson, and C. Bouffard. 2003. Marital and parenting satisfaction and infant care, self-efficacy during the transition to parenthood: The effect of infant sex. *Issues in Comprehensive Pediatric Nursing.* 26 (1): 45–47.

Elkind, D. 1967. Egocentrism in adolescence. *Child Development.* 38: 1025–33.

Ellis, A. 1995. Changing rational emotive therapy (RET) to rational emotive behavior therapy

(REBT). *Journal of Rational-Emotive and Cognitive Therapy.* 13: 85–89.

Erikson, E. H. 1987. *A way of looking at things: Selected papers from 1930 to 1980.* Edited by S. Schlein. New York: Norton.

Eysenck, M. W. and M. T. Keane. 1990. *Cognitive psychology: A student's handbook.* United Kingdom: Lawrence Erlbaum Associates.

Festinger, L. 1957. *A theory of cognitive dissonance.* Stanford, CA: Stanford University Press.

Festinger, L. and J. M. Carlsmith. 1959. Cognitive consequences of forced compliance. *Journal of Abnormal and Social Psychology.* 58: 203–10.

Floyd, R. L. and others. 1993. A review of smoking in pregnancy: Effects on pregnancy outcomes and cessation efforts. *Annual Review of Public Health.* 14: 379–411.

Fontaine, J. H. and N. L. Hammond. 1996. Counseling issues with gay and lesbian adolescents. *Adolescence.* 31: 817–30.

Fraiberg, S. 1959 *The magic years: Understanding and handling the problems of early childhood.* New York: Scribner.

Frankel, L. 2002. "I've never thought about it": Contradictions and taboos surrounding American males; experience with first ejaculation (semenarche). *Journal of Men's Studies.* 11 (1): 37–54.

Freud, S. 1953–1974. *Standard edition of the complete psychological works of Sigmund Freud.* Edited by J. Strachey. London: Hogarth Press and The Institute of Psychoanalysis.

Fuller, R. K. 1988. Disulfiram treatment of alcoholism. In *Alcoholism: Treatment and outcome.* Edited by R. M. Rose and J. E. Barrett. New York: Raven.

Gardner, H. 1998. Are there additional intelligences? The case for naturalistic, spiritual and existential intelligences. In *Education, information and transformation.* Edited by J. Kane. Englewood Cliffs, NJ: Prentice Hall.

Gardner, H. and T. Hatch. 1989. Multiple intelligences go to school: Educational implications of the theory of multiple intelligences. *Educational Researcher.* 18 (8): 4–10.

Gershoff, E. T. 2002. Corporal punishment by parents and associated child behaviors and experiences: A meta-analytic and theoretical review. *Psychological Bulletin.* 128 (4): 539–79.

Gibbs, N. 2002. Making time for a baby. *Time.* April 15: pp. 48–54.

Gould, E., A. J. Reeves, M. S. A. Graziano, and C. G. Gross. 1999. Neurogenesis in the neocortex of adult primates. *Science.* 286: 548–52.

Grossman, K. E. 1984. Fathers' presence during birth of their infants and parental involvement. *International Journal of Behavioral Development.* 7 (2): 157–65.

Hall, J. 1978. Gender effects in decoding nonverbal cues. *Psychological Bulletin.* 85 (4): 845–57.

Hanke, W., J. and others. 1999. Passive smoking and pregnancy outcome in central Poland. *Human and Experimental Toxicology.* 18: 265–71.

Harter, D. 1987. The determinants and mediational role of global self-worth in children. In *Contemporary Topics in Developmental Psychology.* Edited by N. Eisenberg. (pp. 219–42). New York: Wiley.

Harter, S. 1985. Processes underlying the construct, maintenance and enhancement of the self-concept in children. In *Psychological Perspectives on the Self.* Edited by J. Suls and A. Greenwald. Vol. 3. Hillsdale, NJ: Lawrence Erlbaum.

Heider, F. 1958. *The psychology of interpersonal relations.* New York: Wiley.

Henneman, R. H. 1973. *The nature and scope of*

psychology: Introduction to general psychology: A self-selection textbook. 2nd ed. Dubuque, Iowa: Wm. C. Brown Company Publishers.

Hernstein, R. J. and C. Murracy. 1994. *The bell curve: Intelligence and class structure in American life.* New York: Free Press.

Hock, R. R. 2002. *Forty studies that changed psychology: Explorations into the history of psychological research.* Upper Saddle River, NJ: Prentice Hall.

Hoffman, E. 1994. *The drive for self: Alfred Adler and the founding of individual psychology.* Reading, MA: Addison-Wesley.

Horn, J. L. and S. M. Hofer. 1992. Major abilities and development in the adult period. In *Intellectual development.* Edited by R. J. Sternberg and C. A. Berg. (pp. 44–99). New York: Cambridge University Press.

Huyck, M. H. and W. J. Hoyer. 1982. *Adult development and aging.* Belmont, CA: Wadsworth.

Jacobsen, P. B. and others. 1993. The formation of food aversions in patients receiving repeated infusions of chemotherapy. *Behaviour Research & Therapy.* 31 (8): 739–48.

Janis, L. L. 1972. *Victims of groupthink.* Boston: Houghton Mifflin.

Jones, M. C. 1924. Elimination of children's fears. *Journal of Experimental Psychology.* 7: 381–90.

Jung, C. G. 1967–1976. *Collected works of C. G. Jung.* Edited by H. Read, M. Fordham, and G. Adler. Princeton, NJ: Princeton University Press.

Katz, L. C., M. Rubin, and D. Suter. 1999. *Keep your brain alive: 83 neurobic exercises.* New York: Workman Publishing Company.

Kelley, H. H. 1967. Attribution theory in social psychology. In *Nebraska symposium on motivation.* Edited by D. Levine (pp. 192–238). Lincoln, NE: University of Nebraska Press.

Koff E. and J. Rierdan. 1995. Preparing girls for menstruation: Recommendations from adolescent girls. *Adolescence.* 30 (12): 795–811.

Kosterman, R. and others. 2000. The dynamics of alcohol and marijuana initiation: Patterns and predictors of first use in adolescence. *American Journal of Public Health.* 90 (3): 360–66.

Kübler-Ross, E. 1969. *On death and dying.* New York: Macmillan.

Kubrick, S. (Director). 1971. *A clockwork orange.* Motion Picture. United Kingdom: Warner Bros, Swank/16.

Landine, J. and J. Stewart. 1998. Relationship between metacognition, motivation, locus of control, self efficacy, and academic achievement. *Canadian Journal of Counseling.* 32 (3): 200–12.

Lefrancois, G. R. 1983. *Psychology.* 2nd ed. Belmont, CA: Wadsworth.

Levinson, D. 1986. *The seasons of a man's life.* New York: Ballantine Books.

Lightbody, P. and others. 1997. A fulfilling career? Factors which influence women's choice of career. *Educational Studies.* 23 (1): 25–37.

Lott, A. J. and B. E. Lott. 1974. The role of reward in the formation of positive interpersonal attitudes. In *Foundations of interpersonal attraction.* Edited by T. L. Huston (pp. 171–89). New York: Academic Press.

Lowenstein, G. 1994. The psychology of curiosity: A review and reinterpretation. *Psychological Bulletin.* 116: 75–98.

Malpass, R. S. and P. G. Devine. 1981. Eyewitness identification: Lineup instructions and the absence of the offender. *Journal of Applied Psychology.* 66 (4): 482–89.

McClelland, D. C., J. W. Atkinson, R. A. Clark, and E. L. Lowell. 1953. *The achievement motive.* New York: Appleton.

McCrae, R. and P. Costa. 1996. Toward a new generation of personality theories: Theoretical contexts for the five-factor model. In *The five-factor model of personality: Theoretical perspectives.* Edited by J. S. Wiggins. (pp. 51–87). New York: Guilford Press.

Melzack, R. and P. D. Wall. 1965. Pain mechanisms: A new theory. *Science.* 150: 971–79. In *Psychology of problem solving: Theory and practice.* By G. A. Davis. 1973. New York: Basic Books.

Merk. 1997. *The Merck manual of medical information: Home edition.* Whitehouse Station, N.J.: Merk.

Milgram, S. (1963). Behavioral study of obedience. *Journal of Abnormal and Social Psychology.* 67: 371–78.

Miller, G. A. 1956. The magical number, seven plus or minus two: Some limits on our capacity for processing information. *Psychological Review.* 63: 81–97.

Mischel, W. 1968. *Personality and assessment.* New York: Wiley.

Morgan, C., J. Issac, and C. Sansone. 2001. The role of interest in understanding the career choices in female and male college students. *Sex Roles.* 44 (5–6): 295–320.

Morris, C. G. and A. A. Maisto. 1999. *Psychology: An introduction.* 10th ed. Upper Saddle River, NJ: Prentice Hall.

National Advisory Mental Health Council. 1999. Basic behavioral research for mental health: A national investment: Emotion and motivation. *American Psychologist.* 50 (10): 838–45.

Neale, J. M., G. C. Davison, and D. A. F. Haaga. 1996. *Exploring abnormal psychology.* New York: John Wiley & Sons, Inc.

Newcomb, T. M. 1961. *The acquaintance process.* New York: Holt, Rinehart, and Winston.

Ogawa, S. and others. 1997. Behavioral effects of estrogen receptor gene disruption in male mice. *Proceedings of the National Academy of Sciences of the United States of America.* 94: 1476.

O'Leary, K. D. and D. A. Smith. 1991. Marital interaction. *Annual Review of Psychology.* 42: 191–212.

Paley, V. G. 1984. *Boys and girls: Superheroes in the doll corner.* Chicago: University of Chicago Press.

Pavlov, I. P. 1927. Conditional reflexes. Translated by G. V. Anrep. London: Oxford University Press.

Perlman, M. D. and A. S. Kaufman. 1990. Assessment of child intelligence. In *Handbook of psychological assessment.* Edited by G. Goldstein and M. Hersen. 2nd ed. pp. 59–78. New York: Pergamon Press.

Pervin, L. A. and O. P. John. 2001. *Personality: Theory and research.* 8th ed. New York: John Wiley & Sons, Inc.

Phinney, J. and M. Devich-Navarro. 1997. Variations on bicultural identification among African American and Mexican American adolescents. *Journal of Research on Adolescence.* 7 (1): 3–32.

Porter, R. H. 1999. Unique salience of maternal breast odors for newborn infants. *Neuroscience and Biobehavioral Reviews.* 23 (3): 439–49.

Porter, R. H. and others. 1986. Recognition of kin through characteristics of body odors. *Chemical Senses.* 11: 389–95.

Raven, J. C., J. H. Court, and J. Raven. 1985. *Manual of Raven's progressive matrices and vocabulary scales: Standard progressive matrices.* London: H. K. Lewis.

Reed, S. K. 1988. *Cognition: Theory and applications.* Monterey, CA: Brooks/Cole.

Rogers, C. R. 1989. *The Carl Rogers reader.* Boston: Houghton Mifflin.

Rosenthal, N. E., et al. 1985. Antidepressant effects of light in seasonal affective disorder. *American Journal of Psychiatry*. 142: 163–70.

Ross, L. 1977. The intuitive psychologist and his shortcomings: Distortions in the attribution process. In *Advances in experimental social psychology*. Edited by L. Berkowitz. 10: 174–221. New York: Academic Press.

Russ, S. 1998. Play, creativity, and adaptive functioning: Implications for play interventions. *Journal of Clinical Child Psychology*. 27 (4): 4469–80.

Russell, M., T. Mendelson, and H. V. Peeke. 1983. Mothers' identification of their infants' odors. *Ethology and sociobiology*. 4 (1): 29–31.

Saarni, C. 1999. *The development of emotional competence*. New York: Guilford Press.

Saranson, I. G. and B. R. Saranson. 2002. *Abnormal psychology*. 10th ed. Upper Saddle River, NJ: Prentice Hall.

Schaie, K. W. 1990. Intellectual development in adulthood. In *Handbook of the psychology of aging*. Edited by J. E. Birren and K. W. Schaie. 3rd ed. pp. 291–309. San Diego, CA: Academic Press.

Schiffman, S. S. 1983. Taste and smell in disease. *New England Journal of Medicine*. 308: 1275–9.

Schultz, D. and S. E. Schultz. 1998. *Theories of personality*. 6th ed. Pacific Grove, CA: Brooks/Cole.

ScienceNet. 2003. *How many cells does the human body contain?* Dated 5 February; retrieved 13 April from http://www.ScienceNet.org.uk/database/biology/b00307c.html.

Selman, R. L. 1980. *The growth of interpersonal understanding*. New York: Academic Press.

Smith, D. V. and R. F. Margolske. 2001. Making sense of taste (Electronic version) *Scientific American*.

Sogon, S. 1987. Sex differences in emotion recognition by observing body movements: A case of American students. *Japanese Psychological Research*. 29 (2): 89–93.

Sperling, G. 1960. The information available in brief visual presentations. *Psychological Monographs*. 74: 1–29.

Sternberg, R. J. 1982. Who's intelligent? *Psychology Today*. 16 April: 30–39.

——. 1986. *Intelligence Applied*. Orlando, FL: Harcourt Brace Jovanovich.

Stillion, B. D. 1996. Gender differences and facial expressions of emotion. (Doctoral dissertation, Emory University, 1996). *Dissertation Abstracts International*. 56: 5801.

Terman, M. 2001. Internal night. *Archives of General Psychiatry*. 58 (12): 1115–16.

Thomas, A., S. Chess, and H. G. Birch. 1968. *Temperament and behavior disorders in children*. New York: University Press.

Thorndike, E. L. 1911. *The elements of psychology*. 2nd ed. New York: A.G. Seiler.

Till, A., and E. M. Freedman. 1978. Complementary versus similarity of traits operating in the choice of marriage and dating partners. *The Journal of Social Psychology*. 105: 147–8.

Treisman, A. M. 1964. Verbal cues, language and meaning in selective attention. *American Journal of Psychology*. 77: 206–19.

——. 1960. Contextual cues in selective listening. *Quarterly Journal of Experimental Psychology*. 12: 242–8.

United States Bureau of the Census. 1999. *1999 Population Report*, Retrieved 6 May 2003 from http://www.census.gov/population/socdemo.

Veroff, J. J. B. Veroff. 1980. *Social incentive: A life-span developmental approach*. San Diego, CA: Academic Press.

Watson, J. B. and R. Rayner. 1920. Conditioned emotional reactions. *Journal of Experimental Psychology*. 3: 1–14.

Whitbourne, S. K., ed. 1986. *Adult development*, 2nd ed. New York: Praeger.

Wolff, P. H. 1969. The natural history of crying and other vocalizations in early infancy. In *Determinants of infant behavior*. Edited by B. Foss. London: Metuchen.

Wright, D. B., E. F. Loftus, and M. Hall. 2001. Now you see it; now you don't: Inhibiting recall and recognition of scenes. *Applied Cognitive Psychology*. 15 (5): 471–82.

Wysocki, D. J. and M. Meredith. 1987. *The vomeronasal system*. New York: Wiley.

Yates, J. F. and P. A. Estin. 1998. In *A companion to cognitive science*. Edited by W. Bechtel, and G. Graham. Malden, MA: Blackwell.

Zajonc, R. B. 1968. Attitudinal effects of mere exposure. *Journal of Personality and Social Psychology*. 9 (2): 1–27.

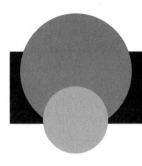

INDEX

NOTES